BUSINESS POWER
AND THE STATE
IN THE CENTRAL ANDES

PITT LATIN AMERICAN SERIES

CATHERINE M. CONAGHAN, EDITOR

BUSINESS POWER
AND THE STATE
IN THE CENTRAL ANDES

Bolivia, Ecuador, *and* Peru *in* Comparison

JOHN CRABTREE, FRANCISCO DURAND,
AND JONAS WOLFF

UNIVERSITY OF PITTSBURGH PRESS

Published by the University of Pittsburgh Press, Pittsburgh, Pa., 15260
Manufactured in the United States of America
Printed on acid-free paper
10 9 8 7 6 5 4 3 2 1

Cataloging-in-Publication data is available from the Library of Congress

ISBN 13: 978-0-8229-4789-9
ISBN 10: 0-8229-4789-7

Cover art of La Paz, Bolivia, by Rodrigo Gonzalez
Cover design by Melissa Dias-Mandoly

Dedicated to the memory of José Francisco (Paco) Durand
(1950–2023)

CONTENTS

PREFACE

The seeds for this book were first sown in the seventeenth-century hall of Lima's San Marcos University at an international conference organized by Francisco Durand and Nicolás Lynch in which both John Crabtree and Jonas Wolff were participants. Entitled "Economic Power, State and Civil Society in the Central Andes and Southern Cone," the conference was a joint endeavor of the Catholic University (PUCP), San Marcos University (UNMSM), and Arequipa's Catholic University Santa María (UCSM). Supported by the Friedrich Ebert Foundation (FES), the Postgraduate Program for Research on Inequalities and Sustainable Development in the Andean Region (trAndeS), and Oxfam Peru, the conference took place on September 12-14, 2019, across all three university campuses. In this project we sought to take the proceedings of the conference forward and to analyze the development of business power across the three Central Andean countries Bolivia, Ecuador, and Peru over the long term, with its determinants, its strengths and weaknesses, in different conjunctures—and to examine its role in consolidating (or not) patterns of democratic politics and economic governance in these three countries. The book you have before you is the result of that initial project.

When we started working on this joint study, we knew it would be difficult to meet frequently given the physical distance between our respective places of residence and work. Yet, we could not have anticipated that a global pandemic would mean, in the end, that we would have not one single in-presence meeting while collaboratively writing, discussing, and revising this book. The result, or so we hope, is still a genuine monograph written by six hands.

Sadly, Francisco Durand passed away on February 1, 2023, shortly after the completed draft of the manuscript had been submitted to the publishers. He had been suffering from leukemia but, despite his illness, had been able to contribute fully to the book. John Crabtree and Jonas Wolff are greatly indebted to his efforts. He was a towering figure in the Peruvian academic community. This book is therefore dedicated to his memory.

There are many people and institutions on both sides of the Atlantic that, in one way or another, supported the three of us while doing the research on which the present study is based. Here, we would only like to acknowledge those that directly contributed to the making of this book: the Friedrich Ebert Foundation in Peru for bringing John and Jonas to the 2019 conference in Lima; Josh Shanholtzer at the University of Pittsburgh Press for supporting our project all along the different stages of the review process; Fernando Molina and Carlos Pástor Pazmiño for commenting on the Bolivia and the Ecuador sections of the draft manuscript, respectively; Cornelia Hess from the Peace Research Institute Frankfurt (PRIF) for helping us prepare the manuscript; and four anonymous readers for offering constructive criticism and extremely useful advice. We are also indebted to Pippa Letsky for her meticulous copy editing.

ABBREVIATIONS
AND ACRONYMS

ADEX	Asociación de Exportadores (Peru)
ADN	Acción Democrática Nacionalista (Bolivia)
AFP	Administrador de fondos de pensiones
ALBA	Alianza Bolivariana para los Pueblos de Nuestra América
Alianza PAIS	Alianza Patria Altiva I Soberana (Ecuador)
ANAPO	Asociación de Productores de Oleaginosas y Trigo (Bolivia)
APRA	Alianza Popular Revolucionaria Americana (Peru)
Asoban	Asociación de Bancos Privados de Bolivia (Bolivia)
BCRP	Banco Central de Reserva del Perú
CADE	Conferencia Anual de Ejecutivos (Peru)
CAF	Corporación Andina de Fomento
CAINCO	Cámara de Industria, Comercio, Servicios y Turismo de Santa Cruz (Bolivia)
CAN	Comunidad Andina de Naciones (Andean Pact)
CAO	Cámara Agropecuaria del Oriente (Bolivia)
CBN	Cervecería Boliviana Nacional (Bolivia)
CEE	Comité Empresarial Ecuatoriano (Ecuador)
CELAC	Community of Latin American and Caribbean States

CEPB	Confederación de Empresarios Privados de Bolivia (Bolivia)
CIDOB	Confederación de Pueblos Indígenas de Bolivia (Bolivia)
CIP	Cámara de Industrias y Producción (Ecuador)
CNC	Cámara Nacional de Comercio (Bolivia)
CNI	Cámara Nacional de Industrias (Bolivia)
COB	Central Obrera Boliviana (Bolivia)
COMEXI	Consejo de Comercio Exterior e Inversiones (Ecuador)
Comibol	Corporación Minera de Bolivia (Bolivia)
CONAIE	Confederación de Nacionalidades Indígenas del Ecuador (Ecuador)
CONAM	Consejo Nacional de Modernización (Ecuador)
CONAMAQ	Consejo de Ayllus y Marcas del Qullasuyu (Bolivia)
CONDEPA	Conciencia de Patria (Bolivia)
Confiep	Confederación Nacional de Instituciones Empresariales Privadas (Peru)
CPCCS	Consejo de Participación Ciudadana y Control Social (Ecuador)
CREO	Creando Oportunidades (Ecuador)
CTE	Confederación de Trabajadores del Ecuador (Ecuador)
CTM	Confederación de Trabajadores de México (Mexico)
DP	Democracia Popular (Ecuador)
ECLAC	Economic Commission for Latin America and the Caribbean
EIA	Environmental Impact Assessment
EITI	Extractive Industries Transparency Initiative
EMBOL	Embotelladoras Bolivianas Unidas (Bolivia)
ENDE	Empresa Nacional de Electricidad (Bolivia)
ENFE	Empresa Nacional de Ferrocarriles (Bolivia)
ENTEL	Empresa Nacional de Telecomunicaciones (Bolivia)
EU	European Union
ExpoCruz	International Trade Fair of Santa Cruz (Bolivia)
Fedecamaras	Federación de Cámaras y Asociaciones de Comercio y Producción de Venezuela
FEPSC	Federación de Empresarios Privados de Santa Cruz (Bolivia)
FES	Friedrich Ebert Foundation
Foncodes	Fondo de Cooperación para el Desarrollo Social (Peru)

FP	Fuerza Popular (Peru)
Fredemo	Frente Democrático (Peru)
FSTMB	Federación Sindical de Trabajadores Mineros de Bolivia (Bolivia)
FTAs	Free Trade Agreements
FUT	Frente Unitario de Trabajadores (Ecuador)
GDP	Gross Domestic Product
GSP	Generalized System of Preferences
HIPC	Highly Indebted Poor Country Initiative
ID	Izquierda Democrática (Ecuador)
IDB	Inter-American Development Bank
IDH	Impuesto Directo a los Hidrocarburos (Bolivia)
IFC	International Finance Corporation (World Bank)
IFIs	International Financial Institutions
ILPES	Instituto Latinoamericano de Planificación Económica y Social
IMF	International Monetary Fund
IPE	Instituto Peruano de Economía (Peru)
ISI	Import Substitution Industrialization
IU	Izquierda Unida (Peru)
LAB	Lloyd Aéreo Boliviano (Bolivia)
MAS	Movimiento al Socialismo (Bolivia)
MEF	Ministry of Economy and Finance (Peru)
MIR	Movimiento de la Izquierda Revolucionaria (Bolivia)
MMG	Chinese-owned international mining company
MNR	Movimiento Nacionalista Revolucionario (Bolivia)
NGO	Non-Governmental Organization
NPE	Nueva Política Económica (Bolivia)
OAS	Organization of American States
OCP	Oleoducto de Crudos Pesados (Ecuador)
OECD	Organization for Economic Cooperation and Development
Petroecuador	Empresa Estatal Petróleos del Ecuador (Ecuador)
PNP	Partido Nacionalista Peruano (Peru)
PNUD	Programa de las Naciones Unidas para el Desarrollo
Podemos	Poder Democrático y Social (Bolivia)
PPPs	Private Public Partnerships
PRE	Partido Roldosista Ecuatoriano (Ecuador)
PRI	Partido Revolucionario Institucional (Mexico)
PSC	Partido Social Cristiano (Ecuador)

PT	Partido dos Trabalhadores (Brazil)
PUCP	Pontificia Universidad Católica del Perú (Peru)
PUR	Partido Unidad Republicana (Ecuador)
SBS	Superintencia de Bancos y Seguros (Peru)
SIN	Servicio de Inteligencia Nacional (Peru)
Sinamos	Sistema Nacional de Movilización Social (Peru)
SNA	Sociedad Nacional Agraria (Peru)
SNI	Sociedad Nacional de Industrias (Peru)
SNMP	Sociedad Nacional de Minería y Petróleo (Peru)
SOBOCE	Sociedad Boliviana de Cemento (Bolivia)
SOE	state-owned enterprises
SPCC	Southern Peru Copper Corporation (Peru)
Sunat	Superintencia Nacional de Administración Tributaria (Peru)
SUTEP	Sindicato Unitario de Trabajadores en la Educación del Perú (Peru)
TCP	Tribunal Constitucional Plurinacional (Bolivia)
TIPNIS	Territorio Indígena y Parque Nacional Isiboro-Sécure (Bolivia)
TSE	Tribunal Supremo Electoral (Bolivia)
UCS	Unión Cívica Solidaridad (Bolivia)
UCSM	Universidad Católica de Santa María (Peru)
UN	Unidad Nacional (Bolivia)
UNASUR	Union of South American Nations
UNES	Unión por la Esperanza (Ecuador)
UNMSM	Universidad Nacional Mayor de San Marcos (Peru)
USAID	US Agency for International Development
VAT	Value-added tax
WTO	World Trade Organization
YPFB	Yacimientos Petrolíferos Fiscales Bolivianos (Bolivia)

BUSINESS POWER
AND THE STATE
IN THE CENTRAL ANDES

INTRODUCTION

Much has been written about the turn to neoliberalism across Latin America during the 1980s and 1990s, about the increasing popular challenges to "neoliberal democracy" since the late 1990s, about the "leftist turn" to some kind of post-neoliberalism in many Latin American countries during the early 2000s, as well as about the less clear-cut pattern of politico-economic development in the region over the most recent years. In doing so, scholars have also tackled the important question of variation: why is it that certain countries adopted and implemented far-reaching neoliberal structural adjustment policies while others moved in this direction only gradually and much more inconsistently? Why is it that neoliberalism was openly challenged by mass movements in certain countries but not to the same extent in others? Why did some countries, after the turn of the century, embark on quite radical attempts to transform the development model, some much more modestly, and others not at all? And how can we make sense of the even more diverse political trajectories that have characterized the region since 2015, the swings from left to right and from right to left in ways that have challenged business power and forced it to adopt ad hoc strategies to maintain its close relationship with the state?[1]

Bolivia, Ecuador, and Peru offer a key puzzle in this regard. On the one hand, they are characterized by a series of commonalities that date back to their colonial and postcolonial history and include similar political, economic, cultural and socio-geographic characteristics. On the other hand, their politico-economic trajectories since the 1980s have varied in unexpected and shifting ways. During the 1980s, attempts to implement far-reaching structural adjustment policies failed in Ecuador and Peru—but Bolivia, with the post-1985 "New Economic Policy," stood out as the exceptional poster child of neoliberal reforms. During the 1990s, with Fujimori in power in Peru, this changed—and Ecuador remained one of the very few Latin American countries that stuck to the mode of gradual (and fairly inconsistent) implementation of market-oriented policies. This pattern notwithstanding, it was Bolivia and Ecuador—but not Peru—that saw a huge wave of anti-neoliberal mobilization taking off in the late 1990s, which culminated in the election of Evo Morales in Bolivia in 2005 and of Rafael Correa in Ecuador a year later. These governments, subsequently, in fact implemented a set of post-neoliberal policies that reinforced state power over market forces and substantially modified the established development model—if refraining from serious attempts to move beyond either capitalism or extractivism.[2] Peru, now, remained the outlier. Even if the country similarly benefited from the global commodities boom and did see the temporary rise of political outsiders, it did not experience any meaningful attempt to implement leftist or post-neoliberal policies that challenged the established development model. Under interim president Jeanine Áñez (2019-2020) and Correa's elected successor Lenín Moreno (2017-2021), both Bolivia and Ecuador saw a marked return to the right, including adoption of openly pro-business policies. Yet, with the election of Luis Arce in October 2020, this return remained a brief interlude in Bolivia, while Ecuador—with the election of Guillermo Lasso in April 2021—seemed to be seeking to consolidate this path. At the same time, Peru found itself in deep political troubles and, finally, saw the unexpected triumph of leftist outsider Pedro Castillo in the June 2021 runoff election and his subsequent removal as president eighteen months later.

In attempting to explain such diverging paths of political and economic development among Latin American countries in general and the Central Andean countries in particular, much research has been devoted to the role of social movements (e.g. Silva 2009; Yashar 2005) and the institutional features characterizing the different party systems and political regimes (e.g. Levitsky and Roberts 2011; Van Cott 2005).[3] Much less attention has been paid to the role played by business elites in its various components. This is precisely the dimension that was emphasized by Catherine Conaghan and James Malloy in their pioneering work *Unsettling Statecraft: Democracy and Neoliberalism in the Central Andes* (1994), which focused on the 1970s and 1980s. Indeed, few observers would doubt that economic elites play an important role throughout the Central Andean region (and beyond). Yet, to date, an account is missing that looks systematically at how the role of economic elites and configurations of business power in all its dimensions have changed in Bolivia, Ecuador, and Peru during the recent decades and how these changes have interacted with dynamics at the levels of the popular sectors and the political regime in order to shape change and continuity in economic policy making and the overarching development model. This is what we set out to do in this book.

AIMS AND ARGUMENT OF THE BOOK

The political role of economic elites and the complex relationship between business power and the state are certainly key issues that merit much more systematic analyses across Latin America and beyond.[4] In this book, however, the focus is deliberately set on the three countries of Bolivia, Ecuador, and Peru, countries that share many structural similarities with one another. Rather than cast the net wider, we believe that a narrower, more focused and detailed historical comparison sheds important light on the role played by economic elites in fashioning political outcomes over the long run. In this, we follow up on the work of Conaghan and Malloy, convinced that there is importance in writing a sequel that takes into account what has happened in the region over the three decades since that book was published.

In the early 1990s, the neoliberal project was but an incipient enterprise whose overall sustainability was the question that Conaghan and Malloy addressed for these three countries in which "unsettledness" was a salient feature. But much water has passed under the bridge since then. Bolivia at that time stood out as the exception to the rule, a country in which the viability of the previous, statist model of development was shaken to the core by the crisis, or "critical juncture," of the early 1980s. As the 1990s drew on, however, the neoliberal model appeared to become hegemonic under the aegis of the Washington Consensus, with business power seemingly sitting well alongside the transitions from authoritarian rule to democracy in Latin America. However, the growing autocracy of the Fujimori regime in Peru (1990–2000) raised serious questions about the extent to which radical economic liberalization was compatible with notions of democratic rule.

The coming of the "pink tide" in the early years of the new millennium further questioned the "settledness" of the neoliberal model, giving rise to the return to more statist and nationalist forms of governance. But while Ecuador and Bolivia stood out as exemplars of that genre, in Peru the business class maintained its political hegemony, achieving what, in an earlier text, Crabtree and Durand (2017) described as being a case of "political capture." But even there, more recent events seriously question the ability of business elites to fashion political life in ways that preserve their leading role while strengthening democratic governance. Looking at the region in the early 2020s, it appeared to be as "unsettled" as ever, if not more so. More than becoming a stabilizing factor that could contribute to the governability of the state and society, business brokers have sought to protect their economic interests and to exert their influence over the state, thus contributing to "unsettledness." We hope in this book to help provide an understanding of why this is so.

In identifying the means by which business elites exercise the resources available to them in different historical conjunctures and in different geographic settings, we seek to harness new academic scholarship in understanding the multidimensional nature of business power. We thus analyse the various forms that such power takes—structural, instrumental and discursive—and how business actors use these different forms of power, in contention with other claimants in society, in attempting to ensure that public policy responds to their interests. In addition to updating the study by Conaghan and Malloy, we thus also enrich the analysis by drawing on the new theoretical and methodological approaches of recent decades that focus on business power and state capture.

We are also concerned to identify those key moments, or critical junctures, when the nature of that power changes and new meanings of "development" emerge. For this reason, we adopt a historical approach to chart variations in business power over time and to explore how that power coexists with, and is shaped by, power exercised by other social actors. The comparisons among the three countries are drawn with reference to long-run historical patterns. There are a number of points in the story when these established patterns suddenly change, whether as a result of exogenous shocks, endogenous developments, or a combination of the two. Our historical narrative thus begins with the impact of the 1929 crash in forcing important changes, giving way to a new period of business-state relations that ended in the debt crisis of the 1980s. The period of neoliberal hegemony was challenged in the early 2000s at least in Bolivia and Ecuador, while—arguably—the COVID-19 pandemic and its socioeconomic consequences may represent a new critical juncture with the weakening of globalization and world growth prospects.

In selecting these three countries for comparative analysis we are convinced that, despite their evident differences, they share enough in common to make such analysis meaningful and illustrative of broader trends that have affected other Latin American countries. It goes without saying that all three formed parts of the Inca empire and, on its demise, of the Spanish empire administered from Lima and were integrated into the world economy through the export of precious commodities, especially minerals. Their societies as well as business-state relations were then forged in the nineteenth century around processes of neo-colonial domination in which indigenous peoples found themselves at the base of the class structure, a historical antecedent that still impacts on society and politics today with their marked inequalities, lack of social and ethnic inclusion, and the privileged relationship that elites enjoy with the state.

All three countries were latecomers in seeking to cast off, or at least modify, this historical inheritance and with it the pattern of oligarchic agriculture (*latifundismo*) and mineral extraction. Although two world wars and the intervening crash of the late 1920s helped stimulate the beginnings of industrial development in the larger economies of Latin America, the end of the dominance of agrarian elites, and the emergence of previously excluded actors into the political sphere, it was not until the 1960s and 1970s that our three countries began to experience these patterns of change. Indeed, the process of industrialization in all three has been relatively modest (and, again, late) when compared to the Southern Cone and Brazil. All three remain heavily dependent for the bulk of their foreign exchange on extractive industries for which international prices are notoriously volatile. This pattern of development has tended to be exclusive, with large populations still living in poverty at the margins of the "modern" economy.

In the political sphere, our three countries struggled to establish and uphold more or less democratic regimes over the course of the twentieth century and into the new millennium. They lacked strong traditions of democracy rooted in public participation and with institutionalized and representative political parties and an organized civil society. In contrast to other parts of the world, party systems have remained shallow and exclusive. Although political democratization since the late 1970s meant more inclusive party systems and stronger forms of social organization, these proved ineffective in providing the institutionalized channels through which the previously excluded could find a voice.

Business elites in Bolivia, Ecuador, and Peru have had to vie with bouts of popular mobilization in ways that have led to periods of both instability and authoritarian rule. As we shall show in this study, the ability or willingness of elites to build strong and sustainable democratic institutions and stable forms of interest representation has been limited in all three countries. Political power has remained highly concentrated, a facet reinforced by neoliberalism, and attempts to broaden the power structure and include previously excluded elements have proven contested and difficult to sustain. All three countries also demonstrate highly unequal territorial patterns of state penetration, with state authority being at best patchy in large swathes of territory, particularly in the Andes and the Amazon lowlands, the latter only "colonized" relatively late on in the twentieth century. Across the Central Andean region, these spaces have witnessed important clashes between extractive industries and indigenous-based social movements in which the ability and will of successive governments to mediate and impose rules of conduct have been lacking. Indeed, institutional development and political stability have been tenuous in all three countries. Building effective state institutions and adopting long-term policies have also been constrained by the difficulty in establishing a strong base of taxation capable of underpinning public spending and facilitating a more equal income distribution.

The Central Andean region is still far from finding the formula for reconciling business power with wider political participation in ways that can underscore stable, democratic governance. This is a difficult balancing act in most capitalist societies. Electoral challenges to the neoliberal pro-business agenda in more recent years have obliged the core economic elite, business groups, and multinational corporations—now strongly intertwined—to decide between seeking compromise with politically strong leftist governments and trying to subvert them.

So, although the three cases studied here share many of the vices or virtues found elsewhere in Latin America, we believe that there are some clear commonalities that make for meaningful comparative analysis. But the differences between them are significant and revealing in the contrasts they elicit. Each country reflects its own social, political, and cultural peculiarities, characteristics that are the product of their historical development since independence two hundred years ago.

OUTLINE OF THE BOOK

In chapter 1 we map out key debates that surround this topic and the relationship between business elites and the state. In line with the overall literature, we identify three dimensions along which that power is constituted and thereafter exercised: (1) structural power, or the ability of economic elites to influence the state through their decisions to invest (or disinvest), made all the more pronounced by the fact that Latin America as a whole (and the Andean countries within it) is an area long dependent on financial inflows from the rest of the world; (2) instrumental power, or the means by which local elites are able to influence political outcomes through domestic institutions of one sort or another; and (3) discursive power, by which elites are able to influence patterns of public opinion and their ideological underpinning in ways that go well beyond the state but which, in turn, influence state policy. We go on to interrogate the idea of "state capture" and the circumstances in which the three strands of business influence combine to become effectively hegemonic. The focus then changes to the cycles that have characterized Latin America's models of economic development and the mechanisms of transition between them from the 1920s to the present day. Configurations of business power and the degree of state capture tend to vary in line with these shifting development models, themselves the product of the emergence of new social and political actors. Such factors can lead to changes in the economic model, and we see how these changes may impact on the political regime and, specifically, on elite support for democracy. The shifts from one model of economic development to another, as we will argue, tend to take place at critical junctures, themselves often caused by cyclical variations at the global level.

In chapter 2 we apply this conceptual framework to patterns of development in Bolivia, Ecuador, and Peru—from the demise of old oligarchic structures, through the various attempts at structural reform that characterized the period between the 1950s and the 1970s, to their final collapse in the early 1980s at the time of the Latin American debt crisis. We begin the chapter with an overview of the period for Latin America as a whole before analyzing our specific case studies. We trace the changing relationship between business elites and the state within the model of state-led development and import substitution industrialization, strategies aimed at widening the boundaries of social inclusion, although these were subject to limitations of resources and capabilities. We identify degrees of regulatory and policy capture by different actors in specific settings. In particular, in this chapter we analyze the economic and political conditions that led to the collapse of the model and the role played in this collapse by business power within the context of changes in the global order.

In chapter 3 we outline the nature of the neoliberal "revolution" as it applied to the Andean region, along with its relationship to the process of democratization. We identify the main detonators of change and the structural transformation that were brought about. Covering the late 1980s and 1990s, we study the domestic forces that pushed for pro-market policies and the degree of external support they enjoyed, as well as the key features of the political economy as it took shape during the neoliberal period. How did business power evolve in this context, and to what extent did it create conditions for capture? We analyse and compare the different trajectories and outcomes within the Central Andean region, with the process of adjustment going faster and further in Peru and Bolivia (as a consequence of the severity of the crises in the 1980s) than in Ecuador.

In chapter 4 we begin by looking at the societal challenges to neoliberalism and the resultant "pink tide" as a broader phenomenon in Latin American politics with all its variants in different countries. We point to the failings in the neoliberal model in generating an equitable pattern of growth, and we focus on the extent to which this led to a challenge to business power across the region. Roughly covering the first decade of the new millennium, we trace the variants in the courses taken by our three countries. We begin with Bolivia under Evo Morales (after 2006) and then compare this with the "pink tide" in Ecuador under Rafael Correa (after 2007). Then, we turn to the rather different trajectory followed by Peru where business power remained entrenched throughout the post-Fujimori era, in spite of challenges to it such as those by the election of Ollanta Humala (in 2011). In the Bolivian and Ecuadorian cases, we examine the practices adopted by business elites in this far less favorable set of circumstances, while also identifying the sources of their residual power. We look at how conventional notions of development were challenged as new actors came on the scene demanding the adoption of new paradigms. With a view to Peru, we address the question of how business elites managed to deflect incipient challenges to their controlling position and, thereby, contributed to preventing Peru from joining the "pink tide" through the first two decades of the new millennium.

In chapter 5 we look at the conservative reaction against the "pink tide" that manifested in the second decade of the new millennium, albeit in different ways. This backlash corresponded, to an important degree, to the ending of the commodity super-cycle that had facilitated the return to more statist and interventionist policies. We chart the restoration of business power and the increased leverage it offered in defining public policy. Again, our three Andean countries pursue different courses, which diverge in important ways, with business elites gaining sway in Bolivia and Ecuador at the expense of the popular organizations that had initially backed the Correa and Morales governments. In each case, we look at the rising influence of business—both during the latter years of these two presidents and then under the more right-wing governments that replaced them. In Peru, by contrast, we see the power of business declining and increasingly contested, in part because of the recurrent episodes of socio-environmental conflict, the delegitimizing effects of the proliferation of corruption scandals in the years after 2016, and the weakening of governments that were initially committed to sustaining pro-business policies.

In the Conclusions, we summarize our main findings and identify overarching theoretical implications before rounding off the historical sweep with a short epilogue. Here, we look at the impact of the COVID-19 pandemic, its economic and social consequences, and the political gyrations as a consequence of elections in all three countries, which brought Morales's Movimiento al Socialismo (MAS) back to power in Bolivia, helped underscore the turn to the right in Ecuador, and led to the surprise victory of a leftist outsider in Peru. In a rather speculative manner, we suggest that the region might be facing a new critical juncture. In the current context, on the one hand, the consequences of the pandemic seem to have further undermined the public appeal and political viability of pro-market policies, weakening business's capacity to shape public discourse and craft broader alliances. On the other hand, rising fiscal deficits and debt levels aggravated by COVID-19, at a moment of increased wealth concentration, also pose important obstacles to a statist agenda and threaten to further aggravate distributional conflicts. At the global level, the world appeared increasingly segmented into competing blocs with growth rates falling and inflation reasserting itself after decades of relative quiescence. In this context, a political climate of "unsettledness" appeared to have returned throughout the Central Andes with business power seeking to use the resources at its disposal to protect its strategic interests.

CHAPTER 1

BUSINESS POWER, MODELS OF ECONOMIC DEVELOPMENT, AND THE STATE

When wealth and income are concentrated in the hands of a small elite of local and international individuals, families, or corporations that operate in poor, socially, and regionally fragmented societies—traits particularly pervasive in the countries of the Central Andes—access to political decision-making tends to become highly unequal.[1] As middle classes and/or popular forces contest economic elites' privilege and their disproportionate influence over the state, patterns of political, social, and economic change unfold. Sometimes such struggles lead to an effective, if usually partial, redistribution of both economic wealth and political power, forcing wealthy businesspeople, foreign investors, and big private corporations to adapt or even to remove regimes that are perceived as threatening their interests. Frequently, however, structural change remains limited, at best, as business elites succeed in maintaining or restoring their control over the economy, their influence over the state, and their ability to disseminate pro-market ideas among the population.[2]

This contestation over economic privilege and political-ideological influence constitutes a dynamic and at times erratic political process. Once capitalist development produces an industrial workforce and a middle class and societies transit from "aristocratic" to mass polities, the political process is driven by an ongoing struggle between oligarchic and democratic principles in the exercise of power, with clear benefits for those who control strategic economic resources and the means of production (Foweraker 2018; Lindblom 1977; Rueschemeyer et al. 1992). Under the conditions of mass politics, business elites—for the sake of their own survival—must face the bottom-up challenges to their power and develop effective ways to secure their political influence and defend their interests. It is a learning process in building and wielding bargaining power and in mobilizing resources to shape the public debate and control the political process in competition with other forces. A core issue that is at stake in these struggles concerns the establishment, transformation, or replacement of competing models of economic development, some of which provide for a greater role for private business and the operation of market forces while others are, rather, state-oriented, interventionist, and/or redistributionist.[3]

Focusing on the political behavior and power of economic elites in Latin America, in this chapter we develop a business-oriented approach to explain the interrelated alternation of political regimes and models of economic development. Our core aim is to improve our understanding of the capacities and strategies developed by elites to navigate in turbulent times with a view to maintaining their privileged position in such unequal societies. This said, the approach developed in this chapter and then applied in the rest of the book is an analytical one. Normatively, we start from the assumption that the privileged influence of business elites in and on capitalist states is in fundamental tension with the key democratic principle of political equality, and empirically, we recognize that this privileged and at times predominant role has been an important cause of the reproduction of extreme levels of inequality throughout Latin America (and beyond). In general terms, we therefore tend to sympathize with attempts, movements, and models that aim at containing business power, balancing the relationship between state and markets with a view to reducing socioeconomic and political inequalities. We feel that reducing levels of inequality—whether social, regional, or ethnic—is important in helping to foster healthy democracies. Yet, in this book, we do not try to identify "appropriate" levels of business power, nor do we normatively evaluate competing models of economic development or the performance of individual governments.

The following conceptual and theoretical considerations open with a discussion of the political power of business from a tridimensional perspective: the existence and mobilization of structural, instrumental, and discursive resources to influence the political and policy process over the long run.[4] We continue the chapter with a discussion of state capture, a situation in which extreme power asymmetries endow business elites with undue or excessive influence over (parts of) the state. Finally, we address the question of economic policy changes in Latin America and their relationship with the evolution of state-business relations. In response to the dynamics of the political cycle and, most notably, to points of crisis or critical junctures, during which correlations of forces change and new ruling coalitions emerge, such economic policy changes give rise to the transformation or reconfiguration of models of economic development. As we show, the various economic models that have taken shape across Latin America and beyond—whether supporting private capital accumulation through market mechanisms or, rather, relying on state intervention to "modernize" and redistribute—have been associated with specific configurations of business power. This approach enables us to observe historical and current variations of business-state relations and gauge the ability of business elites to influence economic policy making.

BUSINESS POWER

A multidimensional approach to business power allows us to understand in a comprehensive manner the strategies adopted by economic elites to deploy their varied resources, adapting such uses in relatively stable political environments or, alternatively, when they are confronted by the challenges of mass politics and the dynamics of inclusion. In such turbulent and contested contexts, the economic models, as well as the political regimes, can be hard to stabilize and are more prone to modification. Historically, and up until the present day, such situations have proved to be not uncommon in the countries of the Central Andes.

Business elites need to protect their privileged position in the economy and society, to defend themselves politically and ideologically, and to legitimize the influence they wield over public decisions. These tasks are particularly challenging when a small, heavily privileged economic elite operates in unequal societies, in unstable polities without strong institutions, and in states with tight fiscal limitations. At its core, the influence wielded by business elites is based on economic advantage, particularly in the case of big business (domestic economic groups and multinationals). Control over material resources including financial assets and land as well as over means of production, combined with more sophisticated forms of organization (as in the case of corporations) and interest representation, helps business construct and defend the political and ideological mechanisms required to influence the political process through individual and collective action (Lindblom 1977). The power of modern business in a Latin American context characterized by deep inequalities accentuates the unevenness of the playing field that generally characterizes capitalist societies. It also tends to generate counter movements that challenge the privileged position of economic elites. Business groups therefore seek to rebalance the market-state equilibrium in their favor while reducing the power of real and perceived adversaries.

Following Lukes's (2005) classic study of power, we can conceptualize business power with more precision, distinguishing between the capacity to influence public decisions, to veto them, and to secure the adoption of policy decisions that—even if other actors do not benefit from them—are accepted with some degree of consensus. In recent decades, scholars of business power have followed this lead, identifying various sources of business power that, together, help explain the political role of economic elites at various levels: at the global level, as corporations have emerged as the most important actor in the process of globalization (Fuchs and Lederer 2007); at the national level, in particular in countries that form part of the global South (including Latin America) where international corporations operate together with national elites (Gates 2009; Fairfield 2015a; Wolff 2016; Crabtree and Durand 2017); and at the local level, particularly in the case of extractive industries (Gudynas 2015) and where organized crime operates as for-profit economic agents (Garay and Salcedo-Albarán 2012).

Systematically, scholars have identified three types of business power that loosely relate to the three dimensions discussed by Lukes. First, in terms of structural power, the control of material resources implies an indirect influence over the state through the latter's dependence on economic investment decisions. With a focus on the external dimension, this structural type of power has been extensively discussed in the politico-economic scholarship on Latin America, most notably by dependency theorists.[5] Instrumental power, second, refers to direct influence over policy making based on access to and representation within the political arena. Finally, a third expression of power is discursive (or ideological) and concerns business influence on the public debate and over society as a whole.

The first two dimensions of power—structural and instrumental—are more evident and can be understood as "hard" forms of power through which influence is exercised. The third dimension is a "soft" form of power. Its impact on political debates and policy decisions is more subtle as it operates through ideas and perceptions, but it is no less influential. As Lukes admits, not all scholars consider it important to include this third dimension of power. Some see it as an extension of instrumental power (Fairfield 2015a; Cárdenas and Robles-Rivera 2020) or, given its weight in short-term political analysis, prefer to focus just on "hard" forms of power (Gates 2009; Bernhagen 2017). We consider the discursive dimension of business power to be significant and analytically distinct from the other two dimensions, even if the three certainly interact in many ways.

STRUCTURAL POWER

Economic or structural business power is based on the control of material resources and, more specifically, on executive decisions as to whether to invest or disinvest (Culpepper 2015). Depending on their perceptions of risk (economic, monetary, or political), business elites decide to develop or to halt investment plans—that is, to expand production and open new plants or to reduce staff and move capital out of a country (capital flight) in search of more profitable markets. All such economic decisions have political consequences since growth rates, fiscal income, and employment levels depend in large part on private investment. In countries with structurally weak currencies, capital flight—as triggered by increasing political uncertainty or specific political decisions that harm investors' prospects—also has immediate effects on the exchange rate (Bailey and Chung 1995). Normally, therefore, the expectation that business might respond negatively to a specific policy shapes the decision-making process, no matter whether business representatives are actually involved in it.

Structural power, as Tasha Fairfield (2015a, 43) has put it, depends on "a credible and economically significant *disinvestment threat*," which can come in two forms (original emphasis). When the mobility of capital is high, as in the case of liquid assets, investors can threaten exit—that is, through capital flight and the search for alternative markets. In cases of fixed assets, however, business may still respond to negative political signals or high perceived risks by withholding investment. As a result, as Lindblom (1977) has argued, business generally has privileged influence over governments.

Structural power is especially pronounced in regions such as Latin America where capital is concentrated and usually in scarce supply (Schneider 2013). Lacking a strong fiscal base, Latin American governments are generally in chronic need of both credit and private direct investment, and this gives big business and foreign sources of credit strong leverage over the state. Traditionally, structural business power in the region has been vested in companies operating in the export-oriented primary sector, including in industrial agriculture and natural resource extraction. However, as internal markets grew, a process evident at least since the mid-twentieth century, a new, more dynamic, urban-based economic pole developed. The relative strength of this pole, which also includes a powerful financial sector controlled by both local and international banks, depends on the level of industrialization, the size of the domestic market, and the extent of privatization (e.g., in the area of social security). At the same time, rising external debt levels, including through internationally issued government bonds, elevate the state's dependence on the global financial markets and international credit ratings, while the increasing mobility of capital enhances the "ability to exit" for both domestic and international investors (Fairfield 2015b, 412).

Structural power in Latin America is thus primarily based on the control exercised by core business elites over two economic poles: agricultural-extractive and urban-financial. In addition, local elites in Latin America have traditionally invested most of their liquid assets abroad as a means to protect themselves from sudden political or economic swings (as well as from taxation). With globalization, capital mobility has increased hugely, facilitating the movement of assets and, thus, the risk of capital flight faced by governments when taking decisions that may be perceived as "anti-market."

In general, structural power is based on market mechanisms and thus does not require collective action. Given the concentration of capital ownership in Latin America and the usually tight (often family) ties that bind national elites together, however, this sort of market reaction can be bolstered through coordination, particularly when elites face economic and political threats or when they want to castigate governments. Changes in the exchange rate and the local stock markets can be quickly generated by a handful of powerful companies selling foreign currency or shares in domestic companies. The political signals can be loud and clear, effectively forcing politicians to make conciliatory gestures and to reassure investors. For instance, when two leaders seen as potential threats to business interests—Luiz Inácio Lula da Silva in Brazil (2002) and Ollanta Humala in Peru (2011)—became election frontrunners, Lula wrote a "Letter to the Brazilian People" and Humala presented his "Roadmap" (*hoja de ruta*), both attempting to calm investors by publicly moderating their own previous stance on economic policy. More recently, the election of union leader Pedro Castillo in Peru in 2021 led to capital flight and posed a threat to currency stability, forcing him to provide guarantees to stabilize the markets. In addition to policy promises, such guarantees typically include the appointment of "market-friendly" politicians or technocrats to the central bank and top cabinet positions.

When it comes to assessing the extent and change of structural business power, throughout this book we first look at the dependence of the state and the economy on individual sectors in which private companies or business groups play a predominant role. Key indicators in this regard concern the macroeconomic relevance of a given economic sector in terms of its share in GDP, its contribution to fiscal income, the (foreign) investment attracted, and the workforce employed; the degree of concentration or diversification of the economy and of important economic sectors; and the type of ownership (private or public, domestic or foreign). Second, in line with Bril-Mascarenhas and Maillet's (2019) distinction between the mere existence and the actual use of business power, as well as Tasha Fairfield's proposal on how to operationalize structural power (2015b), we also identify instances in which economic elites activate their structural power by issuing threats (of disinvestment, suspension of production, or capital flight) and cases in which policy makers respond to such perceived, explicit, or implicit threats.[6]

INSTRUMENTAL POWER

Business can express its interests in various ways. In line with Hirschman's (1970) classical distinction, business can either "exit" when governments are unwilling to listen to its demands or use "voice" to dialogue and negotiate. In contrast to the exit option, which is the base of structural power, voice requires political agency on the part of business elites. Instrumental power—just as is the case with discursive power—depends on the type and level of material resources possessed by business elites. But it is also crucially determined by the degree of their cohesion, coordination, and organization as well as by their formal and informal links to the political arena (Fairfield 2015a; Schneider 2004).

The three main legal political short-term mechanisms used are campaign donations, lobbying, and the use of the so-called revolving door by which private sector executives are brought into influential posts in government (Garín and Morales 2016; Maillet et al. 2016; Durand 2019). Other instruments of influence are developed by such intermediaries as think tanks, business intellectuals, and consulting firms seeking short- and long-term influence in support of pro-business policies (Robles et al. forthcoming) In addition, economic elites can also "cross the line" and engage in conflicts of interest or dubious or illegal activities such as paying bribes or dispensing favors to gain access and influence.[7] In most of Latin America, this "line" is somewhat ill-defined. All these mechanisms—whether legal, dubious, or illegal—can be pursued individually or collectively and mobilized directly or indirectly through intermediaries.

Campaign donations can be channeled formally or informally, as well as illegally. In mass democracies, the principle of one person/one vote in elections (particularly if the vote is mandatory and elections are based on proportional representation) gives considerable political power to the majority. But income inequality also provides an opportunity for the rich and powerful to influence cash-strapped parties and make their candidates dependent on large donations (OAS 2008, 68-70; PNUD 2018, 371-72). Linkages with political parties that represent business interests and pursue pro-business agendas constitute a key source of instrumental power (Fairfield 2015a).

Although rarely studied hitherto, large donors can channel money directly to would-be presidents, sometimes using labyrinthine mechanisms to disguise their origin. Political parties in Latin America face major difficulties in raising the cash needed to fight elections through their membership, so they can become precariously reliant on wealthy donors with agendas of their own. In some cases, as Casas-Zamora (2005) demonstrates, campaign contributions are seen as "insurance" by business elites to mitigate against arbitrary legislative or executive decisions. These donations are usually channeled informally, with payments made in cash and delivered directly to the candidate or party leader.

This "loaded dice" situation has led to discussions of "excessive influence" and political capture, triggering proposals to reform the electoral system by providing public funding to parties and helping with the costs of media publicity (Casas-Zamora 2005; Posada-Carbó and Malamud 2005; OAS 2008). Although regulation of party finances has become stricter, the debate in Latin America continues since big donors tend to accommodate themselves to the changes and continue to use informal donations to maintain their influence.[8] In addition, business leaders and organizations can fund media campaigns in "defence" of the market model and to promote pro-business candidates.

The Car Wash (Lava Jato) scandal in Latin America (2016-2021) provides detailed evidence of how Brazilian construction conglomerates made huge campaign contributions on a regular basis throughout Latin America and elsewhere in almost every election, covering the expenses of both candidates and parties. Contributions were made mostly through informal or illegal means (payments in cash given directly to the leaders and their campaign managers without receipts and not listed as campaign contributions) or through elaborate offshore banking transactions. Once business establishes a connection with leaders and parties, there is a "present and future debt" to use Marcelo Odebrecht's expressive phrase (Cabral and Oliveira 2017; Durand 2018b, 86). As parties and new leaders came to occupy the seats of political power, the Brazilian construction firm Odebrecht reestablished contact to remind them to honor their debt. The connection between bribes and rigged contracts in public works has been a constant in Latin America, as demonstrated by US judicial investigations on Brazil and eleven other Latin American countries (US Department of Justice 2016).

Lobbying is a widely used and well-organized form of political influence, particularly in democracies, whether in the Global North (Gilens 2012, Cagé 2018) or the South. According to Fuchs (2007), political financing has become an effective mechanism of access and influence for international corporations at the global level, which explains why corporations devote ever-larger sums to this end. Indeed, it has become an industry, as specialist firms become internationalized to serve global and local business groups in Latin America and elsewhere. The largest national conglomerates and global firms tend to hire the services of such companies, which in turn hire local lobbyists. In Latin America, even in countries where regulation has improved (like in Chile), lobbying operates mostly in the shadows (Garín and Morales 2016; Castellani 2018).

The "revolving door" is also a widely used mechanism. In this case, business elites place like-minded "experts" in government (as cabinet members, advisors, directors of regulatory agencies, and even in the tax administration) or hire them directly (Castellani 2018; Robles et al. forthcoming). Both "revolving doors" (i.e., those providing entry to government and those providing an exit for former officials into the corporate world) provide business actors with a wealth of information and contacts. They also provide business elites with an understanding of the inner workings of bureaucracies as well as with inside information on how to maximize lobbying efforts. But, given normal practices of democratic turnover, such direct influence within governments requires continuous efforts on the part of business elites. In particular, when governments change after elections, business access can be interrupted—perhaps only temporarily.

As in the case of party campaign funding, both lobbying and the revolving door, although legal, can also easily generate conflicts of interest.[9] Both mechanisms tend to operate in a grey area, a zone of opacity in which it is difficult clearly to differentiate right from wrong, legal from illegal, and the private from the public interest. Whether overstepping the line of legality or not, lobbying and the revolving door generate a transmission belt to establish a direct connection with decision makers with a view to business proposing, influencing, or vetoing legislation or other government decisions (Maillet et al. 2016; Garín and Morales 2016). Another function can be to protect corporations from executive or congressional oversight (Cave and Rowell 2015).

The possibility of being hired by a large company is an effective incentive wielded by the private sector (PNUD 2018, 386–96). Hiring relatives or friends of political leaders happens frequently in Latin America, where getting a job in a big company is a form of access to privilege. This was a practice widely used by Odebrecht in Latin America (Durand 2018b, 280). Favors in the form of gifts (artwork, personalized expensive items) or invitations (to hotels or even as guest speakers) may complement lobbying efforts. These two additional forms of influence are also part of the grey area and can easily become a form of bribery.

Economic elites can enhance the effectiveness of direct political forms of influence by using their social and professional networks. In Latin America's family-based capitalism, in which social circles of friends and relatives are an important asset, such ties are a particularly useful form of social capital (Lazzarini 2011; Bull et al. 2013; Schneider 2004; Cárdenas and Robles-Rivera 2020). Known as the "F connection" (firm, family, and friends), these networks are useful for both business (Ben-Porath 1980) and political dealings. In addition, national and international corporations frequently rely on a professional network of intermediaries (think tanks, law firms, tax consultants, public relations firms) to develop policy proposals and to lobby for them. Since high-ranking officials tend to be recruited from the elites, such networks facilitate access and influence through personal contacts (PNUD 2018).

Cohesion or unity is a key variable in the deployment of instrumental business power, particularly at critical junctures (Fairfield 2015a). Intra-class cohesion and coordination requires leadership and the ability to bring together political factions and business segments of different sizes, sectors, and regions, while avoiding the divisive strategies used by opposing coalitions and governments. Traditionally, this ability to come together was achieved informally through networks. Leading families in control of business groups call private meetings either to access and coordinate with top-level government officials—a common phenomenon in Latin America (known in the Dominican Republic as the *acuerdo de aposentos*)—or to discuss strategies to deal with opposing forces and governments deemed hostile.

Class unity can also be achieved through encompassing business associations, an organizational development of the late twentieth century (Durand and Silva 1998; Schneider 2004). Although there are different levels of interest aggregation (in terms of economic sectors or territorial subdivisions), it is the formation of peak business organizations, bringing together sectoral or regional associations, that makes the difference. These, however, seldom include medium- and small-sized enterprises, which tend to follow different organizational paths and lack the deep pockets of larger business associations. Smaller companies, usually, have less ability to maintain strong sectoral representation, as the Mexican case shows (Shadlen 2000), and their base tends to be diverse. Just as with structural power, therefore, the distribution of instrumental power disproportionally favors larger corporate interests (economic groups and multinationals).

The formal representation of the business sector is basically left to big business and the major associations that speak in the name of the private sector as a whole. Size matters, as well as the social origin of entrepreneurs. Even in cases where some smaller businesses succeed and their directors eventually become millionaires, the social cleavages between the "emerging" *cholo* elites, as they are called in the Andean region, and the traditional elites of European origin, who live and travel in different circles, adds another layer of class separation.[10]

Unity is not only the result of the ability to garner forces to increase pressure on government or support a ruling coalition. It can be developed if business can overcome the divides that separate economic activities (for example, the "sectoral clash" between exporters and industrialists in the 1960s and 1970s) and those between regions (elites from the capital versus those from outside), not to mention the effects of political factionalism. In cases of sectoral clash, economic policy decisions may benefit some business interests and sectors while hurting others. The same can be the case in regions that are favored or disfavored. This cleavage is structural in that it corresponds to different sets of interests.

Unity requires leadership and organizational support to be effective, but most of all it needs causes to rally around. Coming together is easier when there are common problems or a generalized perception of danger, when there are threats from "above" or "below," as O'Donnell (1973) argued in his study on the emergence of bureaucratic-authoritarian regimes in South America. Business unites when faced by social conflicts that can paralyze the economy (general strikes, roadblocks, "sacrifice marches," and the like) or when insurgents attack business elites directly (bombing installations, kidnapping businesspeople, occupying business premises, etc.). Business leaders and organizations thus coordinate to create the conditions to safeguard property and protect owners and executives. Threats "from above" can be generated by nationalist or socialist governments that issue policies that support labor organization and demands, increase taxation, or expropriate or confiscate private property.

Business unity—whether activated by popular challenges from below, by political threats from above, or by a combination of the two—is thus more likely to develop in defense of general class objectives (Durand and Silva 1998; Fairfield 2015a, 37–38; Fazekas and Tóth 2016, 323). It can come about in defense of a market-oriented model of economic development or a pro-business government, or in opposition to a government or a development model that is perceived as harmful to business interests. Frequently, however, cleavages as well as competing interests tend to prevent higher forms of cohesion from taking root within a given business community.

In sum, this theoretical and conceptual discussion provides us with two approaches to empirically assessing instrumental business power. On the one hand, we will look at evidence for each of the three mechanisms of direct business influence—that is, business donations to parties, politicians, and electoral campaigns; at qualitative information on lobbying efforts and successes; and at individuals that directly link the business world and the political arena in line with the revolving door (here, the most important information concerns the representation of businesspeople or like-minded technocrats within cabinets and regulatory agencies). On the other hand, we analyze the organization of the business community. By studying the evolving structure and agency of business associations in the three Central Andean countries, we can assess the unity/cohesion or fragmentation/division of business elites and analyze the strategies and practices of key business associations when it comes to actually influencing political debates and decisions.

DISCURSIVE POWER

The ideological dimension allows us to produce a comprehensive view of the role and agency of business elites in capitalist societies. In contrast to structural and instrumental power, discursive power is not about political influence in a narrow sense but, rather, about the ability of economic elites to shape social values, public discourses, and public opinion—including what Gramsci called the "common sense"—in such ways as to create a climate of acceptance and, indeed, support for their interests and agenda (Durand 2019; Fuchs 2007). Discursive power, thus, includes the capacity to shape broader understandings about the role of private business, "entrepreneurship," and "the market," understandings about appropriate and inappropriate forms of state regulation (Kwak 2014), as well as the ideological transformation of the role of corporations (e.g., in terms of "social responsibility") that enables them to play "a new political role" (Scherer and Palazzo 2011). Generally speaking, both national and international corporations as well as wealthy individuals and families all seek to develop discourses that legitimize their privilege and power and project a positive image to society. This has become increasingly important in more democratic systems in which governments rely on public support and in which the political allies of business groups need to compete electorally with forces that represent other, much more numerous social groups. Several features characterize and shape business's discursive power in Latin America and beyond.

First, whether traditional and oligarchic or more modern and entrepreneurial, pro-business conceptions on how to organize the economy, government, and society are generally based on the idea of the preeminence of private property, concentrated largely in the hands of local and foreign elites. More specifically, corporations and business associations generate and disseminate ideas about the key role they play in the overall process of "development," "modernization," or even "civilization." They project themselves as valuable elites that generate wealth, thus justifying proper compensation for their efforts, as is demonstrated by studies of elite perceptions and attitudes (see Robles et al. forthoming). They are the "indispensable" agents of those strategic economic sectors that contribute most to GDP, employment, and again, to "development" or "modernization." In few sectors is this more important than in the export-oriented primary sector, which occupies a central position in most Latin American economies. Property owners and their organizations have developed a set of concepts (that justify legal provisions) designed to legitimize access to natural resources (land and water), a process initiated in a violent and arbitrary manner at the time of the conquest of Latin America (Mattei and Nader 2013). Such ideas and concepts, initially spread by empires and privateers to justify indigenous dispossession, evolved over time as old and new forms of natural resource-based accumulation developed in the region. Traditionally, hacienda and plantation owners as well as foreign companies portrayed themselves as "civilizers," as agents of modernization and technological progress in a "backward" part of the world, especially where they tended to operate in a poor hinterland with the wealth concentrated in cities. This sort of pro-extractivist discourse has assumed a more comprehensive form since the beginning of the new millennium as "a way of understanding development and nature" to quote Gudynas (2015). Corporations in charge of large investment projects are presented as socially compatible and environmentally responsible, good corporate citizens (Portocarrero and Sanborn 2006).

Second, this notion of the modernizing role of private business is also based on the postcolonial shape assumed by specific Latin American business elites. Given the predominance of investors of European and North American origin in the upper strata of most Latin American societies, local and international elites share a Eurocentric view about the right to rule, based on ideas of cultural superiority—a view that resonates with public sentiments in significant parts of the population (Quijano 2000). Such views have tended to be reinforced by patterns of migration from a variety of European states and the "fusion" of elites when those migrants who enjoyed economic success intermingle with leading local families.

Third, with the spread of economic globalization, modern global corporations have become models for inspiring organizational and discursive changes within the firm and within Latin American economic conglomerates. Latin American executives have assimilated this model, many having received training in new business practice through international MBAs and other forms of foreign study. They seek to replicate international "best practice" (benchmarking) by modernizing their conglomerates and projecting themselves to the international markets, often with the help of consulting companies.

The consolidation of neoliberalism as the dominant economic model in Latin America and its resilience (Madariaga 2020) have underpinned such notions as the central role of entrepreneurs as producers of wealth and employment opportunities and have played a role in rejecting ideas of state intervention in development and redistribution. These views were adopted by national elites in the 1980s as the economic policy of choice, and they have been reinforced over the following decades (López 2019). Unsurprisingly, the rejection of statism and the promotion of private enterprise proved attractive to local elites as they faced interventionist regimes in the 1960s and 1970s, a model that ended in severe economic dislocations and in some cases even hyperinflationary crises. Such views were only enhanced by episodes of expropriation and confiscation of private property and the promotion of powerful state-owned enterprises (Conaghan and Malloy 1994, 70-71).

When it comes to the mechanisms through which business elites shape the public discourse, private media play a crucial role (Hughes and Prado 2011). Private media owners themselves represent economic interests and are often closely linked with other business sectors. A case in point are private media conglomerates that originated from ownership of national newspapers, complemented by control over radio and television networks. Leading families control these conglomerates, which include the likes of Clarín in Argentina, O Globo in Brazil, El Mercurio in Chile, and El Comercio in Peru (Bercerra and Mastrini 2017). In turn, corporations rely on these media conglomerates for advertising, positive coverage of business news, and more generally for presenting them as healthy, honest, and innovative organizations. It is worth mentioning that the richest corporations can buy and establish media outlets, an increasingly common practice. Politically, media organizations have become a de facto power to the point that this has generated discussion of "media capture" (Schiffrin 2017). In addition, business elites also influence social values and public discourses through their influence over education systems, tertiary education in particular. Furthermore, the above-mentioned vehicles of instrumental power are also used to promote general ideas and concepts that support the pro-business agenda and pro-market candidates.

This discursive power not only justifies privilege and influence—the right to affluence—but also encourages non-coercive forms of control or domination over society as a whole. In this line of thinking, Gramsci (1980) convincingly argued that capitalists exercise cultural/ethical power within civil society in order to achieve hegemony. This sort of approach has been adopted in Latin America by (neo-)Marxist scholars to explain patterns of class domination in the neoliberal era that reflect an ideological offensive in a context of the failure of past development projects (Portantiero 1999; Aricó 2015).

As we go on to show, the concept of state capture helps explain in more specific terms the attempts of business elites to establish hegemony in Latin America, basing this on the historical-structural conditions that facilitate business influence over the state and the political instruments used to that end. Not surprisingly, the renovated ideological global corporate discourse, articulated by successful business owners and managers, is capable of leading prominent businessmen to positions of power through electoral victories. Eminent among them have been Gonzalo ("Goni") Sánchez de Lozada in Bolivia (elected in 1993 and again in 2002), Vicente Fox in Mexico (2000), Mauricio Macri in Argentina (2015), Sebastián Piñera in Chile (2010 and again in 2018), and Pedro Pablo Kuczynski in Peru (2016) (Nercesian 2020). A recent case worth mentioning is Guillermo Lasso, a prominent banker, who came to power in Ecuador in 2021 (Macaroff forthcoming).

In a counterintuitive way, business's discursive power is therefore also the product of democratization. As democracy grants to all actors—however unequal their resource endowment—formally equal chances to participate in shaping public and political debates, it enables ideological offensives and electoral campaign drives by privileged minority groups. The result is a new type of "battle of ideas" that takes place on a notably uneven playing field.

When it comes to empirically assessing business power and influence, the discursive dimension is certainly the most difficult one to measure (Fairfield 2015a, 52). In this book, we use a threefold strategy to get a sense of the extent and change of discursive business power across the three Central Andean cases. First, we analyze the discursive strategies employed by business leaders and representatives in order to shape public opinion and political debates. Second, we look at the structure and development of the media sector as the key venue of discursive business power. Third and finally, we rely on existing literature to assess the overall development of public discourses and political debates over time in order to identify the (hegemonic or contested) role of pro-business ideas, concepts and worldviews.

STATE CAPTURE

While the concept of business power helps us identify and assess the ways in which economic elites exercise privileged influence over state policies and society more generally, the notion of state capture turns our attention to the point at which privileged influence becomes effective control. State capture theory, therefore, contributes to the understanding of how effective (or limited) the mobilization of these tridimensional powers can be at the specific or more general level. At the specific level, it helps elucidate the political conditions in which the "normal" privileges of economic elites, in terms of political access outlined above, turn into "undue" influence (to buy laws) and "excessive" influence (to dictate laws) (Hellman and Kaufmann 2001). At the general or societal level, the theory also suggests that economic elites can generate conditions under which business not only shapes but effectively determines (specific segments of) the political debate and public discourse in general. This latter overall projection of business power over the political agenda can be conceptualized as "political capture" (Crabtree and Durand 2017, 12).[11]

The situations that favor business power in enabling state or political capture relate to models of economic development in which market forces prevail. Market-oriented development models (as we shall see later when we recapitulate the economic-political evolution of Latin America over the last one hundred years) can coexist with different types of political regimes, either authoritarian or democratic. Contemporary state capture theory is particularly aimed at understanding the inner workings of (at least formally established) democracies. The liberalization of markets took place at a time when elected governments multiplied globally, during the so-called third wave of democratization between the late 1970s and the early 1990s (Huntington 1991). As Domínguez (1998) argues for the case of Latin America, the expansion of economic and political liberties paved the way for a new era of "market democracies" and governance that combined these two liberal principles, in theory virtuous and self-reinforcing.

In analyzing the forms of influence that de facto lead to control over (specific) policy decisions by particular economic actors, state capture theory questions the positive combination of these two liberal assumptions. It focuses on power rather than governance and suggests that the former prevails, within certain limits, over the latter. It also highlights the presence of oligarchic modes of governance in the context of nominally democratic regimes. In their analysis of state capture in Latin America, both Cañete (2018) and Cortés and Itriago (2018) claim that unequal access expressed in elite privileges generates *democracias capturadas*, or captured democracies. Similar arguments have been made by political scientists who, emphasizing the predominance of oligarchic principles in modern democracies in Latin America, have argued the need for a realistic analysis of liberalism in order to "demystify" democracy (Foweraker 2018). By the late

2010s, the discussion of state capture and its effects on democracy became ever more salient. As Cameron (2021) has argued, complementing Foweraker's theory, Latin America has seen "the return of oligarchy"; the "left turn," initiated by Venezuela in 1998, appeared by around 2016 to be giving way to the return to business-led, oligarchical polities, notably with Jair Bolsonaro in Brazil, Mauricio Macri in Argentina, and both Moreno and Lasso in Ecuador.

State capture theory, initially developed in the 1970s and 1980s, was based on studies of business influence over regulatory bodies (Stigler 1971). The analysis of "regulatory capture" was followed by studies of "rent-seeking behavior" by big industries. Some otherwise pro-market scholars emphasized the negative consequences of business influence over the state in stifling competition and leading to policies benefiting particular industries or groups. Studies on rent-seeking were applied to the critical analysis of the "populist" period in Latin America, characterized by state interventionism and protection of local industries. Hernando de Soto labeled these policies "mercantilist," arguing that big business benefited from legal protections that discriminated against informal businesses, thus criticizing the interventionist model of economic development (De Soto 1986).

Hellman and Kaufmann, who reintroduced the discussion of state capture at the beginning of the twenty-first century to explain "deviations" of market democracies in Eastern Europe and the countries of the former Soviet Union, defined state capture as being the result of "the efforts of firms to shape the laws, policies, and regulations of the state to their own advantage by providing illicit private gains to public officials" (2001, 2). These authors developed this more specific strand of state capture theory with strong institutional backing from the International Monetary Fund (IMF) and the World Bank. The assumption was that the oligarchies that emerged in the postcommunist world used their material power to bribe officials in order to "buy" laws, a practice deemed as a failure of market reforms (Manzetti 2009). Corruption in business-state relations was their main concern.

State capture here expresses the combination of two types of business power (structural and instrumental) and two forms of elite control (to obtain favorable legislation generating particular benefits and to veto or block reforms), which together lead to poor governance: "In particular, we emphasize the importance of mechanisms through which firms seek to shape decisions taken by the state to gain specific advantages, often through the imposition of anticompetitive barriers that generate highly concentrated gains to selected powerful firms at a significant social cost. Because such firms use their influence to block any policy reforms that might eliminate these advantages, state capture has become not merely a *symptom* but also a *fundamental cause* of poor governance" (Hellman and Kaufmann 2001, 2–3; original emphasis).

Although firms of different sizes can use bribes to gain influence over porous states (Hellman and Kaufmann 2001, 6), other scholars identify big business (or the "oligarchy") as the main state captor in Russia and Central Europe (Yakolev 2006; Innes 2014) to the point that it is possible to refer to it as "oligarchic state capture" (Marandici 2017). Studies conducted in Latin America reached similar conclusions, particularly with a view to the 1990s privatization frenzy. In the two regions, surveys and rankings provided empirical evidence of how strong state capture was on a case-by-case basis (Banco Mundial and Vice Presidencia de la República de Colombia 2002). The idea of variations or degrees of state capture, initially arising from differences identified in survey data, later led to the discussion of types of state capture, ranging from "moderate" to "extreme" (Omelyanshuk 2001; Durand 2010b).

Another strand of state capture theory broadened the focus by discussing legal forms of undue or excessive political influence achieved through the three mechanisms of instrumental business power discussed above: the funding of election campaigns, lobbying, and the use of the revolving door. The effects of such influence can be further exacerbated when illegal methods (or corruption) are considered, and the dividing line between legal and illegal forms of influence can be hard to determine with precision. A better understanding of these forms of elite influence requires an understanding of history that takes fully into account the structures and processes emerging at particular times and in specific contexts (García Laguardia 2001; Omelyanshuk 2001; Innes 2014; Fuentes Knight 2016). These studies emphasize the historical-structural factors in both Central Europe and Latin America that generated the conditions for this type of business control over the state to grow. Three main factors can be identified. The first one refers to a high concentration of power in the hands of corporations expressed in the formation of oligopolies in key economic sectors, a concentration of resources that accentuates historical and present inequalities.[12] Second, state capture is facilitated by a weak and easily penetrable state and party system (especially when exacerbated by corruption) in which decision making tends to be concentrated in the hands of the executive and a political class that colludes with business interests. The third factor includes the weakening of labor unions and small business associations as well as other civil society organizations that involve collective action on the part of non-elite groups. This last condition may arise, for instance, because of the demobilizing effects of neoliberal reforms on organized labor, including more precarious forms of employment and the growth of the informal sector (Kurtz 2004; Wolff 2020b).

These general conditions, varying significantly from one country to another (but quite strong in those of the Central Andes), were also present at the time of the traditional Latin American oligarchies—that is, before the advent of mass politics. In the period that followed Independence, these inequalities continued unscathed until the first decades of the twentieth century, with power exercised through elite families directly managing the state or doing so through military leaders. There was a return to rather similar conditions in the post-populist/interventionist periods, with the introduction (from the 1980s onward) of pro-market policies with modern corporate elites assuming some of the characteristics of the old oligarchy and, in some cases, business leaders showing they could win campaigns to achieve power.

These changing patterns (the oscillation between market and state-oriented economic models that is typical of Latin America) reveal periods or moments of resistance to corporate state capture. Preferential access that benefits private interests stimulates countermovements generating political efforts to limit or control it. These efforts can lead to political and economic change. Just as the state has traditionally been "captured" by traditional oligarchies, or recaptured by modern and better-organized business groups, it can also be "liberated" by new ruling coalitions that emphasize state autonomy, stronger regulation, and redistributive policies (Blofield 2011a, 59). This obliges economic elites to adapt their political game to new and more challenging circumstances. In sum, as the political cycles of the region unfolded and as different economic models emerged, business elites learned how to use their tridimensional powers, adapting them to more difficult times, and testing their mettle in responding to such challenges.

MODELS OF ECONOMIC DEVELOPMENT, CRITICAL JUNCTURES, AND VARIATIONS IN BUSINESS-STATE RELATIONS IN LATIN AMERICA

Capitalist economies, whether sustained by authoritarian or democratic governments, are arrangements that, in the terminology of the French regulation school, combine a specific regime of accumulation and a corresponding mode of regulation (Lipietz 1987). Such arrangements are sustained by ruling coalitions. According to the type of political regime and the model of economic development, these coalitions express variations of business-state relations but also elite-labor relations and state-society relations in a broader sense. At this abstract level, it is useful roughly to distinguish between two overarching types of economic development model. In *market-oriented* models, capital accumulation or economic development is mainly left to private business actors that compete on "the market" (both domestically and internationally); state regulation of the economy, here, is primarily aimed at enabling private initiative and competition while offering some protection to the consumer. In *state-centered* models, the state assumes a much more important role in economic matters; this role includes both state intervention in the private economy (through regulation and/or redistribution) and the direct participation of the public sector in the production of goods and services (through state-owned companies).

The topic of changes in economic policies, models, and structures has been the subject of numerous and cumulative comparative studies on the political economy of Latin America and at the subregional level (South America, the Caribbean, and Central America).[13] As has been extensively documented throughout these studies, changes in the economic development model are usually closely related to changes in the political regime, or at least to significant modifications in power relations and ruling coalitions.[14] When it comes to studying periods of politico-economic change, the concept of critical junctures offers a useful tool. As defined by Collier and Collier in their landmark study *Shaping the Political Arena*, a critical juncture is a "period of significant change, which typically occurs in distinct ways in different countries (or in other units of analysis) and which is hypothesized to produce distinct legacies" (Collier and Collier 2020, 29). This definition includes two key elements.

First, critical junctures are "moments of relative structural indeterminism" (Mahoney 2001, 7) or "brief phases of institutional flux" (Capoccia and Kelemen 2007, 341), during which the future trajectory of a country or any other unit is set. In our case, this concerns moments of crisis of an established politico-economic configuration during which "societies" debate and decide about the questions of whether and how to adjust or transform a given model of economic development. Scholars agree that, at such junctures, economic elites (national and multinational) play a key role as supporters or opponents of changes in both the political regime and the development model. For them, the stakes are high with respect to their material interest and privileged position in society.[15]

Second, while the specific outcome that emerges from such a period of contingency is not predetermined (with continuity also being a potential outcome), what makes such junctures critical is that they produce enduring legacies. The decisions taken at a critical juncture "put countries (or other units) onto paths of development . . . that cannot be easily broken or reversed" (Mahoney 2001, 7), as they "close off alternative options and lead to the establishment of institutions that generate self-reinforcing path-dependent processes" (Capoccia and Kelemen 2007, 341). Yet, such legacies are certainly not set in stone. In the case of models of economic development (and political regimes), business elites—and the question whether they form part of viable ruling coalitions—play a key role for the consolidation of a given trajectory.

Based on a long-term view covering Latin American societies over the last one hundred years or so, we can identify patterns of change in the economic development models that define the role of business elites in the economy, their relationship with the state, and the way they participate in ruling coalitions. Four models of economic development stand out: the traditional oligarchic liberal model, the model of import substitution industrialization (ISI), the neoliberal model, and the post-neoliberal model.[16] Given that the first and the third models emphasize private capital accumulation with little state regulation, while the second and fourth provide for a much more active role of the state in the regulation of the market and the process of economic development, the historical sequence follows a pendular movement. In terms of ruling coalitions, this alternation between a market-oriented and a state-oriented development model was accompanied by shifts between elite-centered regimes and others in which emerging or marginalized social sectors were at least partially incorporated (Collier and Collier 2002; Silva and Rossi 2018). The pendular movement suggests that economic elites frequently have been capable of nurturing pro-business policies and development models, effectively mobilizing their tridimensional powers and, at times, even capturing the state. Yet, obviously, they have also faced challenges to their power and, at times, have had to adjust to development models that were not of their choosing. Overall, however, with the partial exception of Cuba, changes in the development model across Latin America have so far not seriously touched the underlying conception of development, either in terms of its overall orientation of capitalist development, its more particular extractivist logic, or its embeddedness in a general ideology of modernization.[17]

The traditional oligarchic liberal model was predominant after Independence in the early nineteenth century. Throughout Latin America, it was based on a small elite initially led by landowners (of haciendas, plantations, *fincas*, *estancias*, etc.) of aristocratic and colonial origin, privileged families who concentrated economic wealth and political power. This core national elite associated itself with foreign-owned, export-oriented companies, banks, and commercial houses as the region's economies opened and became an important source of raw materials during the second industrial revolution and as these elites became significant consumers of imported goods, most notably between the 1880s and 1920s. National elites, with the support of foreign counterparts and external allies, captured the state directly or indirectly in a "natural way." It was supposed to be in the order of things that they be leaders of the economy and society. Two governmental options developed. Either oligarchs directly occupied key positions of state power, operating in a political system characterized by a limited franchise, or they ruled indirectly, thanks to their structural power and direct influence over authoritarian governments.

This oligarchic model was first overturned in Mexico by the revolution (1910-1917), which set a trend that gained traction elsewhere between the 1930s and 1960s. At the heart of this challenge to oligarchic elite power and state capture was a critical juncture produced by changes in the social structure and, in particular, by the emergence of a working class throughout the region (though with different intensities and at different speeds). The result was a period of contested incorporation of this new social group (Collier and Collier 2002). In different shapes and forms, new coalitions emerged based on popular movements, inspired by social justice, nationalism, and anti-oligarchic sentiments. Where these coalitions took control of government, business-state relations were redefined. In these changing circumstances (strongly manifested in the 1950s and 1960s), state powers developed as governments emphasized national sovereignty (often at the expense of foreign companies), and in some cases agrarian reforms, with the support of politically activated and previously excluded popular sectors. In this context, the old economic model supported by latifundista ruling families and company towns, which was heavily outward-oriented, was replaced by a statist, developmentalist one aimed at promoting import substitution industrialization (ISI).

In response to the challenge to the ruling oligarchy, elites tried to defend the old liberal regime, resisting the pressures to "modernize." They remained attached to a model of commodity exports that discouraged industrialization and the growth of domestic markets. In the Central Andes, this was a fairly protracted process, and such oligarchies remained entrenched until the 1950s and, in some cases, well into the 1960s. When this development model inherited from the early liberal period was gradually replaced by more state-centered, developmentalist policies, emerging industrial and commercial elites—alongside a new generation of multinationals—were forced to negotiate with or oppose the new model of economic development. Different business segments had to decide whether to invest or disinvest, to confront or negotiate, searching meanwhile for the opportunity to reverse the trend, recover political influence, and restore a pro-business model of economic development. In these conditions, industrialists—depending on their negotiating abilities, level of cohesion, and the degree of governmental tolerance—were able to participate in the new model of economic development, but mostly in conditions of subordination to the new political class (Conaghan and Malloy 1994). Within these shifting models of economic development, and depending on political configurations, business-state relations took on a new character. Local circumstances defined how distant or close the relationship was between economic elites and the political class and the extent to which business influence could be effectively exercised.

In terms of business elites, the second half of the twentieth century saw economic power shift to family-owned business groups (some run by executives) and international companies. These, in addition to natural resources, also invested in manufacturing, banking, and services. Across the board, the new economic elites exercised strong influence on both authoritarian and more democratic governments, to the point of managing to capture the state when market-oriented economic models prevailed.

In the 1970s, the ISI model entered into crisis in most countries of the region and openly collapsed during the debt crisis of the 1980s. As the state weakened and public and private investment dried up, populations frequently suffered from unusually high levels of inflation and falling real wages. At the same time, business elites had to accommodate themselves to the new political circumstances brought about by the "third wave of democratization" (Huntington 1991; O'Donnell and Schmitter 1986). At this critical juncture, the market- and outward-oriented neoliberal model, sustained by new modern economic elites and external agents, spread throughout most of the region, reinforcing business power. In some cases, as we have seen, the modern business class was even able to run presidential candidates and win (Barndt 2014; Nercesian 2020).

Generally speaking, however, business elites' accommodation with democracy remained an uneasy one given the risks associated with universal elections in contexts of extreme social inequality. This risk became manifest in the early 2000s, as a new critical juncture was ushered in by a wave of anti-neoliberal mass protests that culminated in the election of a series of leftist governments. This "pink tide," once again, led to a (re-)turn to more statist and redistributionist agendas. These agendas have been dubbed "post-neoliberal," as they combined a gradual, diverse, and yet significant turning away from neoliberal recipes.[18] This "post-neoliberal" development model has also been called "neo-extractivist," as it was based on the continued, if not intensified, exploitation of natural resources in the context of a global commodity boom (Burchardt and Dietz 2014; Gudynas 2015; Svampa 2019). The challenge to business interests and power associated with the "pink tide" has led to varying responses on the part of economic elites, ranging from adaptation to outright authoritarian strategies (Luna and Rovira Kaltwasser 2014).

By the end of the 2010s, as the export boom (2003–2014) petered out and governability problems arose, these "pink tide" countries themselves entered into crisis. In most countries, economic elites eventually proved themselves capable of regaining protagonism, building alliances with other social and political forces, and at least partially, reversing the post-neoliberal trend from the mid-2010s onward. Several "pink tide" countries reverted to the neoliberal model, notably Brazil and Ecuador, temporarily also Argentina and Bolivia. However, the reversal was neither complete nor uniform. And even in cases that saw the turn to an explicitly pro-market ruling coalition, the defeated social and political forces continued to mobilize and participate in the political process, engendering an ongoing struggle over the future shape of the economic model. This is an indication that business elites have had difficulties in institutionalizing pro-business regimes and stabilizing political conditions with a new social pact. The result, throughout the region, has been a context of considerable instability.

The movements between different economic development models tend to take place during critical junctures. Economic development models change as a consequence of structural crises, which combine intrinsic dynamics (e.g., the exhaustion of the ISI model), socio-structural changes that undermine a given ruling coalition (e.g., the emergence of a working class), and external shocks and changes in the global context (as in the case of the 1980s debt crisis). As a consequence, established ruling coalitions weaken, as newly emerging or previously marginalized actors demand voice. In these "moments of relative structural indeterminism" (Mahoney 2001, 7), key actors—with elite groups usually playing a crucial role—use their structural, instrumental, and discursive power as well as their connections (both domestic and external) to support or oppose, to negotiate or accommodate themselves to changing circumstances, and depending on the outcome, to activate their structural power in deciding whether to invest or not.

Table 1.1 presents a list of key characteristics that typify the different models of economic development, indicating variations in the forms of government, the nature of ruling coalitions, their options in terms of popular sector inclusion (or exclusion), their ideological leanings, their connections with external agencies, and the type of firms (private and non-private) concerned. Transitions from one economic model to another are, therefore, also accompanied by the formation of a new political coalition, with business elites and associations playing varying roles (Schneider 2004). Depending on the case in point, a more or less well-defined pattern of political inclusion and exclusion of various social classes develops (Collier and Collier 2002). At times, the military becomes a key component of the ruling coalition, as witnessed by the conservative and repressive dictatorships of the Southern Cone studied by O'Donnell (1973) in the late 1960s and early 1970s.[19]

In economic terms, the development models define access to resources and the types of firms (private/non-private) that receive privileged treatment in the process of capital accumulation. In much of Latin America, priority has been given in recent decades to the production of commodities, often in areas populated by indigenous peoples. Policy defines forms of inclusion or exclusion, thus affecting income and economic opportunities for underprivileged social groups. Model type can determine access to a basket of natural resources: gas, oil, hydroelectric energy, mining, fishing, forestry, and agriculture. Private access to land or territory as well as decisions regarding infrastructure such as roads and dams can have a major impact on the lives of communities and indigenous peoples (Gudynas 2015). This is a particularly significant issue in countries such as those of Central America and the Andes with large indigenous populations and where good, arable land is in scarce supply.

Statist models base their power on the ability of the state to gain relative autonomy from private business. A key strategy in the region has been to expropriate or renegotiate access to natural resources, particularly gas and oil. Also, state-centered models tend to rely on publicly owned enterprises at the expense of private ones. By contrast, market-oriented models favor private property and the concentration of land and concessions in the hands of local and international corporations. State-centered models typically use the state's bargaining and regulatory powers to place limits on private ownership and develop policies to protect communal lands, national parks, or public land.

A ruling coalition—whatever its preferred model of development—seeks political support not only domestically but internationally. Each economic model has different sources of international support (see Table 1.1), often involving participation in schemes of regional cooperation (Quiliconi and Rivera 2022). In the 1960s the Economic Commission for Latin America and the Caribbean (ECLAC) and Instituto Latinoamericano de Planificación Económica y Social (ILPES), both located in Santiago de Chile, provided the intellectual muscle and training capacity to promote the statist model of economic development. As part of its industrialization programs, ECLAC backed subregional integration through such mechanisms as the Andean Pact (Comunidad Andina de Naciones, CAN) and the Central American Common Market. ECLAC, which played a central role in the development of dependency theory, sought to steer Latin America away from relying on the United States for capital and markets by developing local industries and nationalizing foreign-owned firms to create state monopolies in "strategic" sectors of the economy.

Those countries that identified with the "pink tide" at the beginning of the new millennium also sought to build supranational ties. The Alianza Bolivariana para los Pueblos de Nuestra América (ALBA), led by Venezuela, sought to establish regional institutions and its own regional market. Mercosur, the trading bloc founded in the Southern Cone by Brazil, Argentina, Paraguay, and Uruguay in the context of the neoliberal model, developed similar integration objectives. In parallel, the governments leading the "pink tide" formed the Community of Latin American and Caribbean States (CELAC) and the Union of South American Nations (UNASUR) to offset US influence over the region. In the case of Cuba after 1959, the Soviet Union and the Warsaw Pact countries became the main sources of international support and trade after the imposition of the 1962 US embargo. In the new millennium, many Latin American states have sought to develop ties with China. While deepening of economic and, in part, also polit-

TABLE 1.1. MODELS OF ECONOMIC DEVELOPMENT: MAIN ATTRIBUTES

Economic Model	Key Business Actors	Role of the State	Regime Type	Ruling Coalition	Popular Incorporation	International Support
Early Liberal (oligarchic)	Latifundia, company towns	Low/guardian state	Elitist democratic or authoritarian	Landed elites, company towns, upper middle class, military	Low (exclusion)	United Kingdom/USA, pan-Americanism
Import Substitution Industrialization (ISI)	Industries, state-owned enterprises (SOE)	Moderate to high	Populist democratic or authoritarian populist	Middle class, industrialists, labor (and peasant) unions	Moderate (controlled inclusion)	ECLAC, Instituto Latinoamericano de Planificación Económica y Social (ILPES)
Neoliberal	Business groups, international capital	Low	Authoritarian or democratic liberal	Business groups, international capital, upper middle class, emprendedores	Dispersion, low to moderate (electoral inclusion)	US-led neoliberal internationallism, IMF, World Bank, OECD
Post-neoliberal	SOE, international capital with renegotiated contracts	Moderate to high	Democratic, strong executive	Middle and popular classes, accommodating business groups	Moderate to high	Bolivarianism, ALBA, UNASUR, CELAC
Socialist Central Planning	SOE, international capital in some sectors	Very high	One-party system, centralized planning	Nomenklatura, popular classes	Highly controlled incorporation	USSR

ical relations with China was not limited to "pink tide" governments, these in particular used increasing trade with China, as well as investment, loans, and aid, as means to counterbalance the traditional dependence on the United States (Stallings 2020, 39–64; Wise 2020).

In similar fashion, pro-market models of accumulation involve support from outside the region. Historically, alliances with Western powers, the United States in particular, have been important in this regard, as has been support from the Organization of American States (OAS) and international financial organizations such as the IMF and the World Bank. More recently, as an extension of this alliance, market-oriented governments have sought support from the Organization for Economic Cooperation and Development (OECD), with several countries now accepted as members (Mexico, Chile, Colombia) and others hoping to be accepted (such as Peru and Brazil). The free-market model of economic development is also underpinned by free trade agreements (FTAs) and legislation to safeguard foreign investment and to discourage regression toward statism. Governments in such schemes become rule takers. Governments guided by state-oriented models change the rules as well, attempting to become rule makers.

CONCLUSIONS

Business-state relations in Latin America can be best observed analyzing the political role played by economic elites (both national and foreign) as they display their tridimensional powers (structural, instrumental, and discursive) to influence political decision making or even capture (at least parts of) the state. Throughout the history of Latin America, business elites have been generally quite successful in this regard, as the continuities in the extreme social inequalities that characterize the region to this date would seem to demonstrate. Still, business power has also frequently encountered significant challenges that went far beyond the inevitable disruptions caused by the normal succession of one government to another. As capitalist development advanced in Latin America, transforming the region's social and economic structures, new popular-sector organizations, social movements, and mass-based parties emerged, giving rise to demands for redistribution and for inclusion of the poor. As a result, economic elites have had to adapt and respond to changing correlations of forces, shifting models of economic development, and changing political regimes.

The study of the change of economic models across time highlights the fluctuations in business-state relations in ways that tend to repeat themselves. When the neoliberal development model was established in the 1980s (a transition that took place in almost the whole region with the exception of socialist Cuba), elites found difficulty in implementing the sound policies and establishing the solid institutions necessary to generate governability, overcome deep socioeconomic inequalities, and build consensus. Then, with the incipient "pink tide," established elites faced increasing difficulties in sustaining the neoliberal model and maintaining sufficient influence to exercise long-term control of the political process. With few exceptions to the rule, the long-term course of changes in the economic development model in Latin America reveals patterns of deep-rooted instability where neither policies nor institutions can grow and put down strong roots.[20] This was referred to by Conaghan and Malloy (1994, 14) as a question of "unsettled statecraft" as new market democracies struggled to find a firm footing in the early 1990s in Bolivia,

Ecuador, and Peru. Until today, this "unsettledness" expresses itself in the failure to stabilize a coherent model of economic development, including a stable ruling coalition and a set of institutions needed to sustain it. With a view to business elites, the very notion of "unsettledness" is indicative of the difficulties in exercising hegemony in the Gramscian sense of the word—that is, an inability to move beyond mere influence and domination over state and society and to develop more effective and lasting forms of political capture based on sustained discursive power. At the same time, and notwithstanding the challenges to business power under the governments of Evo Morales in Bolivia (2006-2019) and Rafael Correa in Ecuador (2007-2017), popular movements have so far similarly proved unable to establish an alternative and durable hegemony with economic elites relegated to less influential roles (Wolff 2016).

Even in cases of strong popular challenges to business power, economic elites have remained a powerful actor, well connected nationally and internationally, and capable of mobilizing their structural, instrumental, and discursive power. Yet, there are also structural limits to the power of business elites. One of the key problems is that their very success reinforces conditions of unequal political access that are structurally embedded in material inequalities, but which sit awkwardly with the very logic of democracy and the "power of numbers" that comes with electoral politics. The fact that pro-market economic models have experienced difficulty in developing governability and generating consensus is indicative of the limits of business power in Latin America. The pendular movement between left and right, statism and the free market, is thus symptomatic of both the limits and the strengths of business power in the region. And it arguably also reflects the persistent weakness of institutions and the lack of political arrangements and agendas that would bring together viable cross-class alliances.

In sum, the ways in which business could access and influence decision making and develop a privileged relationship with the state that at the same time excluded other social groups can be best observed by tracing instances of economic model changes in the region over the second half of the twentieth century and the first decades of the twenty-first century. Studying the processes behind the swings of the economic pendulum in a long-term perspective allows us to analyze the changing patterns of business-state relations. This helps us to deepen our understanding of the role of business elites from the tridimensional power perspective (structural, instrumental, and discursive), and to estimate their political impact and efficacy.

CHAPTER 2

BUSINESS POWER IN THE ERA OF STATE-LED DEVELOPMENT

The period between the 1930s and the 1970s for Latin America as a whole was one of transformation: economic, social, and in terms of the region's politics. Although with different speeds and to different extents, Latin American countries embarked on a process of industrialization, guided and fostered by a quantum increase in the role of the state in the economy. Old, oligarchic systems, based on laissez-faire systems both nationally and globally, gave way to a much more interventionist economic model, concerned with forging patterns of development that would lead the region to "catch up" with the developed countries. Within this model, private sector investment—both domestic and foreign—would play an important part, leading to the growing power of new business elites in exerting influence over the direction of state policy. However, such influence had also to contend with countervailing forces, notably from organized labor.

This process of economic transformation was at once the result of changes in the global economy as well as the political changes in Latin America which these brought about. As Rosemary Thorp has aptly commented (1998, 97): "Structures shifted, new forces and coalitions emerged, experience accumulated, and attitudes and strategic thinking were reshaped." The coalitions that emerged in the 1930s in much of the region ended displacing those of the previous period based on and around extractive industries and agriculture. Reflecting different economic interests, these new regimes opened up access to political power, bringing new political actors to the fore and creating new areas of contention.

The economic growth generated during these four decades proved rapid (faster than the expansion of the world economy as a whole), enabling a significant increase in GDP per capita, despite also significant demographic growth. The period produced marked social changes with the growth of a professional middle class as well as the emergence of a more powerful working class. And perhaps most germane for our purposes, it led to the appearance of a business class linked to the growth of new forms of enterprise as well as to labor unions concerned both to give workers a voice and to protect and project their class interests. Both sought, in varying contexts and with varying degrees of success, to influence public policy as administered by a burgeoning class of technocrats working within an increasingly active and interventionist state.

These changes came about through a combination of changing domestic political conditions and interruptions in the international economic environment that produced a crisis of the old order. This was a critical juncture in which old elites found themselves displaced by new social and political actors (Collier and Collier 2002). The first country to undergo such changes was Mexico, whose revolution (1910–1917) had a strong impulse over the rest of Latin America. The stability of the old order was then further undermined by the three external shocks of the first half of the twentieth century: two world wars and, between them, the effects of the 1929 Wall Street crash. Of these, the depression of the late 1920s and early 1930s probably had the most decisive impact on Latin America. Although the two world wars led to interruptions in patterns of trade (especially imports from European countries), the 1929 Wall Street crash brought about major changes in the region's politics and economic policies, especially in the larger economies. Faced with a collapse in prices for just about all Latin America's commodity exports, the crash provoked a crisis of the old order, as one country after another entered into economic turmoil that led, in many, to changes in economic orientation (Thorp 1998).

Up until the 1920s, the economic policies of most of Latin America had broadly adhered to the liberal principles set in place in the mid-nineteenth century. These were based on the primacy of agricultural and mineral commodity exports, mainly to Europe but increasingly to the United States. This was a model that fostered enormous differences in income, asset holding, and access to political power. In most cases, the narrow oligarchic interests that prospered under this model of economic development maintained control over their country's political establishments. Though not unchallenged, these interests upheld control up until the 1930s, but the transformations engendered by the Wall Street crash corroded their sources of income and power.

The dislocations of this period led to the development of a new and more assertive type of state. The impulse for greater state interventionism had begun back in the 1920s when many of the region's central banks were first established. Such institutional development was prompted, in part, by the United States, whose "money doctor" Edwin Kemmerer was a forceful advocate of such institutional changes (Drake 1989).[1] As more interventionist policies gained sway in the 1930s, there were significant increases in the size and scale of state institutions, particularly as states entered into the terrain of productive activities by nationalizing sectors that were regarded as strategically important. Again, Mexico took a lead in this by nationalizing its oil industry in 1938. But it was in the 1950s, under the influence of the Economic Commission for Latin America and the Caribbean (ECLAC), that the ideology of state-led modernization coalesced, based around the policy of import substitution industrialization (ISI).[2]

The change in the political complexion of Latin American governments, or at least in the larger countries, became more evident by the 1930s and 1940s. Building on the growth of an increasingly articulate middle and working class, more broadly based regimes replaced narrowly constituted oligarchic ones. Popular sectors became incorporated into the body politic (Collier and Collier 2002). Although Mexico was perhaps a special case, both Brazil and then Argentina saw new military-backed regimes take control with transformative agendas. In Brazil, Getúlio Vargas ruled for a total of eighteen years from 1930, seeking to build a corporatist regime (the Estado Novo) that extended worker rights and promoted social reform amid policies of state intervention and industrial development. In Argentina, Juan Perón, a former general and three times president, pursued similar policies in the 1940s, seeking to respond to the interests of labor and business through the promotion of industrial development. In Chile, different reformist governments (not all explicitly leftist) emerged that also challenged the status quo.

Whether ISI policies were the most adequate has been a topic of unending debate, but there is no doubt that they had an important impact on the pace of industrialization and consequent social change in many Latin American countries.[3] This varied greatly from one country to another with those most dependent on commodity exports (especially the smaller countries of the Central Andes and the Central American isthmus) lagging behind. Those countries in which industrial development went furthest included the larger economies of the region, notably Brazil, Argentina, Mexico, and Chile, but also some smaller ones such as Uruguay. All these countries experienced rapid growth in manufacturing output over the years after 1930, not only in consumer durables but also in intermediate inputs and even capital goods. The period saw the installation of new state enterprises, but it was also characterized by powerful new private sector interests that sought to make their voices heard.

The relationship between emerging business elites and the state varied considerably among different countries depending on their own specific political contexts and degrees of economic development. But in general terms, the period saw an increasing interdependence of business and government. As time went on, this often turned out to be more a question of "business intervention in government rather than government intervention in business."[4] By the 1960s these new elites had managed to consolidate their economic power and, in doing so, had developed mechanisms of influence over state decision making that helped them define the rules of the game in ways that further favored their strategic interests.

Business elites vied with other actors in determining government policy, using the various sources of power at their disposal—structural, instrumental, and discursive—that we outlined earlier. Not only seeking to influence macro policy, they had to contend with the power of organized labor, itself enhanced by industrialization. In two countries, in particular (Chile and Argentina), the power of organized labor, alongside other popular sectors, was such that it made for a highly conflictual relationship with business, especially when politics moved to the left.[5] In Brazil and Mexico, where more corporativist regimes took root, the power of popular movements proved more easily manipulated and co-opted.[6] In both countries too, the entry of mainly US multinationals in the 1950s and 1960s added further complexity to the patterns of influence exercised.

In the Central Andean countries, as we shall see, the picture differed substantially from those countries that led the way with ISI and state intervention. These were countries in which agrarian elites managed to hold on to power longer, where industrialization was only incipient, and in which laissez-faire policies persisted longer.

But even in these countries, by the 1950s, the picture was beginning to change.

BOLIVIA

Of the three Andean countries reviewed here, Bolivia, at the time of the 1952 revolution, was by far the least developed. For much of its history since Independence (see Klein 2003), political power had been wielded by a small oligarchy in which mining interests predominated. The beginning of the twentieth century saw the replacement of silver mining by tin as the main link with the global economy and Sucre by La Paz as the center of political power.[7] The mining economy was dominated by the so-called three tin barons—Patiño, Aramayo, and Hochschild—whose firms produced untold wealth for their owners. The agrarian economy was controlled by large-scale landowners whose holdings had expanded since the middle of the nineteenth century at the expense of indigenous communities. Up until the 1930s, these groups exercised political power through traditional party structures based on the narrowest of franchises, mainly through the Liberal Party. The basis of their power was essentially structural in the sense that they (especially the tin barons) commanded inflows of foreign exchange and export revenues. However, in instrumental terms, the "tin barons" relinquished control over policy making to a largely middle-class elite of lawyers whose policy options broadly followed the interests of the mining sector.[8] Discursively, they adopted much of the racist ideology that was common at the time (Klein 2003, 159). But, as in Peru and Ecuador, the economic effects of the 1929 crash challenged the hegemony of this narrow elite.

The 1930s and 1940s in Bolivia saw the rise of new social forces that clashed with patterns of oligarchic governance. The disastrous Chaco War against Paraguay (1932-1935) brought with it the emergence of new political actors, particularly in the military, who were critical of previous forms of government and their failure to rescue the nation from its problems. The governments of David Toro and Germán Busch saw important attempts to recalibrate policy along lines designed to modernize the economy and reform antiquated systems of government. In March 1937, Busch nationalized the holdings of Standard Oil in Bolivia to create the state-owned Yacimientos Petrolíferos Fiscales Bolivianos (YPFB), a full year before President Lázaro Cárdenas established Pemex in Mexico. The following year, a new constitution was approved that, among other things, challenged the sanctity of private property, introducing the notion of social utility as a criterion of landownership.

The period between the fall of Busch in 1939 and the victory of the Movimiento Nacionalista Revolucionario (MNR) in 1952 was one of struggle for control of the state between reformist groups—backed by a small professional middle class and an increasingly assertive and radical labor and peasant movement—and conservative interests concerned to maintain the liberal status quo. The tin barons, led by Carlos Aramayo, sought unsuccessfully to orchestrate an alliance of traditional parties in opposition to those of the nationalist left. It was also, of course, the period of the Second World War when demand for tin was extraordinarily high, an export boom that was to last until the Korean War in the early 1950s. This can be construed as a transitory phase in which the protracted struggle for dominance was fought out but not finally consolidated.

While the old oligarchic elite saw its power reduced on all three dimensions with the emergence of new actors in the 1930s, the labor movement had emerged as a significant force (Lora 1977). The Mineworkers Union (FSTMB) was established in 1944 and quickly provided the political backbone of a small working class, composed mainly of workers in small-scale industry and public sector employees. The radicalization of the mineworkers came about as a result of successive strikes and mobilizations, as well as a consequence of Trotskyist influences in the leadership derived from the exile of leaders to neighboring Argentina and Chile (John 2009). The Thesis of Pulacayo, adopted by the FSTMB in 1949, advocated the creation of a workers' state and put forward the idea of permanent revolution. In the rural sector, meanwhile, the peasant unions that emerged in the 1930s and 1940s took advantage of absentee landlordism to occupy haciendas and destroy the last vestiges of servile labor relations. Although the old oligarchy sought to wrest back control from the nationalist reformism of the Toro-Busch years, notably under the so-called Concordancia in the early 1940s, it failed to restore the status quo.

By the late 1940s, notwithstanding buoyant demand for tin, the profitability of the industry was in serious decline. The quality of the ore grades in Bolivia's underground mines was falling fast and the country's monopoly of tin mining was increasingly challenged by cheaper production costs in open pit mines in countries such as Malaysia and Indonesia (Crabtree 1987). It would take massive investment to restore the health of the Bolivian mining industry, the costs of which the tin barons were unprepared to shoulder. Meanwhile, in the agrarian sector, the inefficiencies of domestic agriculture, based on the hacienda system, were increasingly clear to see, with the country becoming ever more dependent on imported foodstuffs. In this context, landlords increasingly resorted to living in the main cities, abandoning their estates or putting them in the hands of local managers.

The efficacy of the private sector in driving the economy thus came increasingly into question. Bolivia remained a country with scant levels of industrialization outside the mining sector.[9] What industry existed in 1952 was largely in the hands of European immigrant families for whom the country's isolation from key ports and trade routes provided a degree of natural protection (Molina 2019, 79). Industries like printing, food manufacture, brewing, and textiles grew up in the first half of the twentieth century but remained small both in terms of output and the numbers of workers they employed. The growth of state-led activity over this period also led to a small bureaucratic and managerial elite emerging in La Paz, but it was highly dependent on government patronage. However, while providing a modicum of employment, the state at this period was a largely ineffectual structure with extremely limited outreach beyond one or two centers of administration. The tax system was mostly based on export and import duties and excluded oligarchic interests from its reach.[10]

The 1952 revolution proved to be a key turning point, significantly changing the structure of power within the country by destroying the economic base of the old oligarchic elite and opening the way to a broader coalition of interests. Although the revolution was of short duration (if compared, for example, with the Mexican revolution), lasting only days rather than months or years, its speed was illustrative of the weakening of the old elite, a process that had begun two decades earlier. It resulted in the destruction of the traditional army and its replacement by workers' militias (Dunkerley 1984), thus depriving the elites of a traditional resource for maintaining political dominance. It brought about the nationalization of the assets of the tin barons and the formation of the state mining company, the Corporación Minera de Bolivia (Comibol). It led to a wide-ranging agrarian reform that formally abolished serfdom and redistributed land previously belonging to haciendas in the Altiplano and the inter-Andean valleys. It introduced universal suffrage, in so doing providing a notion of citizenship and citizen rights for the first time. Finally, it brought to power a coalition of nationalist reformists (from within the MNR) and representatives of the labor movement under the auspices of the newly created Central Obrera Boliviana (COB) over which the mineworkers maintained effective control. Within the government led by MNR leader Víctor Paz Estenssoro, the COB gained control of three ministries. Moreover, within the mining industry, the unions exercised what was known as *co-gestión obrera*, an important degree of worker control over management. In short, the revolution led to the destruction of the remnants of oligarchic power in structural, instrumental, and discursive terms.

If this was a form of state capture "from below" with workers and their union representatives wielding unprecedented power, it was at best only a partial capture and of short duration as well. The coalition that brought Paz Estenssoro to power, and which led to a dramatic reduction in business influence on policy making, quickly dissipated in the months and years that followed the enactment of key reforms (Malloy and Thorn 1971). Already in the immediate aftermath of the 1952 revolution, pressure on the part of the US government—which in turn lent economic support to the postrevolutionary government (Heilman 2017, 53–86)—had successfully pushed the Paz Estenssoro government to refrain from also nationalizing the private banks (Molina 2017, 22). Later, a power struggle quickly emerged between the MNR leadership and the leader of the COB, Juan Lechín Oquendo. The socialist objectives of the miners were never shared by the middle-class reformists who made up the main leadership of the MNR. Divisions emerged between them over the extent to which workers would exercise control over the mining industry, the country's main source of foreign exchange and the main provider of resources for the MNR's developmentalist agenda. This split was exploited, particularly by the United States, under Paz's successor after 1956, Hernán Siles Zuazo.[11]

The end of the Korean War in 1953 brought with it an abrupt fall in tin prices, exacerbating the economic dislocation caused by the 1952 revolution. The export income generated by the mining industry declined, while state spending increased. The collapse of the old agricultural system left Bolivia critically dependent on food imports. Concerned to curtail the sort of radicalism and nationalism that 1952 brought to the surface, the United States moved in with large-scale food and fiscal assistance. It is estimated that between 1957 and 1961, US assistance accounted for up to one-third of the Bolivian budget. By 1956, under external pressure from the United States, the system of *co-gobierno* had been brought to an end with the expulsion from the cabinet of representatives of the COB, although the battle for control over the nationalized mining industry continued to rage for several years. Faced with hyperinflation and a bankrupt state, the

MNR governments had little option but to seek outside assistance. A US advisor, George Eder, devised the plan for Bolivia's recovery based on strict monetarist principles and fiscal discipline. Although this inevitably involved tensions and noncompliance, by the early 1960s Bolivia found its economic priorities effectively dictated from outside, through a scheme known as the Plan Triangular.[12]

It was therefore external structural pressure rather than that of a domestic business elite that pushed policy to the right in these years. However, the revolution was eventually to give rise to the growth of domestic business power in the years that followed. At the time, though, business elites had little political leverage, and the power of the old elite had collapsed.[13] Although the revolution represented an abrupt change for the private sector, focused up until then on mining and latifundista agriculture, the destruction of the private sector was never the policy of the MNR governments. In the years that followed, both under Siles Zuazo (1956-1960) and then again under Paz Estenssoro (1960-1964), the MNR governments sought to implement policies that would lead to a gradual recovery in the role of the private sector, especially in agriculture and agribusiness, a process that would eventually lead to fruition in the 1970s. During the 1960s, notably after the MNR government was supplanted by a military regime under General René Barrientos, government policy encouraged the development of a private mining sector that vied with the state sector. This revival of private enterprise led to some diversification and the development of significant family groups, but not such (as elsewhere) as to promote objectives of industrialization (Conaghan and Malloy 1994, 45).

The so-called *marcha hacia el oriente* (march to the east), first contemplated in the US-sponsored Bohan Plan of 1942 as a way of diversifying the economy, aimed to lay the basis for a dynamic expansion in agricultural production centered on the eastern department of Santa Cruz (Roca 2001). The growth of the *cruceño* economy, hitherto a relative backwater, was facilitated by the eventual completion in 1954 of the highway linking the city of Santa Cruz to Cochabamba and the rest of Bolivia. In the years that followed, the MNR governments and then their military successors channeled large amounts of aid money and the surplus still derived from mining toward Santa Cruz and its increasingly prosperous agricultural elite. This began with loans to build infrastructure in the lowland departments of the Oriente and, subsequently, with credits to develop regional agriculture through the Banco Agrario. Loans were granted on favorable terms and much of the money was never repaid. As a consequence, new forms of agricultural production grew rapidly, especially in areas such as cane sugar and cotton. The development of hydrocarbons production also helped fuel the *cruceño* economy.[14]

The city of Santa Cruz and its surrounding towns grew rapidly during these years as the seemingly unlimited agricultural frontier expanded. Government plans brought in surplus labor from the Altiplano to colonize the land being developed for agriculture. And the city also attracted inward migration, much of it from Eastern Europe. The result was the development of a new business elite, self-confident in its ability to prosper and increasingly resentful of any economic dependence on the rest of the country. Emblematic of this was the Comité Pro Santa Cruz, the regional civic committee, first established in 1950. Its key members included an amalgam of traditional local families with powerful sectoral organizations rooted in agriculture and agroindustry. These effectively captured the state at the local level and lead institutions such as the regional development corporation, Cordecruz, known until 1978 as the Comité de Obras Publicas de Santa Cruz. Cordecruz was responsible for building the infrastructure on which regional development was based, and it became a powerful interlocutor of local business interests. A public institution largely financed by oil rents, it helped provide the infrastructural basis on which the private sector in Santa Cruz could expand. As Conaghan and Malloy point out, the new business elites were to a large extent the "creations of state intervention and development policies" (1994, 45).

The revival of private sector mining in the 1960s and 1970s saw the more profitable mining concessions awarded to influential business groups. Chief among them was Comsur, the company owned by the Sánchez de Lozada family. The private sector prospered while the state sector under Comibol languished for lack of public investment and falling ore grades in key mining centers. At the same time, the business sector more generally, represented by the Confederación de Empresarios Privados de Bolivia (CEPB), began openly to criticize what it saw as the overbearing public sector crowding out private enterprise (Conaghan and Malloy 1994, 63). It was in the 1960s that new economic groups began to emerge, mainly organized around the ownership of commercial banks. The Banco de Santa Cruz was established in 1966, bringing together different productive sectors in Santa Cruz. Other major banks brought together economic interests in La Paz. However, little by way of investment went into import substitution industrialization, and the manufacturing sector of the economy remained underdeveloped and restricted largely to consumer nondurables (Morales 2001).

The memory of 1952, however, created a lasting nervousness among business leaders about democracy given their paucity in number and the risks of what they saw as majoritarian "populism." These risks were accentuated in the late 1960s in the gyrations between military regimes of both the right and the left, creating problems of chronic instability, not least in terms of access to decision making. The internal instabilities of the Bolivian state meant that it remained prey to clientelistic and patrimonial practices that made it difficult to establish clear rules of the game (Whitehead 1975). The proclamation of the short-lived left-wing Asamblea Popular in 1970 as an alternative popular-based parliament that revived the traditions of 1952 did nothing to assuage such fears.

The economic power of this new elite reached a peak during the military dictatorship of General Hugo Banzer Suárez (1971-1978), himself from Concepción in Santa Cruz, who toppled the leftward-leaning military government of General Juan José Torres and brought the Asamblea Popular to an abrupt end. Although in no way seeking to reverse the underlying statism of the economic model of the time, Banzer was energetic in extending the benefits of state interventionism to the private sector.[15] Buoyed up by a temporary boom in tin and oil prices, he used Bolivia's newfound improved international credit rating to tap foreign loans and to channel these into agricultural development projects. The Banco Agrario pumped unprecedented resources into the private sector, especially in Santa Cruz. However, as Conaghan and Malloy (1994, 80) note from interviews they conducted only shortly after, the business sector participated in government as individuals, not as sectoral representatives in a corporativist structure. This was a far cry from any sort of state capture based on structural power. Nor did the elite exercise much by way of instrumental power. Indeed, the business sector as represented by the CEPB became increasingly critical of the Banzer dictatorship and its attempts to make policy decisions without consultation. Business thus began to maneuver in favor of a democratic opening in which it would be a key actor.

It was not until 1985 that the model of state-directed developmentalism finally collapsed with Víctor Paz Estenssoro returning to the presidency, espousing policies designed to reverse those he had set in motion after 1952. However, the economic and political crisis that led to this critical juncture had long been in gestation.

The external borrowing binge of the Banzer years, as elsewhere in the Central Andes and in Latin America as a whole, had been premised on a combination of high commodity prices and low dollar interest rates that favored borrowing countries, especially in the wake of the petrodollar crisis of the early 1970s that forced international banks to find new customers to lend to. By the late 1970s, commodity prices had fallen while US interest rates had risen. Debt repayment became increasingly onerous, and Bolivia's ability to contract new loans disappeared. The situation was made worse by the suspension by Argentina of purchases of Bolivian oil. The hyperinflation of the early 1980s was the reflection of the adverse balance of payments situation as well as the inability of the Bolivian state to finance its activities.[16]

In domestic politics, the fall of Banzer in 1978 gave rise to extremes of political instability with short-lived civilian governments interspersed by military interludes, culminating in a series of military regimes between 1980 and 1982. In 1982, with the reinstatement of democratic rule, Siles Zuazo returned at the head of a left-of-center government in which, as in earlier times, the MNR (or at least Siles's branch of it, the MNR-Izquierda) vied with pressures emanating from the left and the union movement that sought to reinstate the socialist-oriented agenda of *co-gobierno* abandoned in the 1950s but briefly revived in 1970 by the Asamblea Popular. In the unfavorable economic circumstances of the time, reminiscent of the mid-1950s, Siles and his ministers struggled against the political odds and finally were forced to bring forward the date of presidential elections to 1985.

In this context, a more politically active private sector played an important role in destabilizing the Siles Zuazo government and, thereby, preparing for the about-face in economic policy in 1985. Increasingly the private sector exerted its structural power and expanded its instrumental leverage. Acting as the key representative of a domestic bourgeoisie unified in its rejection of Siles Zuazo, the CEPB attacked the record of the Siles government and its dependence on the goodwill of the COB. Among its members was the Association of Medium Miners, representing the private mining industry. Under Fernando Illanes's leadership, the CEPB became a more focused and effective organization, not only in voicing a private sector ideology (as opposed to that of the COB) but in mounting mobilizations designed to pressure the government and—ultimately—destabilize it.[17] Against a backdrop of spiraling prices and consequent falls in real living standards in the domestic sphere and the rise of the discourse and practice of structural adjustment in the context of the regional debt crisis, it was an appropriate moment to be launching a right-wing alternative to so-called populism. This neoliberal alternative would become manifest when, shortly after Paz Estenssoro took office with Gonzalo Sánchez de Lozada as his planning minister, the all-important Decree Law 21060 was published, initiating a new phase in which private investment and other financial flows managed to stabilize the economy.

In sum, the final collapse of the oligarchic power in Bolivia in the 1950s ushered in a period in which the state enjoyed a degree of autonomy, structurally curtailed more by external than domestic pressures. The subsequent development of business power was itself largely the creation of the state, and the economic elite only became a significant actor in the formulation of public policy in the late 1970s and early 1980s. The interaction of structural factors, domestic dynamics, and global dynamics contributed to a significant growth in structural and instrumental business power at this time. This simultaneously enabled an increasingly unified and "modern" economic elite to use its discursive power to shift the dominant narrative in a direction that was more conducive to private-sector interests. Influenced and supported by thinking from abroad, the CEPB thus sought to construct an economic alternative that combined a liberalizing agenda on economic matters with a commitment to liberal democracy in the political sphere. In Santa Cruz in particular, there were innovative attempts to seek to build consensus around a private-sector ideology including the establishment of a private university and the opening of new media outlets reflecting clearly pro-business views. The most strident individual force behind this incipient crusade was Gonzalo Sánchez de Lozada who brought his US connections and his own personal wealth to bear in giving leadership to the movement to oust Siles Zuazo from power and to shift this on to more compliant shoulders.

PERU

As in Bolivia, Peru's traditional oligarchy maintained tight control over politics well into the twentieth century, although within an economy far more diversified and better integrated into the capitalist world economy.[18] The so-called Aristocratic Republic, initiated in 1896 and lasting until 1919, was founded on the wealth of agrarian interests derived from a range of products that responded to increased international demand (especially in the United States, including copper, oil, rubber, wool, cotton, and sugar). Elections were held on a regular basis but on a narrow franchise. The oligarchy effectively controlled the workings of the state and acted collectively through the powerful Sociedad Nacional Agraria (SNA) and its leader, Pedro Beltran, a hacienda owner from Cañete. But, unlike Bolivia, foreign interests played a much more important role, notably in the shape of the Peruvian Corporation.[19] Political power both national and local, however, lay squarely in the hands of economically powerful families, mostly those whose wealth was based on sugar and cotton on the coast and wool and traditional crops in the highlands. The Pardo family played a key role in the Aristocratic Republic. Years of relative economic prosperity underscored political stability, with civilian-led governments elected on an exclusive franchise. Two parties, the Partido Civilista and the Partido Demócrata, vied with one another more as oligarchic clubs than competing political projects, and elite power—along all its dimensions—remained entrenched. The dictatorship of Augusto Leguía (1919-1930) brought an end to this period of limited elected government, but his government pursued many of the same policies that favored capitalist modernization and foreign investment, albeit with some genuflections in the direction of accommodating social tensions. But it was an authoritarian regime that was notably corrupt, involved in extending mining concessions to foreign companies and building expensive public works (especially roads) financed by international banks.

Whereas in much of Latin America the 1929 economic crises helped generate an opening up of the political regimes, this did not happen to the same extent in Peru. The ouster of Leguía in 1930 ended up in the election of a proto-fascist government under Luis Sánchez Cerro, supported by the SNA with Beltrán the power behind the throne (Jansen 2017). In subsequent years, the military either ruled directly or through civilian proxies, excluding more progressive parties like APRA (Alianza Popular Revolucionaria Americana) and perpetuating basically laissez-faire economic policies that favored oligarchic interests. The electoral defeat of APRA in 1931 was to lead to two decades of political ostracism in which its supporters were victims of intermittent persecution. Whereas countries like Brazil, Argentina, and Chile embarked on policies designed to promote industrialization behind protective trade barriers based on new coalitions of support, Peru stuck to orthodox policies that sought to marginalize incipient left-wing challenges. For most of the 1930s up until the outbreak of the Second World War, APRA and the Communist Party were outlawed. Between them, the agrarian oligarchy and the army, with the support of foreign investors, controlled the operations of the state.

This was to continue, except for a brief and more democratic interlude in the immediate postwar years, up until the 1960s.[20] The dictatorship of Odría (1948–1956) was supported by similar interests, although the government of Manuel Prado (1956–1963), a banker and industrialist with strong ties with the country's leading families, was somewhat more liberal. The Odría regime benefited from the 1950s commodity boom and set about maximizing Peru's mining potential through concessions to foreign companies (Thorp and Bertram 1978). The fishing industry boomed in the late 1950s and early 1960s, attracting new capital and adding another commodity to an already diversified export economy (Klarén 2000, 309). The coastal landed oligarchy retained political power, but export diversification diminished its control over the economy. Although sugar continued to be an important source of revenue, cotton production declined following the Korean War as synthetic fibers gradually took over the market. Urban growth, particularly in Lima, generated new business opportunities to a small but growing bourgeoisie (Dietz 2019, ch. 3).

But by the early 1960s, with the postwar export boom petering out, there were moves afoot to try to pursue alternative policies promoting industrialization. Prado's 1959 Industries Law was a step in that direction. This offered generous subsidies to manufacturing companies across the board, while tariffs introduced in the early 1960s offered a modicum of protection to firms. However, policy was guided more by the influence of lobbies than by any overall sense of planning. Most of the investment that took place came from abroad, with US multinationals using the space offered to sell to the growing domestic market and US banks controlling the financial system (Thorp and Bertram 1978, 266). At the same time, incipient industrialization and the growth of a working class led to the development of organized labor.

Compared with Bolivia and Ecuador, Peru possessed a relatively large industrial sector by the 1960s, but it was small compared with those of Latin America's initial industrializers, notably in the Southern Cone.[21] Back in the 1920s, there was a nascent industrialization, much of it the work of European immigrants, especially from Italy. The largest companies were in the textile industry, but other industries also developed to supply local demand, especially producing basic consumer goods. However, the maintenance of free trade principles made it difficult for Peruvian firms to compete with imported items from Europe or the United States. Meanwhile, this incipient industrialization gave rise to the growth of labor unions and left-wing parties, but whose influence over policy making was severely limited by the exclusive nature of the political system. Up to this point the political power of the old elite, reinforced by foreign investors, remained largely intact; between them they maintained their structural power by controlling the country's exports and its supply of foreign currency, and the SNA remained as the dominant business association, exercising strong instrumental power. State policy largely continued to follow laissez-faire principles that had been abandoned in many other Latin American countries. But things were about to change as the old model failed to satisfy the aspirations of new political actors entering the scene.

The mildly reformist Belaúnde government, which was elected in 1963, identified closely with the "modernizing" agenda of the US Alliance for Progress and was timidly supported by the more reformist Sociedad Nacional de Industrias (SNI). It built on the process of change initiated under Prado, but the scope of reform was hampered by political opposition from the right.[22] A construction boom, brought about by urban growth and public works, created a cluster of industrial companies, together with assembly plants producing cars and household items for a growing middle class. Many firms were foreign owned or the property of immigrant families, but domestic elites began to invest in industry, taking advantage of the government subsidies on offer. Meanwhile Belaúnde began a program of agrarian reform. This formed part of a development strategy but without confronting the rural oligarchy and the still powerful SNA. The SNI refrained from openly challenging the SNA to become the leading trade association. Belaúnde's agrarian reform left intact the prosperous landed estates of the coastal valleys producing for the global market. Strident right-wing opposition from the supporters of Odría and APRA in Congress used their instrumental power to block Belaúnde's modernization plans, reducing the scope for reform. The tax system remained highly regressive, becoming rather more so during the Belaúnde years (Kuczynski 1977, 80-86). So, in spite of its reformist impulses, the Belaúnde government failed to break the business power still wielded in all three dimensions by Peru's conservative landed elites.

The coup that ousted Belaúnde in 1968 ushered in Peru's most determined and bold effort to introduce structural reforms under the presidency of General Juan Velasco Alvarado.[23] This involved the nationalization of much of the country's traditional industries, including most of the foreign-owned mining sector and petroleum industry, as well as foreign banks; a radical agrarian reform that did away with the old hacienda system and replaced it with worker cooperatives; the introduction of a system of worker co-participation in industry and of social integration of previously excluded sectors of the population; support for labor unions; and trade policies designed to speed up industrialization and productive diversification. It also did away with the formal trappings of democracy such as Congress and political parties and ended up confiscating the press and other media. Unlike the changes that came about in Bolivia in the early 1950s, this was essentially a top-down authoritarian project based fundamentally on military force. Peru's military rulers sought to put the state at the very center of a development model to transform the country and rid it of its residual oligarchic characteristics.[24] The state was there to serve the public interest, not simply the interests of a narrow (and wealthy) minority. It was envisioned as "autonomous," one beholden neither to elites nor workers, famously "neither capitalist nor communist" (Contreras and Cueto 2000, 309). The regime initially sought the support of the new class of industrialists in eliminating the old oligarchy, but some of its reforms (notably worker participation and support for unions) generated distrust in business circles. The SNI initially supported the reforms, but by 1973, when industrial interests were threatened by the reforms and the growing power of trade unions, it shifted to a more confrontational position (Conaghan and Malloy 1994, 60-62). The role of civil society pressure groups or specific lobbies was subservient to the general public interest as interpreted by the military and its technocratic advisors.

At its heart, the Velasco regime sought to engineer the transformation of a largely agrarian society into a modern industrialized country in which the private sector was expected to play an important part. A system of incentives was created to encourage the transfer of capital from the traditional sectors, now largely under the control of the state, to nontraditional ones in which private enterprise would be respected, indeed encouraged (Fitzgerald 1979). However, the regime was less than successful in convincing domestic economic elites of its benign intentions. The violation of norms of private property, both in the agrarian sector and with the establishment of worker-based industrial communities, did little to reassure investors. Industrialists found themselves divided between confrontational and more accommodating strategies. Many sought to take their money abroad through capital flight rather than invest it in new domestic enterprises. Attempts to integrate the business sector into discussions over policy failed to convince most of those involved as to the government's good intentions. However, there were cases in which the military government was successful in steering investment into new sectors where business elites were willing to accept the new rules of the game in ways that opened up lucrative activities. The newly established Asociación de Exportadores (ADEX), representing highly subsidized exporters of nontraditional products, supported the government. The growth of the Romero group during these years into Peru's top business conglomerate stands as an outstanding example of collaboration in response to the exchange of benefits (Durand 2013).

Policy toward the private sector varied according to the sectors involved and how they responded to the incentives on offer. In this sense, government policy was more pragmatic than it is usually credited for (Crabtree and Durand 2017, ch. 3). Points of contact with business leaders were established, such as the annual conference for executives (CADE). Some of the nationalizations of foreign companies announced provided opportunities for local entrepreneurs, not least the introduction of rules limiting foreign ownership of banking institutions. But such moves only went so far in mollifying the business class. Many executives remained highly suspicious of the Velasco regime's intentions, fears that were confirmed by the 1970 Industrial Communities Law (Knight 1975). This not only gave workers a share in the profits of the companies that employed them but also offered them representation on their management boards. Of all the reforms of this period, this was the one most viscerally disliked by company executives.[25] The business elite also looked nervously at the attempts at social mobilization undertaken by the regime (such as the Sistema Nacional de Movilización Social [Sinamos]) and the stimulus it gave to an increasingly radical discourse on the left that by this time had gained sway in the labor movement.[26]

Probably the Achilles heel of the Velasco regime and its attempts to build an effective and socially responsive state was its failure to put the state on a sustainable financial footing. As in Bolivia and Ecuador, the expanded role of the state was funded, primarily, on foreign borrowing. As we have seen, these were times when it was relatively cheap to borrow, and foreign lenders had excessive liquidity that they were willing to offer to what looked like relatively stable regimes in South America. Foreign borrowing increased more than threefold under Velasco, from just under US$1 billion in 1970 to US$3.5 billion in 1976 (Banco Central de Reserva del Perú 1980, 158). But by 1974, the strains of foreign borrowing became manifest as the debt service ratio ballooned and Peru's credit rating came under scrutiny as the strains of repayment became evident.[27] It is significant that among the reforms introduced at this time, little was done to overhaul the tax system to make it more progressive and socially redistributive.[28] Financial dependence ended up neutralizing the autonomy of the state.

In sum, the Velasco regime sought reforms to finally break the power of Peru's landed oligarchy and to engineer a transition toward a more modern industrial economy under the auspices and control of the state. They severely reduced the instrumental power of the business sector while not entirely eliminating it. The nationalization of key companies reduced the structural power wielded by Peru's hitherto powerful business groups. And through its takeover of much of the media (Gargurevich 2021), the regime denied these groups the influence that they had previously wielded over public opinion. But while it managed to create a more "autonomous" state, it was unable to put this on a sustainable trajectory, either politically or economically.

The following decade, the state under two governments—the military regime led by Francisco Morales Bermúdez (1975-1980) that ousted Velasco in 1975 (to the delight of the business community) and the return of a democratically elected government under Belaúnde (1980-1985)—saw attempts to row back from the statism of the Velasco years.[29] This was a process dictated both by external global conditions and by domestic political pressures in which the disgruntled private sector played an important part. This was a period in which the notion of state-led development was rejected across much of Latin America and in which the seeds of neoliberal discourse were planted. However, in the Peruvian case, the neoliberal response proved half-hearted and failed to bring about a significant reengineering of public policy. As we shall see, dissatisfaction with the shortcomings of the Belaúnde administration led directly to the reassertion of the more statist and protectionist variant in 1985 with the election of Alan García to the presidency. It was the failings of his government and his frustrated attempt to nationalize the banking sector that effectively buried the notion of state interventionism for at least another generation.

On seizing power in 1975, Morales Bermúdez, who had been Velasco's finance minister, found little alternative but to seek the assistance from international banks and (subsequently) the IMF in correcting what proved to be large fiscal and balance of payments imbalances.[30] A combination of massive increases in state spending with the turnaround in international credit markets created an unsustainable macroeconomic situation. And as was to be expected, the banks and then the IMF demanded tough conditions that involved jettisoning the interventionist approaches of the previous period.[31] The fiscal year 1975-1976, therefore, proved to be a critical juncture that altered the structural power of business and brought about a sharp about-turn in policy orientation. The Velasco government had failed to mobilize sufficient political support among the beneficiaries of its reforms to keep itself in power. Policies that had challenged notions of private property such as the agrarian reform and the industrial communities were summarily wound up, as was Sinamos. In the economic sphere, orthodox policies based on tight monetary and fiscal policies were introduced, and reforms liberalizing the labor code were adopted. Privatizations took place in some sectors such as the media, fishing, and agriculture (Stallings 1983, 170-71).

The rollback of state intervention, which began under Morales and continued with the return of Belaúnde in 1980 was the consequence, primarily, of external economic pressure. The extent of direct business influence over government decisions at this point was limited since policy disagreements over the speed and depth of the liberalization process divided the business sector. The structural power of the private sector was guided by Peru's external vulnerabilities, and its instrumental power at this point was strictly limited, although it is true that appointments to key economic posts after 1975 provided greater access. In terms of discourse, the prevalent ideology continued to be influenced strongly by interventionist ideas, though this would change after 1980.[32]

The social cost of the transition proved high, however, which had the effect of curbing growth and domestic demand. The transition also triggered widespread political conflict. Arguably, the late 1970s represented the highpoint of labor unrest, with general strikes taking place in 1977 and 1978. Business organizations were circumspect in their dealings with the state and the military at this point, with a preference for a return to civilian rule. As in Bolivia at much the same time, these organizations began to press for a full democratic opening in which they hoped to become key actors. In 1977 the government announced its plans for a political transition, involving a rewriting of the country's constitution by an elected constituent assembly and then the holding of direct elections. Although the constitution contained some elements the business sector found distasteful (it sought to strike a balance between labor and capital, albeit shifting toward a market economy), it provided for the reemergence of party politics through which business interests could assert their influence. Significantly, twenty-seven years after Bolivia, the constitution provided for universal suffrage by giving illiterate people the vote for the first time.

The establishment of democratic rule brought the return of Belaúnde in 1980, this time, however, with a more explicit commitment to economic liberalization. Belaúnde chose as his prime minister and economy minister Manuel Ulloa, a wealthy businessman exiled under Velasco. And within Ulloa's team came a number of US-trained economists dubbed "the Dynamo," schooled in a commitment to push back the frontiers of the state in favor of market forces. In the first two years of the new administration, liberalizing reforms and privatization initiatives were introduced that aimed to deregulate the economy, reduce protective tariffs, and encourage foreign investment in sectors previously under the aegis of the state. The private sector was well placed to increase its instrumental power over decision making through the restoration of a number of lobby organizations that had been sidelined (if not banned outright) under the military government. Among them were the SNI and the Sociedad Nacional de Minería y Petróleo (SNMP). In 1984 a new umbrella organization came into being in the shape of the Confederación Nacional de Instituciones Empresariales Privadas (better known as Confiep).[33] A unifying factor was the fear caused by insurgent groups and union activity. Still, not every business sector was happy with the direction of policy. Reductions in tariff protection and the removal of export subsidies provoked opposition, especially in sectors like textiles that were exposed to foreign competition under a more liberal tariff regime and nontraditional exporters.

However, the liberalization crusade espoused by Ulloa and the Dynamo was soon knocked askew by three developments that seriously complicated governance at the time. The first was the 1982 debt crisis, which cut new lending to Peru and thus paralyzed the program of public works promised by Belaúnde in 1980 (Wise 2003). As in 1975, Peru found itself in serious balance of payments difficulties and was forced by the IMF to cut back on public spending. The second was the effects in 1983 of serious climatic difficulties, caused by the El Niño phenomenon (Crabtree 1992, 27). The third was the proliferation of rural violence perpetrated since 1980 by Sendero Luminoso, exposing the government to criticisms of failing to maintain law and order.[34]

In 1983 the Peruvian economy slumped a full 12.6 percent in GDP (Banco Central de Reserva del Perú 1990, 145). From 1982 through to 1985, amid rapidly falling popularity rates, the Belaúnde government floundered between the demands of orthodoxy and the need to regain popular support. With inflation rising rapidly, economic liberalization had patently failed to put Peru on a new course of growth and prosperity. The liberalizing discourse with which Belaúnde was elected gave rise to calls for a return to a more interventionist approach, both in the municipal elections of 1983 (in which the left-wing Izquierda Unida [IU] won the city of Lima) and in the 1985 elections in which

APRA and the IU were the two most-voted groupings. The Belaúnde government failed to build a viable coalition with popular support; elected in 1980 with 47 percent of the vote, Belaúnde's ruling Acción Popular party won a meagre 6 percent five years later (Crabtree 1992, 70). The shifts in the structural and instrumental power of business were not complemented by any decisive shift in discursive power; the battle for ideas had yet to be fully engaged. From the business angle, perhaps one of the more significant developments was the foundation of Confiep and its attempts to unify business interests in the midst of a prevalent social and economic crisis.

The government of Alan García and APRA (1985 was the first time that APRA had won office since its foundation in Peru in 1930) brought a clear shift in policy making back toward the orientations of the Velasco regime (Crabtree 1992, ch. 2). The state resumed a central role in spearheading development amid economic policies that parted clearly from orthodox formulae. Peru broke with IMF and creditor bank-supported policies, unilaterally suspending some debt repayments. As under Velasco, the private sector was invited to take part in this project on the understanding that the (hoped for) return to growth would lead it to invest in industrial expansion. García's "Twelve Apostles" included the country's largest economic groups, headed by the Romero group.[35] In this relationship, however, García sought to ensure that it was the state (or perhaps more accurately, himself) that was in the driving seat (Durand 2017a). When the various groups, mostly headed by financial institutions, failed to provide the investment necessary to keep the economy on a growth track, García took the bold decision in July 1987 to try to nationalize the country's leading banks.

This proved a pivotal decision that broke asunder a fragile ruling coalition. Up until this point business elites and Confiep had given grudging support to García's heterodox schemes. The return to growth and a fall in inflation in 1986 helped create a more favorable business climate and boosted profits. With the bank nationalization, however, the country's main business groups turned on García with a vengeance. With Confiep contesting the decision in the courts and pro-business members of Congress challenging it in the legislature, García was eventually forced to abandon the idea altogether. In ways that had not happened previously, the business sector became directly involved in political confrontation, using its structural and instrumental power while seeking to articulate a discursive narrative about the evils of state intervention. Brought together by Confiep, the business community acted as a united force. For the first time business executives led demonstrations on the streets of Lima. They rallied behind the campaign to safeguard their properties in the financial sector by supporting the creation of a political movement led by novelist Mario Vargas Llosa. Libertad, as the movement was known, revived the pressures that emerged in the late 1970s for both economic and political liberalization. Garcia, like Velasco before him, was portrayed as an unhinged authoritarian nationalist who eschewed the sanctity of private property in favor of state-centered corporativism.

The Garcia government led to the final collapse of the state-centered economic development model, a critical juncture that opened the way to neoliberalism and new forms of state capture, as the private sector regained structural power (through the reprivatization of the banks), while building up instrumental power. In the last two years of its five-year term, the government struggled against increasingly negative economic conditions. Isolated internationally, Peru was starved of capital (a situation made worse by capital flight) and suffered extreme balance of payments problems and the evaporation of its foreign currency reserves. Like Bolivia a little earlier, the country experienced hyperinflation leading to plummeting real incomes, massive unemployment, and an ever-growing fiscal deficit, which brought the viability of the state itself into question.[36] But unlike Bolivia, the challenge to state authority came also from the expansion of Sendero Luminoso and its campaign of extreme violence, which had begun in rural Ayacucho in 1980 but by 1989 had spread through much of the country, a direct challenge to public order and, indeed, political stability. In such circumstances, the model of state-led development initiated in the 1960s appeared increasingly redundant, its supporters were marginalized politically, and public opinion prepared to accept an alternative whatever the social cost. Whereas the return to economic liberalism in the mid-1970s had brought half-hearted measures that proved difficult to consolidate, the 1990 elections set the scene for a massive and enduring shift in policy that was to bring huge benefits to Peru's business class. All three sources of business power militated in the same direction.

ECUADOR

As in Peru, it was agrarian interests that dominated the era of oligarchic politics in Ecuador during the first decades of the twentieth century (Ospina 2016, 40–48; Quintero and Silva 1998a, 255–399). With the liberal revolution in 1895, the export-oriented agrarian elites effectively established their control over the state. Unlike in Peru, however, Ecuador's export sector was much less diversified; it was focused at that time on one single product, cocoa. It was, therefore, the "cocoa oligarchs" (Guerrero 1980) that effectively dominated the scene, in close articulation with a banking elite that had emerged in the wake of the cocoa boom. Also, the division between the coastal region, around the city of Guayaquil, with its thriving export-oriented economy and the *sierra* with the capital of Quito and its domestic- and state-oriented economy added an additional twist to the "political takeover by Guayaquil's export elites" (Conaghan and Malloy 1994, 26). This takeover by an alliance of large agro-exporters and coastal bankers included the control of the financial system, which was now used to fund a government that responded to the export-led boom by increasingly borrowing from domestic private banks (see Quintero and Silva 1998a, 257-61).

In Ecuador, it was the crisis of the cocoa economy in the early 1920s that effectively undermined the oligarchical state (Ospina 2016, 43). Simultaneously, the rise of cocoa production in other countries led to a plunge in world market prices, while cocoa plantations in Ecuador were seriously affected by crop diseases (Acosta 2003, 81-82). In addition to weakening the power of the agro-exporting elites in Guayaquil, the ensuing economic crisis also made debt-financed public spending unviable. In 1925 a military coup overthrew the government of liberal president Gonzalo Córdova and ushered in the short-lived Revolución Juliana. Backed by "a heterogeneous alliance of highland landowners, incipient industrialists, and middle- and lower-class groups," the Julianista officers embarked on a series of reforms that were meant to modernize the state and build a certain "regulatory capacity vis-à-vis dominant groups" (Conaghan and Malloy 1994, 29-30). This period of reform proved short-lived. And even if the Revolución Juliana left relevant discursive and institutional legacies (such as the Central Bank and a series of regulatory agencies), the laws introduced to promote and protect industrialization did not significantly transform the mode of accumulation. In structural terms, the 1930s and 1940s saw a gradual diversification of the economy, but the coastal agro-export sector remained predominant, and the overarching regional cleavage between the export-oriented economic elite centered on Guayaquil and the more traditional hacienda-based elite in the *sierra* persisted (see De la Torre 1993, 55-76; León Trujillo 2003; Maiguashca and North 1991, 95-108).

Up until Ecuador's transition to democracy in 1979, it was military governments that attempted to reduce business control over the state, enable some kind of relatively autonomous policy making, and push through some (mostly mild) economic reforms in order to "modernize" both the state and the economy (Isaacs 1993; North 2006). In addition to the Revolución Juliana, these experiences included further brief episodes of military-led reformism in 1937-1938, between 1963 and 1966, and most notably, during the 1970s (see below). By contrast, elected governments during these decades were mostly conservative as well as directly and/or indirectly controlled by (competing) domestic economic elites.[37] Between the 1930s and the 1970s, elected civilian governments in Ecuador came mainly in the form of the specific type of populism that characterized the five presidencies of José María Velasco Ibarra (1934-1935, 1944-1947, 1952-1956, 1960-1961, 1968-1972). While Velasco Ibarra's populist discourse was decidedly anti-oligarchic and deliberately appealed to the poor masses, his moralistic agenda of change did not include any redistributive aims and, thus, did not significantly challenge any vital business interests (see De la Torre 1993; Maiguashca and North 1991). As a result, before universal suffrage was introduced in 1979, electoral competition in Ecuador was increasingly shaped by appeals to the popular sectors, but official politics and policy making largely remained an intra-elite affair, in which economic elites had an important say.[38]

Since the 1950s, state-led developmentalism along the lines of ECLAC thinking had found increasing support among both state actors (in particular, within the bureaucracy and the military) and within society (among middle classes and popular sectors as well as in parts of the business community). But no powerful sociopolitical coalition emerged that was able to promote a developmentalist strategy of industrialization. Among other things, this reflected the persisting dominance of the agro-exporting elite, which, in the years after the Second World War, became increasingly centered around bananas as the new primary export commodity (Acosta 2003, 98-105). Reflecting the regional division of the country, which included a multiple fragmentation of the economic elites along both regional and sectorial lines, however, the overall pattern that characterized Ecuadorian politics during the twentieth century was not one of simple oligarchic predominance but, rather, one of constant negotiations and unstable equilibria (see León Trujillo 2003; Ospina 2016).[39] This pattern concerned, on the one hand, the relations between the competing (regional) elites, which dominated politics either directly or indirectly through like-minded political parties; on the other, also subaltern groups, including new social and political forces that emerged as a consequence of structural socioeconomic change. These were normally not excluded by force but incorporated politically, if in subordinated ways and mainly through informal mechanisms (clientelism, co-optation). As a consequence, Ecuador experienced what Pablo Ospina (2016, 14) has called "a slow and cumbersome path of molecular capitalist modernization, which dismantled the oligarchic order." Even during the most reformist military governments, business elites in the end always proved capable of translating their structural and instrumental power into political influence in order to slow down "the strategies of modernization advanced by the military governments" (Chiasson-LeBel 2020, 102). Yet, their multiple fragmentation—in terms of regions, sectors, and economic groups—also meant that economic elites could neither unite to defend the old oligarchic order nor push through some common agenda of capitalist development.

The banana boom in the aftermath of the Second World War did bring significant societal changes: an increased role of the state in particular with a view to the construction of the physical infrastructure necessary for the expanding agricultural frontier, a spread of capitalist modes of agricultural production, and important demographic changes in terms of migration to the coast and urbanization (Acosta 2003, 102–5; Conaghan 1988, 37–41; Maiguashca and North 1991, 111–31; Quintero and Silva 1998b, 7–74).[40] This trend toward socioeconomic diversification was intensified during the 1960s. As agrarian exports—and banana trade in particular—stagnated, "many agroexporters began to diversify into industrial investments," and even "a significant segment of the traditional landholding class were either making the transition to modern capital-intensive ranching and dairy farming or moving their capital out of agriculture altogether" (Conaghan and Malloy 1994, 39–40; see also Ospina 2016, 54–71).[41] As in Peru and (less so) in Bolivia, this process of diversification among economic groups was supported by state efforts to promote industrialization through credit and tax exemptions.

It was during the 1970s, however, that Ecuador embarked on the most notable attempt at state-led development (see García Gallegos 2003; Isaacs 1993, 35–65). In 1972 the military led by General Guillermo Rodríguez Lara toppled Velasco Ibarra and resumed its push for state-led developmentalism. Between 1972 and 1976, public sector investment and consumption increased from 16 to 23 percent of GDP, the number of public servants rose from 61,000 in 1970 to almost 110,000 in 1976, and a series of public enterprises were created. An overvalued (fixed) exchange rate, combined with tax reductions for exporters, promoted the expansion of capital-intensive manufacturing plants, which depended on the import of (cheap) capital goods, while business simultaneously benefited from a series of price controls and subsidized fuel and electricity prices (Conaghan and Malloy 1994, 51–57). Economically, these policies were based on the newest boom in primary goods exports, inaugurated by the launch of oil exploitation in Ecuador's Amazonas region in 1972 (Acosta 2003, 119–27). Given this new oil wealth, the Ecuadorian state for the first time could count on significant economic resources independent from the country's business elites (Burbano de Lara 2006, 298). The military government, thus, could use oil revenues to promote industrialization, while reducing the influence of the private sector on economic policy making (Chiasson-LeBel 2020, 103; Conaghan 1988, 47–52). Yet, Rodríguez Lara proved much less able than Velasco in Peru to form a stable ruling coalition and implement reforms even in the face of business resistance.

Even if the bulk of the developmentalist policies implemented by the military regime actually benefited big business (Acosta 2003, 131–36), the business community hardly supported Rodríguez Lara (Isaacs 1993, 69–84). In addition to the overall developmentalist discourse and the shutdown of previous channels of instrumental business power (through corporatist institutions and parliament), it was efforts to increase state regulation of the private economy and, most notably, the 1973 Agrarian Reform Law that met with fierce and united resistance from the business community (see Conaghan 1988, 76–101). Unified opposition from business contrasted with the lack of any attempt to mobilize popular support on the part of the regime, even if the communist Confederación de Trabajadores del Ecuador (CTE) explicitly backed the government (Conaghan and Malloy 1994, 62–63). In contrast to the Peruvian experience under the Velasco regime, therefore, "private-sector opposition to reformism in Ecuador was generally effective, often resulting in embarrassing policy reversals by the regime (for example, regulation of foreign investment) or a quiet abandonment of policy implementation (such as democratization of capital, agrarian reform)" (Conaghan 1988, 105).[42]

In the end, therefore, the implementation of left-leaning state-led developmentalism in Ecuador "fell far short of Peru's structural reforms" (Conaghan and Malloy 1994, 49). Despite this largely successful resistance by the business elite, "the absence of formal institutional channels for voicing their grievances, plus the lack of clarity in the rules of the game for the opposition," impeded a rapprochement between the economic elites and the Rodríguez Lara regime (Conaghan 1988, 105–6). In 1976, Rodríguez Lara was replaced by a new military triumvirate, which terminated the reformist project, readjusted the relationship between the state and the economic elites, and initiated the process of democratization (see Conaghan 1988, 112-15; Isaacs 1993, 97-115).

In sum, between the Revolución Juliana in 1925 and the turn to democratic rule in 1979, economic elites generally dominated Ecuadorian politics.[43] They did so using all types of business power: (1) their structural power, based on the state's dependence on the financial resources and exports generated, in particular, by the coastal agribusiness; (2) their instrumental power, through their direct influence on, and presence within, political parties, via the corporatist system of business chambers, as well as through informal, family-based, and clientelist elite networks; and (3) their discursive power, based on their privileged access to public debates, including through their influence on and in private media outlets. At the same time, the multiple fragmentation (regional and sectoral) of the economic elites meant that their capacity to directly shape governmental policies in their interest was limited. The general picture is, thus, not one of political capture but one of elite-dominated negotiations. Decisive collective action on the part of the economic elites was primarily negative—that is, in defense of common business interests against threats of all-too-reformist initiatives taken by military governments.

This pattern also persisted under democratic rule. During the first democratically elected government led by Jaime Roldós (until his death in 1981) and Luis Osvaldo Hurtado (1981-1984), which struggled to preserve its relative autonomy vis-à-vis economic elites, business chambers and their allies among the traditional political parties organized a sustained campaign of opposition and resistance (Chiasson-LeBel 2020, 112; Hey and Klak 1999, 71-72).[44] But already under Hurtado, the sense and direction of "economic reforms" started to take a new—neoliberal—shape. When oil prices declined and the Mexican default triggered the regional debt crisis in the early 1980s, Ecuador's level of foreign debt, which had increased significantly since the mid-1970s, became increasingly unviable. Hurtado responded by turning to austerity measures, negotiations with the IMF and private creditors, and the adoption of an adjustment and stabilization program (see Conaghan and Malloy 1994, 111-13; Hey and Klak 1999, 70-72; Thoumi and Grindle 1992). As a consequence, it was not so much business but the Ecuadorian labor movement that seriously challenged the Hurtado government. After having grown significantly during the 1970s and unified their forces in 1980 under the Frente Unitario de Trabajadores (FUT), in the early 1980s labor unions allied with various leftist political forces and other popular sector organizations to resist the austerity measures adopted by the Hurtado government (León Trujillo and Pérez 1986). It is in response to both the Hurtado government and this upsurge in popular mobilization that the coastal business leader León Febres-Cordero temporarily managed to unite the economic elites as well as a broad range of center-right parties behind a neoliberal agenda (see Burbano de Lara 2006, 303; Conaghan and Malloy 1994, 131-36; Thoumi and Grindle 1992, 49).

Febres-Cordero, who had led the resistance against the Rodríguez Lara regime as president of the Guayaquil chamber of industry and a direct representative of the (coastal) business elites, finally occupied the presidency of the country. Similar to Belaúnde's second government in Peru (1980-1985), however, he failed in his attempt to implement a coherent set of economic reforms along neoliberal lines (see Burbano de Lara 2006, 303-7; Conaghan and Malloy 1994, 162-202; Hey and Klak 1999, 72-74). On the one hand, he faced stiff opposition from center-left parties in Congress as well as popular resistance on the streets, led by the labor movement. This impeded "a complete takeover of the state by the right" (Conaghan 1988, 130). On the other hand, the business community, the political right, and technocrats in the government themselves were hardly united when it came to the actual implementation of economic reforms. With a view to economic elites, Felipe Burbano de Lara (2006, 305) has emphasized "the absence of a business community willing to compete in the free market, to respect its rules and not to rely on the state to obtain extraordinary economic rents." Given his trajectory as a business leader in the industrial sector, Febres-Cordero himself, although "ideologically committed to neoliberalism," believed "in a more gradual approach to economic restructuring" (Conaghan and Malloy 1994, 159). In the face of external shocks (the collapse of international oil prices and a devastating earthquake) and increasing political threats to the stability of his government, Febres-Cordero ultimately abandoned the emphasis on austerity measures and structural adjustment (Conaghan and Malloy 1994, 147-59, 166-72; Hey and Klak 1999, 73).

Overall, neoliberal reforms in Ecuador were implemented gradually, and inconsistently, by a succession of elected governments: from the exchange rate deregulation and the lifting of interest rate and price controls under Febres-Cordero (1984-1988), through trade liberalization under Rodrigo Borja (1988-1992) and financial liberalization under Sixto Durán-Ballén (1992-1996), up until the deep economic crisis of 1999/2000 gave way to official dollarization and a new set of austerity and structural adjustment reforms in the early 2000s (see

Acosta 2003, 161-95; Hey and Klak 1999; Thoumi and Grindle 1992). This particular trajectory, which differs from both Bolivia and Peru, is the result both of conflicting interests among business elites along regional and sectoral lines and of popular resistance, which were also reflected in almost continuous power struggles between government and parliament. As far as business elites are concerned, these have remained unable to develop a strong peak association that would transcend sectoral differences. In particular, unity proved hard to establish given the deep regional cleavage between the coast and the Andean highlands. This persisting fragmentation has limited both the instrumental and the discursive power of Ecuador's economic elites and, thus, prevented any kind of sustained political capture on behalf of a somewhat coherent pro-business agenda.

CONCLUSION

While the post-Second World War period in Latin America saw significant industrialization in the larger economies, particularly those of the Southern Cone, this was much less the case in the Central Andean countries, where despite important variations, the old elites managed decisively to shape political decision making for longer, reflecting their structural power based on the importance of traditional commodity exports to their various economies. This was particularly the case in Peru and Ecuador, less so in Bolivia. In Peru, the agricultural elites of the coast maintained their grip on political power, successfully repressing political challenges from sectors representing a growing middle and working class. In Ecuador, the growth of the banana industry in the postwar years gave new impetus to the coastal elites, castigated (well before the 1929 crash) by the decline of cocoa production. In Bolivia, where agriculture was much less significant in relation to exports, the power of the traditional mining elites was diminishing, in part because of the long-term decline in the quality of mining ores.

However, by the early 1950s and more so by the 1960s, new political actors were coming to the fore in each of these countries, reflecting changes in the economic structure that provided new sources of political pressure on the direction of state policy. Of the three, industrial development was strongest in Peru—though by no means comparable to that in countries such as Brazil and Argentina. The 1959 Industries Law provided a fillip, though most industries were not import substitutive as such. Similarly, in Ecuador in the early 1960s, with banana production stagnating, government policy sought to encourage industrialization. Still, the results were modest at best. Bolivia remained the least industrialized country, with government policy in the 1950s and 1960s focused on the development of cash-crop agriculture (largely for export) in the eastern lowlands of Santa Cruz. In all three countries, much of the industrialization achieved was related initially to the processing of primary products for export rather than substituting for imports. It was only in Peru that the internal market was strong enough to sustain manufacturing indus-tries, particularly in the consumer goods sector.

The relative structural weakness of an industrial bourgeoisie in the Central Andean countries delayed the point at which their po-litical influence would become a decisive factor in political decision making and opened up the possibility of state institutions gaining an important degree of autonomy, enabling social reforms to take place. In all three countries, the scope of state activity increased sig-nificantly. This began earlier in Bolivia than in Ecuador and Peru, but the nationalizations that took place in the 1970s (especially in Peru) saw the rapid development of state functions, buttressed by the military governments of the time, which closed down spaces for political influence by elites. The boom in commodity prices at the time increased this degree of autonomy. In Ecuador the development of the state-led oil industry helped enhance state autonomy, at least while world prices for crude held up.

It was the crisis of the state-led model of development in the late 1970s and early 1980s that saw the flourishing of business power. This structural shift, made most evident with the debt crisis provoked by the Mexican default of 1982, provided political instruments through which business elites were enabled—often in conjunction with exter-nal actors such as creditor banks and international financial insti-tutions (IFIs)—to influence the course of policy in very direct ways. In Peru, this was evident well before the Mexican default, with the overturn of the Velasco regime and its replacement by a government committed to structural adjustment and economic liberalization. Al-though such policies were forced on Peru by international banks and the IMF, they were also pushed by local business interests that had increasingly opposed the pro-labor reforms of the Velasco period. Although there were business sectors harmed by trade liberalization, the process of ISI had not advanced sufficiently to empower these to resist successfully. Still, although business interests were influ-ential behind the scenes, they only became overt political actors ten years later when fears about the havoc wreaked by Sendero Lumi-noso helped unite the business sector around a single organization,

Confiep, and when the García administration's plans to nationalize the banking system brought them out on to the streets. Similarly, business power in Bolivia grew in the early 1980s in response to the macroeconomic dislocations of the time and the effective collapse in the relative autonomy of the state. Such dislocations were less evident in Ecuador than in Peru and Bolivia, but even there by the early 1980s the civilian governments of the time were susceptible to growing pressures from an increasingly self-confident private sector and institutions associated with it.

Across Latin America, the debt crisis exposed the weakness of the state-led ISI model and, in particular, the failure to mobilize the domestic resources required to fund a greatly expanded state presence, increasingly viewed as both corrupt and inefficient. The discursive attack on the role of the state and the importance of market-led government action gained salience as the 1980s progressed, with the restoration of democratic politics and the need to win "hearts and minds" among the electorate. This intellectual offensive was encouraged by external influences, such as the Chicago School and its influence over economic thinking in the United States (not least in the US Treasury and the IFIs). But changing modes of economic thinking were quick to gain force in the three Central Andean countries where the deficiencies of the state came under attack from institutions connected to the private sector and from a media closely aligned to business. As both the 1929 crash and the debt crisis fifty years later were to show, dominant ways of thinking are swift to establish themselves as new orthodoxies at moments of crisis.

CHAPTER 3

BUSINESS POWER IN THE ERA OF NEOLIBERALISM

The 1980s ushered in an abrupt change in the direction of policy making and governance in Latin America. The region decisively moved away from the model of state capitalism based on ISI strategies and toward a much more liberal, less interventionist model of development. This critical juncture brought to an abrupt end the ISI model that had taken root in much of the region from the 1930s onward, which had given rise to a period of relatively sustained economic growth. The transition in Latin America went parallel to that of democratization in the political sphere, as authoritarian systems of government (many of them military dictatorships) gave way to elected civilian regimes.

The ostensible trigger for these changes was the debt crisis of the early 1980s (specifically the 1982 Mexican debt crisis), which revealed the weaknesses of the state-led model of development and of its ability to fund its activities when sources of foreign capital were suddenly closed off.[1] This shift reflected major changes in the dominant forms of economic thinking, spearheaded initially by the Chicago School but given common currency by the market-oriented models of Thatcherism and Reaganomics with the priority that these afforded to the role of private enterprise and free competition.

The region's huge increase in foreign indebtedness had come about over the previous decade as a consequence of the expansion of commercial borrowing with the recycling of oil money by Western commercial banks. The new, more democratic regimes that emerged did so trammeled by the severe economic constraints imposed by the debt crisis, not least the policies laid down by the IFIs as conditions for the resumption of foreign credit. The gamut of these reforms became known as the Washington Consensus (Williamson 1990).

The twin transition was widely assumed at the time, especially among its intellectual supporters, to represent a self-reinforcing project (Diamond and Plattner 1995; Edwards 1995). Renewed economic stability would help embed new civilian regimes, with more open and democratic forms of government providing the legitimacy to pursue neoliberal restructuring. Free enterprise was considered the correlate of political freedom, as economic actors shook off the burdens of state regulation and control. However, it was also a contradictory process in that the effects of economic liberalization tended to exacerbate inequalities in already highly unequal societies, not just inequalities of income and asset holding but inequalities in access to political power (Oxhorn and Ducatenzeiler 1998; Smith et al. 1994). Arguably, then, the twin transition promised to be inherently problematic: Would not those who lost out to restructuring use the voice and tools offered by democratic society and use them to challenge the policies on offer? Would the model prove politically viable over the medium and longer term?

In practice, the policies associated with what became known as neoliberalism varied considerably over time. In countries with the most serious macroeconomic situations—associated with balance of payments crises and high levels of inflation—they began with the fiscal, monetary, and exchange rate adjustments typical of IMF-imposed stabilization packages (Pop-Eleches 2009). Karen Remmer (1998) has highlighted the role of hyperinflation in creating the circumstances conducive to radical change. Such relatively short-term measures then gave way to longer-term policies associated with structural adjustment: privatization, financial deregulation, trade liberalization, sectoral reforms to encourage investment, and so on, reforms that effectively redrew the frontiers between the public sector and the private sector in favor of the latter (Edwards 1995).

Later on—in many cases in the 1990s—structural adjustment was complemented by "second generation" reforms designed to improve the workings of institutions and to provide political support to the new development model. These included political reengineering, the reinforcement of property rights, reforms to the justice system, and decentralization. Indeed, the policy priorities of organizations such as the IMF and the World Bank evolved over these years, conditioned to no small extent by their involvement in rebuilding and integrating post-Communist polities in the former Soviet Union and Eastern Europe (Freeland 2000).

Within Latin America, the neoliberal "revolution" varied greatly in terms of its speed and degree of radicalness. As many authors have observed, the domestic conditions in each country varied a great deal, in terms of both the conditions provoking the shift and those that helped sustain the new model of economic development. In some countries, like Bolivia (in 1985), Argentina (in 1989), Nicaragua (in 1990) and Peru (in 1990), the shift was sparked by major economic crises, producing situations of hyperinflation that demanded swift and radical changes. In other countries, like Venezuela (1989) and Brazil (in 1990), the external pressures were much weaker, leading to a more gradual economic transformation (Weyland 2002). In Colombia, which had long had a more open, liberal economy, the transition was especially smooth.

Similarly, the nature of the political regimes that introduced liberalizing reforms varied considerably. In Chile, the first country to adopt neoliberalism in 1973, it was the right-wing military dictatorship of General Augusto Pinochet that initiated such policies. In Mexico, it was a one-party state, with the democratic transition taking place only in the latter part of the 1990s. In the case of Peru, it was the semi-authoritarian government of Alberto Fujimori that spearheaded change, though its left-of-center predecessor, the administration of Alan García, had been forced down this route under duress in the years immediately before Fujimori took office (Crabtree 1992, ch. 5). Both Colombia and Venezuela were more conventional democracies, having avoided the earlier period of military dictatorship. Bolivia had just recently returned to democracy when it embarked on economic liberalization in 1985. In several cases such as in Venezuela (under Carlos Andrés Pérez), Argentina (under Carlos Menem), Brazil (under Fernando Henrique Cardoso), and Peru (under Fujimori), governments elected on one ticket adopted very different neoliberal strategies once they reached power (Stokes 2004).[2] Overall, the most drastic neoliberal reforms were introduced by elected presidents who succeeded governments that had openly failed in their attempt to implement heterodox adjustment policies, with Bolivia (after 1985), Argentina (after 1989), and Peru (after 1990) being cases in point (Haggard and Kaufman 1995, 199).

The literature on the twin transition has sought to make sense of these different trajectories and the reason the experience of some countries proved so markedly different from those of others. Scholars have also sought to explain why ostensibly unpopular policies proved acceptable to public opinion, not only at the time they were first introduced but also as time wore on. Some explanations have placed emphasis on external pressure, concretely that of the IMF and World Bank as policy drivers. Some place the focus more on the local domestic situation and the prevalent structure of incentives (Remmer 1998, 25). The power of external actors was probably greater in smaller, more economically vulnerable countries, although in all cases, the two factors both have explanatory power, albeit in different combinations. Some domestic explanations place emphasis on the weakness of opposing constituencies, others on the growing political power of those groups that benefited (Haggard and Kaufman 1992; Pop-Eleches 2009; Weyland 2002).

Many of those writing on the sustainability of neoliberalism—mostly at the end of the 1990s and the beginning of the new millennium—failed to anticipate the reasons that new political challenges emerged in the 2000s, beginning with Venezuela but then spreading to much of the region. There are clearly dangers involved in analyzing contemporary events and failing to see where they might lead. The causes of the "pink tide" revealed shortcomings in the policy design of institutional reforms and the failure of neoliberal governments to meet the promises of growth, employment, and increased well-being with which they were launched.

The focus here is on the rise of national and foreign business power that facilitated, accompanied, and grew as a consequence of the transition to market-led economies in the context of more democratic polities. This took the form of structural power, related to the increased power and the ability of the private sector to influence the direction of capital flows at the moment that newly established political regimes sought to consolidate themselves in power. In Latin America as a whole, this structural power was probably most important at the initial point of redirecting economic policy, especially in those countries most exposed to the vagaries of the international economy. However, the increasingly mobile nature of capital (e.g., portfolio finance), the growth of underregulated tax havens (Zucman 2014), and the economic strengthening of big business as the reforms opened new avenues for capital accumulation made the threat of "exit" more credible, as did (later on) the increasing role and activities of the so-called "*multilatinas*" (Karcher and Schneider 2012).

Instrumental power, the ability of business elites to steer policy in directions that favored their own interests, undoubtedly grew as the period of neoliberalism developed and new institutional mechanisms (formal as well as informal) developed to that end. When organized labor—as well as labor-based political parties, ideologically in retreat following the fall of the Berlin wall—saw themselves weakened as a consequence of both economic crisis and neoliberal restructuring, the balance of instrumental power shifted decisively in favor of business associations and representatives (Kurtz 2004; Oxhorn and Starr 1999). At the same time, economic stabilization and adjustment policies were accompanied by a growing influence of technocrats and of transnational technocratic elite networks in the realm of economic policy making, whose ideological predispositions were generally market-oriented and business-friendly (Conaghan and Malloy 1994).

Similarly, the spread of democratic governance throughout Latin America in the 1980s made it important for business elites to legitimize their new position socially. This was achieved to a remarkable degree throughout the region—in some places more than others—generating widespread acceptance of the new economic model as "the only show in town." Latin America was not alone in this respect, as neoliberal narratives gained acceptance globally, and the fall of communism was certainly a major factor in enabling the emerging discursive hegemony of neoliberal, business- and market-friendly thinking across Latin American and beyond (Castañeda 1993). Many parties on the left—impacted by the fall of the Soviet Union, the troubles afflicting the Cuban regime, the collapse of state-led development models, and the weakening of labor power during the crisis—came round to an acceptance of market principles and the central role of the private sector. The extent to which these overall changes have meant that business achieved state capture in our three countries is a key theme.

Faith in competitive efficiency as the key criterion for economic management appeared to have established itself, displacing redistribution of property and income and the creation of a less unequal society. For much of the 1990s, then, business groups seemed willing to accept democratic norms, particularly if these provided guarantees of relative economic stability and the protection of property rights, two key considerations (Bartell and Payne 1995, 265). Up until the end of the 1990s, the prospects for market-led democracy appeared fair in Latin America. The clouds of uncertainty had yet to make themselves visible both to business and to those studying business preferences.

PERU

Few countries in Latin America, with the possible exception of Argentina, experienced the speed and the depth of the neoliberal transformation as happened in Peru (Gonzales de Olarte 1998). This transformation reflected the extremes of economic dislocation experienced in the last two years of Alan García's government when the economy underwent both a major contraction in GDP and a hyperinflation that peaked at 400 percent a month in the early years of 1990 (Paredes and Sachs 1991). As a consequence, demand in the economy collapsed, rates of unemployment soared, and the informal economy came to account for around 70 percent of the workforce. At the same time, Peru experienced the growth in insurgency from the Maoist-inspired Sendero Luminoso whose armed attacks had spread over much of the country and, most significantly, to the heart of economic and political activity in Lima. The state—and its ability to respond to multiple challenges it faced—appeared to be on its knees, while the heady days of economic heterodoxy initiated back in 1985 seemed a distant memory (Crabtree 1992).

Alberto Fujimori took office in July 1990. The quintessential outsider (few had heard of him even three months before the elections that year), at the polls he beat Peru's famous novelist Mario Vargas Llosa, whose recipe for recovery involved a savage orthodox economic program that threatened to gut living standards even further. Fujimori was elected on a much more moderate ticket, a gradualist program that he was to disregard as soon as he was elected to office. The process of this transformation, an egregious example of "bait and switch," was immediately attributable to the influence of Hernando de Soto, the author of a classic manifesto for deregulation and the affirmation of property rights (1986) and the visits he helped organize for Fujimori in New York and Tokyo in the period before the latter assumed office. Having met with bankers, potential investors, and the leaders of multilateral banks, Fujimori returned to Lima convinced of the need for a thorough restructuring of the economy if the international financial community was to help bail out the Peruvian economy (Boloña 1993).

The sequence of reforms was to stretch out over the first few years of his period in office, but they began with a classic stabilization program, the so-called Fujishock, designed to combat inflation, restore fiscal balance, and facilitate payment of the foreign debt (Gonzales de Olarte 1998, ch. 3). The essence of this radical price adjustment was announced in August 1990 within days of Fujimori's taking office but was substantiated by further measures at the beginning of 1991 when Carlos Boloña, a convinced neoliberal, took over the reins of power at the finance ministry (MEF). Under him, the price liberalization gave way to policies associated with structural adjustment: deregulation, privatization, trade liberalization, and so on. The pace of reform was facilitated by Fujimori's *autogolpe* in April 1992 and the closure of Congress, a measure casting doubt on the notion that economic and political liberalization ran along parallel tracks. A third phase began when Boloña was replaced at the MEF by Jorge Camet, formerly president of the private business confederation (Confiep), with the World Bank playing a key policy-making role (Durand 2003, 430). A new constitution was introduced at the end of 1993, which concentrated political power in the hands of the president while introducing important changes in the economic sphere designed to enshrine the new liberal development model legally and to make it irreversible.

The macroeconomic policies associated with stabilization—fiscal, monetary, and exchange rate—were especially tough, more so than those promised by Vargas Llosa. They led to a sharp rise in unemployment and poverty, somewhat mitigated subsequently as inflation fell and growth picked up. The scrapping of multiple exchange rates led to a piecemeal lowering of tariffs that triggered the closure of many manufacturing firms. Financial liberalization brought the liquidation of state development banks. Labor market reforms made it easier for firms to hire and fire at will. The privatization of public companies, which began in mid-1991 and ran for much of the decade, was probably the most drastic anywhere in Latin America, with almost all large public companies sold to the private sector, mainly to foreign investors (Gonzales de Olarte 1998, ch. 3; Durand 2003, ch. 7; Arce 2010). A new system of private pensions came into existence, in great part modeled on the Chilean scheme of private pension funds (AFPs, administradores de fondos de pensiones), creating a new and powerful business sector and expanding stock market activities. The neoliberal "revolution" also brought into play new institutions designed to complement economic reforms, such as the creation of a new tax authority (Sunat, the Superintendencia Nacional de Administración Tributaria), a network of regulatory offices designed (at least in principle) to protect the consumer from market abuses, and new agencies (such as Foncodes, the Fondo de Cooperación para el Desarrollo Social) designed to mitigate poverty and deprivation.[3]

The reforms produced a massive change in the structure of ownership in the Peruvian economy, sharply reducing the share of the public sector and greatly increasing that of the private sector (in old and new areas), especially that pertaining to foreign capital. This was to lead to a transformation in patterns of societal influence, with the private sector exercising greatly enhanced influence over decision making. Peru became an emblematic case of state capture (Crabtree and Durand 2017, 108).

Peru's economic transformation during the course of the 1990s went hand in hand with an increasing level of authoritarianism in the political domain, one underpinned by the marginalization of representative political parties and popular organizations, together with the introduction of patterns of top-down clientelism that proved effective in winning elections. In the convoluted politics that emerged with Fujimori in 1990, the key power actors were hardly democratic: the security forces, the private sector, and the multilateral banks (Conaghan 2005). The *autogolpe* of April 1992 effectively removed the constraint of an elected Congress in which Fujimori's party, Cambio 90, had only a minority of seats. Under international pressure, Fujimori was obliged to convene elections for a new Congress in which his supporters won an absolute majority of seats. The Congress set about rewriting the 1979 constitution, and this sought to give solid legal guarantees to the new neoliberal model. It also removed the barrier to Fujimori's reelection, achieved with a fulsome majority in the 1995 elections.

Fujimori had won significant popularity by his success in confronting the twin demons of hyperinflation and political violence (the capture of Sendero Luminoso's leader, Abimael Guzmán, in September 1992 led to the dismantling of much of what was left of this insurgent group). This popularity was enhanced by the use of fiscal resources to curry support among the poorest populations of Peru through Foncodes and other social programs that aimed at reducing rural and urban deprivation. Fujimori's ability to rally opinion in opposition to traditional political party elites—he labeled them the *partidocracia*—has been referred to by several authors as "neo-populism" as a concomitant to neoliberalism (Roberts 1995; Weyland 1996). Once reelected in 1995, he turned his attention to how to overcome constitutional barriers to a further reelection in 2000, a quest that led him in an increasingly autocratic direction (Conaghan 2005, 117–40). Indeed, the fatal weakness of Fujimori's style of governance was its destruction of the institutional mechanisms in ways designed to ensure the sustainability of the model. This anti-institutionalism, which led Fujimori to seek repeated reelection, finally proved his undoing when he was forced to resign in the wake of overtly fraudulent polls.

There can be no doubt that privatization, deregulation, and the reorientation of the economy toward export-led growth, which helped attract a new generation of international corporations (especially in mining), greatly enhanced the power of the private sector, along with repressive policies unleashed on the unions and the effects of labor-market reforms (termed "flexibilization"). The domestic private sector had previously benefited from the return to a more liberal economic approach under Belaúnde but had suffered the consequences of the economic crisis that escalated during the rule of his successor, Alan García. The private sector had emerged as a strident political actor in opposition to García's government, especially in its support for the Movimiento Libertad, established by Vargas Llosa to oppose García's abortive bank nationalization in 1987. Business groups also gave fulsome financial support to Vargas Llosa and his Fredemo (Frente Democrático) coalition in the buildup to the 1990 elections. Further, business power was significantly enhanced through the role of Confiep, which brought most business organizations together into a united front after 1984.[4]

At the same time and, as a consequence of the neoliberal reforms, international capital came to play a major role again (albeit behind the scenes) in the strengthening of the private sector as a whole. One of the striking features of business power as it emerged in the 1990s was the convergence of the interests of foreign investors with local business groups. Yanacocha, one of the earliest open pit mining projects, became a symbol of the new extractive era, as it was developed in 1991 as a joint project between the giant US company Newmont Mining and the locally owned Benavides group.

The structural power of the private sector emerged with clarity in the period prior to Fujimori under the García presidency. García's heterodox approach had been premised on the construction of an alliance with the key private sector economic groups, the so-called Twelve Apostles, with a view to these providing the necessary investment to promote growth (Durand 2017a). Without that investment, the model was doomed to fail. The model thus depended crucially on the economic support of local business groups. The 1987 bank nationalization was partly designed as retribution for the failure of the private sector to engage with a government with which it otherwise felt little affinity (Crabtree 1992, 121-24).[5]

During the second half of García's presidency, characterized by growing fiscal and balance of payments problems, the need for capital became ever more pressing. García and his ministers were obliged by circumstances to turn to the IFIs, especially the IMF, in the bid to restore inflows and thus remedy the macroeconomic imbalances. The IMF's repeated refusal to grant García the necessary seal of approval, due in part to his previous unilateral limiting of debt service payments to commercial banks, helped drive the hyperinflationary price spiral that took root in his last year in office. The structural pressures to shift away from the model of state-led development were therefore present well before Fujimori's election in 2001, pressures that García was unable to heed.

Fujimori's about-turn on his policy program came about when it became clear to him, following his election, that the price of external support was a wholehearted reversal of policy and the acceptance of far-reaching liberalizing economic reforms. It was also clear that any sustained recovery of the economy would depend on the economic support from international and local business groups, even though these had been smitten by the preceding crisis. Those in Fujimori's initial entourage who were less committed to this objective were given short shrift, and with Boloña's appointment to the MEF at the beginning of 1991 the scene was set for the *cambio de rumbo* favored by the new finance minister and supported by leading business groups (Boloña 1993). Fujimori's prompt decision to service Peru's foreign debt fully in 1991 helped convince the international business community that the new government was committed to this new path. And Boloña's almost fundamentalist zeal in pursuit of his restructuring program, notwithstanding the interests affected by trade liberalization, reportedly even took officials at the IMF and World Bank by surprise (Iguíñiz 1998). His was a fervor that helped reinforce international business confidence. Indeed, given the lack of a clear domestically designed policy blueprint during the early years of adjustment, policy followed closely the blueprints emanating from the Washington-based financial institutions. Most of the economic reforms were enacted by executive decree, bypassing congressional scrutiny and approval and adopting procedures supposedly designed for use only in extraordinary circumstances.[6] The authoritarian interval between the 1992 presidential coup and the election of a new Congress in 1993, saw a sudden increase in the use of decree laws. An outstanding example is the creation of a private pension fund (AFP) system inspired by the Chilean model and pursuant to World Bank recommendations.

The private sector thus emerged as an enthusiastic supporter of the adjustment strategy, especially when the short-term pain it engendered gave way to macroeconomic benefits as GDP began to grow again (albeit from a low base) and inflation rates fell away. The domestic investment climate improved as a result of this policy, and some capital—which had fled massively in the late 1980s—began to return, thus helping domestic firms expand their activities. Private investment as a proportion of GDP accelerated quickly during the first five years of the 1990s (Wise 2003, 240). Fujimori scooped the rewards for his privatization policy, which led to a massive inflow of capital from abroad. In the period between 1992 and 1997, sales of public companies are estimated to have generated revenues totaling more than US$7 billion, the bulk of it from foreign companies investing in Peru.[7] However, as the state gained a certain degree of autonomy due to the sharp improvement in its fiscal position and consequent decrease in its dependence on investment inflows, this structural aspect of business power diminished. This was more than made up by the increase in instrumental power achieved during these years.

As a consequence of Fujimori's liberalizing reforms, Peru witnessed a large shift in the structure of ownership. Whereas, in 1975, the public sector accounted for 21 percent of GDP, by 2000 this was reduced to only 6 percent, whereas the share of the business sector (foreign plus domestic) increased from 38 percent to 56 percent (Crabtree and Durand 2017, 108). The cooperative sector all but disappeared. The Peruvian companies that had been dominant among García's Twelve Apostles retained their influence, but Peru's top companies by 2000 came to be dominated by foreign companies and a handful of Peruvian groups such as Romero, Brescia, and Benavides, especially in the all-important mining and financial sectors, although in many cases with close links (interlocking shareholdings) to domestic interests. The establishment of alliances with local capital provided foreign-owned companies with valuable local political connections.

The accumulation of instrumental business power in these years perhaps begins with the direct rapport achieved between Confiep and Fujimori in the days immediately after his election, when the president-elect met with Jorge Camet, its president, and members of its managerial board.[8] Whereas Hernando de Soto became the intermediary with the foreign business and banking elite, Camet—who was to replace Boloña as minister of economy and finance in early 1993—was the link with the domestic business community. Confiep became a crucial mechanism for building unity within the heterogenous world of Peru's business organizations and for promoting the business agenda at the level of the state. Whereas Boloña gave guarantees to the international business community, Camet's appointment in January 1993 cemented the organic link between the government and the domestic private sector. Camet was to remain minister until June 1998, becoming a key member of the power troika along with Vladimiro Montesinos (who ran the security establishment) and General Nicolás Hermoza (the commander in chief of the armed forces). Through the social programs of the Ministry of the Presidency, Fujimori focused on building an electoral base among the rural poor. Power was thus not only focused on the executive (to the exclusion of Congress) but also within the executive in the hands of the president.

In this context, the MEF became a *superministerio*, the guarantor of economic policy continuity, controlled then (as subsequently) by appointees enjoying the full confidence of the business and banking communities. Not only did it control budgetary expenditure and thus the activities of other ministries, regulatory authorities, and local administrations but it also supervised flows of foreign assistance, building a close and lasting relationship with neoliberal technocrats hired to conduct studies. Similarly, the presidency of the central bank, the superintendency of banks and insurance, and the heads of the various regulatory agencies were allotted to people with proven commitment to the neoliberal model. Following the "revolving door" mechanism, many of them were recruited either from the private sector or from Peruvians working for foreign banks, returning to these jobs when their allotted time working for the state elapsed.[9]

Closely tied in with these state agencies were corporate law firms, private consultancy firms, lobbyists, and opinion polling agencies, usually also led by people with close connections into economic policy-making spheres and recruited from *limeño* elite circles. The boundaries between these various influential functions were often blurred. A good example is the Instituto Peruano de Economía (IPE), set up by Roberto Abusada in 1994, a former vice minister in the MEF in the early 1980s with strong personal ties to the World Bank. Abusada worked as an advisor to Camet on issues of trade and taxation. Under his aegis, IPE published numerous influential papers on policy issues. When Camet resigned as minister in 1988, he became a board member of IPE. He was replaced as minister by Jorge Baca, an IPE economist. At the same time, Fritz Dubois, an advisor to Camet at the MEF, became a manager at IPE. Similar sorts of linkages provided contact points between other consultancies, such as Apoyo SA, which was involved in both research activities and opinion polling and was closely integrated into policy-making circuits under both Fujimori and the Toledo administration from 2001 to 2006 (Durand 2010a).

Throughout the Fujimori era and subsequently, Confiep thus

provided the key link between big business and the state. It brought together sectoral business gremios led by the biggest firms, providing them with a single voice. In this respect Peru's business elite represented a much more unified force as a pressure group than was the case in either Bolivia or Ecuador. Confiep brought together business leaders from the financial sector, mining, energy, agroindustry, and fishing, all with a keen interest in maintaining the export-led strategy.[10] Bankers and miners were particularly dominant, reflecting the new economic power structure. Some other gremios, like the association representing manufacturing (the SNI), eventually broke with Confiep in 1998, after sensing that its interests were not being properly represented, which led to a loss of policy influence. Some provincial business interests never did join Confiep, in part because they did not form part of the exclusive *limeño* elite. Confiep's predominance, however, did not diminish.

One of the characteristics of the Fujimori years was the ostracism of political parties and their leaders from spheres of decision making. The influence of parties, which might have challenged the hegemony of Fujimori and those in his circle, was effectively truncated by the 1992 *autogolpe*. Fujimori's style was to promote "technical" solutions and to marginalize political debate. Whereas his own party—which underwent several changes of name—enjoyed business support at times of election, other parties were largely excluded. His preference was for personal relationships rather than institutional ones. The extent to which business interests funded his election expenses is unclear, but the pattern became well established under his successors as the Lava Jato revelations were to show. Right up to the end of his government, prominent business interests maintained their support, despite clear evidence of illegal activity and the risks to political stability that these portended.

The historical record for these years indicates the multiplicity of ways in influencing state decisions, but much of that influence was conducted through informal channels that bypassed formal democratic institutions. Domestic business enjoyed privileged access to the state and deference in much of the media, and it saw its interests prosper as a consequence. Foreign investors were less evident in the instrumental influence they wielded, but they saw their interests protected both by a compliant state and through alliances with domestic firms. Organizations like Confiep catered for their needs too, creating a harmony of interests absent in previous periods. Other groups in society, which benefited much less from neoliberalism and were effectively shut out of key decision-making circles, were unable to muster anywhere near the degree of instrumental power wielded by the dominant business organizations during these years.

In spite of its drastic nature and the initial social upheavals caused by the Fujishock in 1990, the neoliberal model gained a remarkable degree of acceptance in society as a whole, more so than in Bolivia and Ecuador. It is fair to say that the Fujimori regime generated a degree of hegemony with widespread acceptance within civil society. This owed much to the government's success in overcoming the disastrous situation it had inherited, a situation that affected all sectors of society, and most of all the poorest. The twin scourges of hyperinflation and terrorist violence produced a deep yearning for stability, a stability that the authoritarian Fujimori regime was able to provide. Few countries had experienced two such traumas at the same time, and this goes a long way to explaining the success of the government in helping to create a narrative that supported the neoliberal agenda and provided it with the necessary legitimation.

The institutions we have identified as having strong instrumental power also played an important role in exercising discursive power, however. During these years think tanks, consultancy organizations, and lobby groups influenced public opinion through their various ties with the media. These linkages constituted a dense network of political power, based on elite family ties and friendships, with the capacity to inform and influence public opinion. The idea of Peru as a *país minero* that justified the economic privileges given to powerful mining groups gained common currency, in part because of the activities of pro-mining lobby groups and relayed through the media. The El Comercio group, by far the most powerful media organization in Peru, was closely tied into this nexus of business power, constituting a stout defender of the market economy. Not only was *El Comercio* Peru's most influential newspaper, but it owned titles that directed themselves toward low-income groups as well as controlling major television channels. The Fujimori government also encouraged the growth of sensationalist tabloid newspapers that routinely defended his government's actions. It did much to stifle opposition media (Conaghan 2005, ch. 7). The media were successful in these years in fostering the idea that there was no alternative and that to preach otherwise was simply to invite a return to a past in which left-of-center political parties had brought Peru to the brink of ruin. Private universities, which multiplied during the Fujimori years, also played an important role in shaping an intellectual climate that was favorable to the new economic model.

The diffusion of such narratives was greatly facilitated by the lack of any powerful counternarrative. Left-wing parties had been discredited by the upheavals of the late 1980s, and they performed weakly in the electoral contests during the 1990s and beyond. The media shunned those advocating any critical or opposition views. The trade union movement, which had provided an institutional bedrock for the growth of the left in the late 1970s and 1980s, was badly undermined both by hyperinflation and by its failure to protect workers' living standards as well as by privatization and the labor reforms pursued by Fujimori. Those that opposed the dominant neoliberal narrative were effectively shut out of policy-making circles. The main labor confederation could organize strikes and demonstrations, but such opposition that it could muster failed to find much echo in the wider society.

The extent of state capture achieved by private-sector interest groups is notable in the Peruvian case, more so than in Bolivia and Ecuador. Capture was achieved principally through control of key institutions governing the conduct of economic policy—not just the MEF but also the central bank (BCRP), the Superintendency of Banks and Insurance (SBS) and the regulatory agencies. State capture involved the insulation of these institutions from democratic pressures, while the political reforms engineered by Fujimori attempted (unsuccessfully, as it turned out) to keep power in his hands indefinitely. Still, in spite of the growing rejection of Fujimori's plans for reelection and in a context of extended corruption and repression, the neoliberal model continued to flourish, and state capture became even more complete under his successors. The space afforded for alternative narratives to neoliberalism to prosper in this context was extremely limited, leading to what we have described elsewhere as "political capture," a form of capture that went way beyond just the state and in which business culture became practically hegemonic (Crabtree and Durand 2017).

The development of opposition to the Fujimori government in its last few years did not represent a rejection of the neoliberal agenda as such but, rather, a protest movement against the increasingly authoritarian demeanor and practice of the president. Unable to find an institutional route toward a succession that would guarantee policy stability in the economic sphere, Fujimori was forced into a series of expedients of doubtful constitutionality in order to keep himself in power after 2000. Although the impact of the Asian crisis of 1998 impacted Peru and contributed toward his declining popularity, the campaign to challenge the results of fraudulent elections in 2000 drew its inspiration from growing disquiet about the degree of political manipulation used to perpetuate the Fujimori regime. Business organizations were not actively involved in the attempt to stem Fujimori's grip on power. Most, and Confiep in particular, remained loyal to Fujimori right up until the end; yet they quickly accommodated themselves to post-Fujimori governments while remaining attached to the followers of *fujimorismo* in the political sphere.[11]

BOLIVIA

The process of economic liberalization in Bolivia preceded that of Peru by a full five years. In 1985, with the election of Alan García, Peru saw the initiation of an ill-fated exercise in economic heterodoxy explicitly aimed at countering the limited neoliberalism initiated but never consolidated under Fernando Belaúnde. In Bolivia, by contrast, the 1985 elections brought Víctor Paz Estenssoro back to power, and he initiated a radical process of pro-market economic reforms, the antithesis of the statist polices introduced by the very same politician in the years after 1952. Bolivia was undergoing the same sort of macroeconomic crisis with hyperinflation that was to take place five years later in Peru, a crisis that shook society to its foundations, a critical juncture that upset the previous order and resulted in a sudden and radical change in policy making. Recently elected, the Paz Estenssoro government pronounced its Decree Law 21060, which sought to stabilize the economy on the back of an orthodox package of measures that would reduce the role of the state and profoundly shift its relationship with the private sector.

Over the following two decades Bolivia would come to be seen as a poster child of neoliberal restructuring in Latin America, showing just how an ill-functioning highly statist system could be turned around (at considerable social cost) into a more market-oriented one within the maintenance of formally democratic institutions (Gamarra 1994; Crabtree and Whitehead 2001). The person with whom this transition is most associated is Gonzalo Sánchez de Lozada, who became Paz Estenssoro's planning minister in 1985, succeeded him as leader of the MNR party, was president between 1993 and 1997, and then returned to the presidency in 2002. As owner of Bolivia's largest private sector mining company (Comsur), Sánchez de Lozada typified the shift toward the private sector becoming one of the first "business presidents." It was his ouster in 2003 that effectively ended the neoliberal cycle in Bolivia, giving rise two years later to the election of Evo Morales and the initiation of another state-led period of development. As well as being a key intellectual author of the decree (DL 21060) initiating the politics of stabilization and structural adjustment, Sánchez de Lozada was also the author of the Plan de Todos, the 1993 policy blueprint that introduced important and innovative second-generation reforms designed to underpin the liberalizing policy changes in the economic sphere politically.

DL 21060 gave birth to what became known as the Nueva Política Económica (NPE), which was, in essence, a major fiscal corrective designed radically to reduce the scope of the state and its activities while at the same time freeing the exchange rate from government manipulation, contracting the money supply, and ending various forms of economic regulation. As Conaghan and Malloy have argued (1994, 145), the NPE deviated from traditional orthodoxy in neither leading immediately to a resumption of foreign debt payments nor including an explicit commitment to privatization. It led, however, to a severe reduction in the economic role of the state, most particularly in the tin mining industry where the state mining corporation (Comibol) withdrew from all but a handful of mining operations, releasing some twenty-five thousand mineworkers from the state payroll.[12] Layoffs were also made throughout the public sector to reduce the deficit, while fuel prices rose, along with public sector tariffs and some taxes. The package was successful in reining in inflation and eventually in restoring growth (Morales and Sachs 1990; Dunkerley 1990). The Paz Estenssoro government was also able to shrug off opposition from both organized labor and some business sectors and to sustain its policies through political deals between the MNR and Banzer's Acción Democrática Nacionalista (ADN).[13]

Indeed, it was the ability of Bolivia's political elite to establish pacts to ensure continuity in the economic sphere that helped underscore the relative political stability of these years. Under Jaime Paz Zamora, who succeeded his uncle in 1989, the model remained in place, helped by an alliance between his previously left-wing Movimiento de la Izquierda Revolucionaria (MIR) and the right-wing ADN. Paz Zamora's government did little to deepen the reforms, although his government presided over the privatization of a few state companies. It was the Plan de Todos under Sánchez de Lozada that took pro-market reform into new areas, fundamentally seeking to extend the beneficiaries of the model and to promote its political sustainability.

A centerpiece of the plan was Sánchez de Lozada's scheme for "capitalizing" selected public companies, a part-privatization by which foreign companies would invest up to just over 50 percent over their supposed value, taking management control and, with the income generated, funding a universal pension (the Bonosol) for those over sixty-five (Bowen and Bauer 1997). As Sánchez de Lozada acknowledged, a full-scale privatization would have proved politically incendiary. By far the most important company "capitalized" was the state oil company Yacimientos Petrolíferos Fiscales Bolivianos (YPFB), but "capitalization" also included the state-owned telecommunications (Empresa Nacional de Telecomunicaciones, ENTEL), electricity (Empresa Nacional de Electricidad, ENDE), airline (Lloyd Aéreo Boliviano, LAB), and railway (Empresa Nacional de Ferrocarriles, ENFE) companies (Molina 2021, 83–84). Another key reform included the Popular Participation program, a policy of administrative decentralization and municipal democratization with community oversight, designed to promote a state presence at the local level in rural areas where it had previously hardly existed and to channel resources through a multitude of new municipalities (Gray Molina 2001). These two key measures were complemented by other institutional reforms designed to improve education, enhance legal security, improve land tenure rights, and counter corruption.

All these more institutional reforms sought, in one way or another, to strengthen the linkages between neoliberal economic order and improved democratic governance (Crabtree and Whitehead 2001). But as with DL 21060, they parted company with standardized and tailor-made reform packages recommended by the World Bank and others. Indeed, initially at least, they ran into some criticism in multilateral bank circles. Sánchez de Lozada maintained, however, that their political acceptance related to their being seen as "Bolivian" measures, not ones imposed by creditors or the Washington-based financial institutions. In this respect, policy making in Bolivia demonstrated more flair and innovation than was the case in Peru. Yet, the ability of the neoliberal order to sustain itself proved far less durable in Bolivia than in Peru.

As in Peru, the liberalizing reforms played to the advantage of private business, although business remained more fragmented and less politically dominant than was the case in Peru. Private business interests increased in number and influence in the period preceding 1985, playing a not insignificant role in the ideological battles that finally forced the Siles Zuazo government to retire early and allow fresh elections. However, their economic strength and political muscle was much weaker than in Peru. The business sector was still small, heterogenous, and characterized by divides between regional elites in the highlands and those of the lowlands whose economic power had grown in the 1960s and 1970s. Unlike Peru, there was no powerful institution representing Bolivia's business sector with a single voice. The business sector was extremely well organized and cohesive in the lowland department of Santa Cruz around the Federación de Empresarios Privados de Santa Cruz (FEPSC) and the local sectoral chambers representing different branches of the economy. Santa Cruz developed in the 1960s and 1970s almost as an "island" of free enterprise, with the local civic committee (the Comité Pro Santa Cruz) providing strong political leadership. These institutions acted autonomously from the CEPB at the national level and business groups from other regions in the pressure they brought to bear on government (Eaton 2017; Peña Claros 2010).[14]

The NPE was broadly welcomed by the private sector as a positive response to an otherwise disastrous situation. Although these policies were effectively designed by businesspersons and like-minded technocrats, including Sánchez de Lozada himself (Molina 2021, 45-46, 51-86), not all sectors of the economic elite were enthusiastic, especially with the trade and exchange rate policies that threatened many local businesses exposed to international competition. The reduction in tariffs and the overvaluation of the exchange rate together encouraged imports. The manufacturers' association, the Cámara Nacional de Industrias (CNI), and agricultural interests in Santa Cruz represented by the Cámara Agropecuario del Oriente (CAO) both lobbied the Paz Estenssoro government for policy changes, but to little effect (Conaghan and Malloy 1994, 156). The umbrella business organization CEPB acknowledged these criticisms but did little to mobilize for change. Business was more dependent on government in La Paz than in Santa Cruz. The removal of the left-wing Siles government and the achievement of relative price stability by 1986 and 1987 did much to allay private sector qualms, especially when an uplift in growth and consequent domestic demand was achieved toward the end of the 1980s.

The effects of liberalization and the restoration of economic and political stability did much to favor the private sector. Corporate interests grew in economic power, structured around the consolidation of private banks and reinforced by their links to the real economy, especially the dynamic agroindustry of Santa Cruz. As Fernando Molina has argued (2019, 190), the fortunes of the business class—traditionally unstable and dependent on variations in commodity prices—grew steadily. The nature of the private sector also changed substantially with the entry into Bolivia of foreign firms, the main beneficiaries of privatization, first under Paz Zamora and then more consistently under Sánchez de Lozada, and the knock-on effects these had in stimulating complementary economic activities throughout the private sector.

Foreign investment in former key state-run industries as a result of the "capitalization" program stimulated production of goods and services within the domestic economy, especially in the hydrocarbons sector in Santa Cruz and Tarija. Even then there were no more than fifty or so relatively large economic and financial groups with a combination of local and foreign capital that dominated the economy, mainly concentrated in mining, finance, and agribusiness. Bolivia's main companies, during the second half of the 1990s, were former state-owned enterprises such as YPFB and the national telecommunications company ENTEL, which had been sold to foreign investors. Further important companies included the brewery Cervecería Boliviana Nacional (CBN) and the cement firm Sociedad Boliviana de Cemento (SOBOCE), which at that time still were under the control of wealthy families (Molina 2019, 42). Most companies in the manufacturing sector, however, were small and technically less developed than in neighboring countries. At the bottom of the pyramid were an estimated five hundred thousand *microempresas* with very low levels of productivity (Grebe López 2001). The neoliberal phase in Bolivia strengthened the private sector, but its level of influence over policy making was less than in Peru, whereas the influence of multilateral banks and foreign donors was a good deal more.

The structural power of the business sector during these years was less important than its instrumental power. The ability of private enterprise to threaten government by the withdrawal of investment or through capital flight was limited by the fact that investment was largely in assets such as land (agribusiness) and extractive industries that were more difficult to liquidate than financial assets. Moreover, during the two decades between 1985 and 2005, during which policy making continued to be led by neoliberal principles, there was little need for businesses to feel threatened by adverse state policies. At the very beginning of this period, the NEP was guided by (and largely accepted) the fact that Bolivia urgently needed to increase levels of private investment given the effective bankruptcy of the state. DL 21060 led to the return of some capital that had sought refuge abroad during the turbulent times of the Siles government. At the end of the period, structural power became a factor as the threat of the model being overturned became a reality with the rise of the Movimiento al Socialismo (MAS). Two measures introduced in 2004 and 2005 elicited such fears: the tabling of legislation to introduce a wealth tax (strongly opposed by domestic elites) and the passage of legislation to raise the tax threshold on hydrocarbons production (opposed by foreign investors in the gas industry as well as by domestic interests connected to the hydrocarbons sector). The fear that foreign gas companies would respond by halting future investment due to proposed increases in taxation forced the government of Carlos Mesa (2003–2005) to back off from implementing the more radical policies demanded by the MAS and others (Fairfield 2015a, ch. 8).

Bolivia's higher dependence on foreign aid inflows during these years set it apart from Peru and Ecuador. The design of the NPE was influenced (though not dictated) by policies approved in the Washington-based institutions. Jeffrey Sachs was dispatched to Bolivia to assist with implementation. Macroeconomic stabilization was aided by the inflow of resources from outside, especially from USAID, which, along with others, sought to mitigate some of the dire social costs of adjustment.

As in the 1950s, foreign aid played an important part in Bolivia's fiscal survival during these years, reflecting the lack of an effective system of taxation. By the late 1990s, Bolivia was receiving more aid per capita than any other Latin American country. In 1999, it accounted for 30 percent of central government income (Klein 2003, 252). A substantial slice of these aid flows was destined not for the relief of poverty but for the elimination of coca production in the Chapare and its substitution by other crops. USAID was a particularly important donor during these years (Heilman 2017). Foreign donors were keen to promote neoliberal development in Bolivia and were generous in their lending policies. These culminated in highly favorable debt relief arrangements with write-offs totaling US$1.35 billion in the period between 1999 and 2006, including debt to the IMF, the World Bank, the IDB, and bilateral donors (Morales 2008). It was a move that was later to assist Evo Morales in his quest to rid Bolivia of policy conditionalities.

In terms of instrumental power, business sectors enjoyed access to decision making through the political parties that dominated these years and the pacts between them that sustained policy continuity. Both the MNR and ADN were parties that enjoyed close contact with economic elites.[15] Initially, the ADN encapsulated many of the interests that had prospered during the Banzer dictatorship in the 1970s, but the MNR also brought such elites close to power, including mining magnates such as Sánchez de Lozada himself. As a consequence, between 1985 and 2005, business interests were directly represented in government by individual businesspersons and like-minded technocrats.[16] At the same time, collective business influence was also limited through much of the period by the strength of technocratic governments that had some considerable success in isolating economic policy making from the political sphere, thereby resisting organized lobbying on the part of vested interests. Given the scale of the crisis inherited in 1985 and the drive to reduce state influence over the economy, government policy enjoyed general support within the business community. Moreover, the way in which elections operated in Bolivia reinforced the ability of party leaders to maintain control over Congress and thus reduce the scope for business to influence decision making through the Congress.[17]

This relative executive autonomy also characterized Sánchez de Lozada's period in office in the mid-1990s, allowing the president to enact the proposals contained in the Plan de Todos relatively free from interference from business lobbies and other sources of pressure. By no means all of his policies were welcomed, especially in Santa Cruz where there was growing resistance to the historically rooted centralizing instincts of the MNR. The decentralizing measures contained in the Popular Participation scheme averted giving greater influence to regional bodies dominated by local elites in Santa Cruz, channeling resources instead through newly created municipal structures, mainly rural.

The ability of central government to maintain its dominant position began to unravel after 1997 when Banzer became president again. He proved more beholden to elites in Santa Cruz than his predecessor, among other things lowering their tax burden. Also, business elites began to worry for the protection of their interests, especially over property rights, as a new wave of popular protest began to develop. In 2000, the so-called water war (*guerra del agua*) in Cochabamba, which led to the expulsion of the US company Bechtel from Bolivia, stoked growing concerns in the business community that "pacted democracy"—the elite-centered system of rotating party alliances in power—was perhaps no longer acting as guarantor of their interests.

Such fears were confirmed in 2002 when Evo Morales of the MAS won a surprising 21 percent of the vote in the presidential elections, almost the same level as Sánchez de Lozada who was later elected president by Congress. These presidential elections signaled the demise of "pacted democracy" and dealt a particularly severe blow to the ADN. As a consequence, Sánchez de Lozada's second government (2002-2003) found itself having to take measures that went against the business community's collective interests. Faced with a large fiscal deficit, Sánchez de Lozada introduced proposals for an income tax that were keenly resisted by the CEPB and other private sector institutions. Despite strong lobbying, the business community was unable to force the government to jettison the proposals; they were finally dropped because of popular protest on the streets that owed nothing to business lobbying (Fairfield 2015a, ch. 8).

The ability of governments to foster societal support for the neo-liberal agenda during these years was limited, at least on a national scale. The trauma of hyperinflation led to a grudging acceptance of the need for a change in policy direction, and the ability of civil society organizations to challenge the new regime was limited. Bolivia's previously powerful union movement was gravely weakened by the crisis and the measures that ensued from it. A series of strikes and demonstrations failed to push the new policy agenda off the government's chosen course. But, as the indigenous Marcha por el Territorio y la Dignidad (March for land and dignity) in 1990 signaled early on, popular sector movements were not destroyed but, rather, underwent a process of transformation and started to resurface with full force starting with the *guerra del agua* in 2000 (Van Cott 2005, ch. 3; Yashar 2005, ch. 5).

The reforms enacted by Sánchez de Lozada in the 1990s were designed to build political support for the model in the wider society through measures like the Bonosol, for example, and the channeling of state resources to the local level through Popular Participation. But such measures did little to stem the growing climate of societal rejection of neoliberalism that became evident in the late 1980s, particularly as the promises made of employment generation and improved living standards for the poor proved wildly exaggerated.[18] The arguments fielded by the CEPB (typically that higher taxation would penalize the formal sector and thereby reduce employment) cut little ice beyond the circle of its own members.

Where discursive power proved most effective was in Santa Cruz. Here the dense network of business-related institutions that had long dominated local politics proved adept at building up a regional identity designed to counterpose the supposedly centralizing efforts of politicians in La Paz. According to this narrative, the economic wealth of Santa Cruz had been plundered by successive governments in order to subsidize other less prosperous parts of the country and their less enterprising citizens. This line of argument had a strong racial connotation that compared the success of Santa Cruz and its adherence to business values with the rest of the country where development was retarded by the dominance of indigenous ethnicities (Bowen 2014; Eaton 2011). This racist, conservative, and regionalist discourse, disseminated by local media, sought to unify all *cruceños* around the defense of their local institutions against inroads from outside. The salience of this sort of xenophobia depended greatly on specific conjunctures and was deployed with particular virulence against leftist governments in La Paz with their supposedly "social-ist" agendas bent on attacking the sanctity of property rights valued so highly in Santa Cruz by landowning elites (Peña Claros 2010). In the early 1980s, this discourse had been aimed against Siles Zuazo, seen at the time as the "enemy" of Santa Cruz. It was to reemerge with even greater force against Evo Morales after his election in 2005. But even in the neoliberal interlude, civic leaders inculcated the no-tion of the *cruceño* identity, seeking also to extend this discursive effort to other parts of lowland Bolivia whose economic and political interests aligned themselves with those of Santa Cruz.

Much lauded at the time within multilateral bank circles for pol-icy successes in bringing a degree of macroeconomic and political stability that followed a bout of extreme instability, the Bolivian road to liberalism ended up proving hard to maintain. Although the return to a more statist model under Evo Morales was unforeseen by com-mentators at the time, it took root with a vengeance after 2005. As the market-based model failed to provide the material benefits to the mass of the population, particularly as the global economy went into downturn at the end of the 1990s, political reforms proved unable to incorporate the poor and indigenous majority of the Bolivian popu-lation. "Pacted democracy," which remained an elite-centered affair, therefore failed to stem the development of new social movements that were critical of both neoliberalism and real existing liberal de-mocracy.[19] Simultaneously, it failed to provide for the long-term needs of and guarantees demanded by an evolving private sector. Bolivian "exceptionalism" thus proved relatively short-lived.

ECUADOR

In contrast to Bolivia under Siles Zuazo and Peru under Alan García, Ecuador did not see the emergence of a left-of-center government adopting heterodox measures in response to the economic crisis of the early 1980s. Nor did the country experience anything similar to the dramatic about-turns initiated by Paz Estenssoro and Fujimori, which were facilitated precisely by the open failure of the preceding attempts at heterodox reforms. These two features are clearly relat-ed, setting the Ecuadorian case apart. In terms of social power rela-tions, the pervasive fragmentation of Ecuador's sociopolitical landscape prevented the emergence of a coalition both willing and able to implement either a set of heterodox or a comprehensive package of orthodox neoliberal reforms (Burbano de Lara 2006, 306).

Still, this is not a story of complete political deadlock either. In the end, each and every president elected in the 1980s and 1990s pushed for some type of market-, outward-, and business-oriented economic reform. And, even if most of these attempts met with significant resistance from within Congress, on the streets, and partially also from business elites themselves, Ecuador did gradually experience a neoliberal transformation of its development model that generally corresponds to the regional pattern (García Pascual 2003; Hey and Klak 1999; Mejía 2009; Thoumi and Grindle 1992).

During the 1980s the presidency of León Febres-Cordero (1984-1988) was the closest Ecuador came to the conformation of a business-led government willing to embark on comprehensive neoliberal reforms. Yet, in line with the overall assessment of the eventual failure of the attempt to impose neoliberalism under Febres-Cordero (Burbano de Lara 2006, 303-7; Conaghan and Malloy 1994, 162-202), comparative assessments of structural economic reforms in Latin America do not attribute significant changes to his period in office. According to data from ECLAC (Morley et al. 1999), Ecuador saw a gradual reduction in capital controls throughout the 1980s and early 1990s, important steps toward trade liberalization under Rodrigo Borja (1988-1992), and significant financial liberalization under Sixto Durán-Ballén (1992-1996). It was under Durán-Ballén that a whole series of neoliberal reforms were initiated and, at least in part, implemented.[20]

As a result, by the mid-1990s, Ecuador was scoring about the same as Bolivia and Peru when it comes to most areas of economic reforms. The one key area that continued to set Ecuador apart from Bolivia, Peru, and other "top reformers" was privatization (Lora 2001; Morley et al. 1999). There was persistent resistance to privatization in Congress, from trade unions as well as among the general population. This opposition slowed down and, in part, successfully prevented attempts to privatize public enterprises, most notably in the case of the state oil company Petroecuador.[21] Still, while Petroecuador remained under state control, even the oil sector was gradually opened up to the participation of private capital. In the 1980s foreign companies were allowed to participate as service providers; reforms in the 1990s allowed for the transition to production-sharing contracts; and in the early 2000s the construction of a new pipeline (Oleoducto de Crudos Pesados—OCP) by a consortium of foreign companies brought significant investment and additional participation by private transnational capital in the oil sector (Rosales 2020, 81–83).

Generally speaking, domestic business elites supported—and benefited from—the transition from a state-led to a market-oriented development model. This overall ideological agreement with neoliberal reforms notwithstanding, business groups and associations frequently opposed specific measures such as cuts in subsidies and tariffs. Their dissent, however, mostly remained "confined to concerns about the *pace* of reform" (Hey and Klak 1999, 88; emphasis in the original).

At the same time, as James Bowen (2014, 108) has argued, the late, gradual, and inconsistent implementation of neoliberal reforms has meant that in Ecuador a much more important segment of the country's economic elite remained "dependent on state protection and rent-seeking behavior" than in Bolivia (or, indeed, Peru). In contrast to thriving export-oriented sectors (such as agribusiness in the coastal region, but also flower production in the highlands), other economic sectors, mostly concentrated in the highlands, continued to depend directly or indirectly on public investment, state expenditure, and/or supplies from state-owned enterprises (e.g., in the oil sector). This helps explain why explicitly neoliberal governments that initially counted on broad business support, such as those led by Febres-Cordero in the 1980s and Durán-Ballén in the early 1990s, confronted resistance from business sectors, not just opposition parties and popular-sector forces. Having initially benefited from relative unity and success in their adoption of neoliberal reforms, both governments were significantly weakened by conflicts that erupted within the alliance of political parties and elite sectors that ideologically shared the neoliberal agenda.[22]

The gradual implementation of neoliberal reforms was facilitated by—and further intensified—relative increases in business power across the three dimensions, reinforced by international support for the neoliberal agenda. Yet, while the weakness of domestic support for political alternatives (in terms of both actors and ideas) contributed to this shift in power relations, popular resistance throughout the 1990s remained much stronger than in Peru. Furthermore, unlike both Bolivia and Peru, the mutually reinforcing fragmentation of business elites and party politics imposed serious limitations on the instrumental and discursive power of business, preventing the formation of a viable policy coalition around the pro-market agenda.

The oil boom of the 1970s significantly increased the relative autonomy of the state by reducing the macroeconomic relevance of the domestic private sector and, thus, structural business power. Oil extraction remained the most important export sector and source of fiscal income throughout the 1980s and 1990s. But the relative weight of the industry declined gradually as oil prices collapsed in the mid-1980s and other traditional (banana, coffee) as well as nontraditional export goods (flowers, shrimps) (re)gained importance.[23]

With a few notable exceptions such as flower production, structural power remained mainly vested in the coastal economy, with its export-oriented agriculture and agribusiness as well as in the related banking sector. In structural terms, other sectors—even if economically relevant—depended more on the state than vice versa. Yet, at the same time, the 1980s saw the consolidation of economic groups (*grupos económicos*), normally owned by a single family and encompassing a range of companies across several economic sectors (Pástor 2019, 105–33). Together, these came to dominate large parts of the country's economy. According to a study by Luis Fierro Carrión (1991), for instance, three coastal groups (Noboa, Maspons, and Marchán) dominated the regional agro-export, agribusiness, and fisheries sectors, with important participation of foreign capital in the latter (Pástor 2019, 120–21). Overall, Fierro identified twelve economic groups, most of them associated with foreign capital, that controlled almost half of Ecuador's national economy (Pástor 2019, 123).[24] Generally speaking, the 1980s and 1990s saw an increasing role of foreign companies in several sectors, including agribusiness, albeit mostly focused on the oil sector (Acosta 2003, 202–22).

In shifting the balance of power in a pro-market and pro-business direction, external constraints and actors (notably the IMF and international creditors) played an important part (García Pascual 2003; Hey and Klak 1999, 81–87). Burdened by a high foreign debt and continuous debt service obligations, between 1983 and 1994 Ecuador signed seven Letters of Intent with the IMF and six agreements with the Paris Club of major creditor countries (Acosta 2003, 371–72). Yet, the fact that Ecuador failed to comply with all but one IMF agreement (Burbano de Lara 2006, 306–7) testifies to the limited impact of such external constraints and incentives when it came to implementation of politically costly reforms. In this overall context of macroeconomic instability, accompanied by chronic exchange-rate instability, the financial liberalization of the early 1990s led to massive increases in both the usage of offshore funds and the de facto dollarization of the Ecuadorian economy (Beckerman 2002).

Although the increase in structural business power was only gradual throughout the 1980s and 1990s, democratization brought a significant and durable boost in the instrumental power of domestic business elites. Business associations under Hurtado in the early 1980s still *"felt* shut out of his policy making circles" (Hey and Klak 1999, 71; emphasis in the original), but this decidedly changed afterwards. Observers agree that, under all democratic governments up until that of Rafael Correa (2007-2017), Ecuador's economic elite—individual technocrats and business leaders, the small club of powerful economic groups as well as the business associations (*cámaras*)—had a disproportionate influence on political decision making, especially when compared to that of the weak and fragmented trade-union federations (Wolff 2018b, 81).

Business influence in this context was wielded in a variety of ways. First, a key instrument was the activity of business associations. Building on efforts at strengthening and uniting organizational structures in response to the Rodríguez Lara regime (Conaghan et al. 1990, 7-8), business associations significantly gained in the power they wielded under democratic rule (Naranjo 1993). Second, political parties provided influential channels in the political arena, or at least those in which business leaders played an important role. Indeed, two of the four main parties that dominated national politics during the 1980s and 1990s represented business interests: the Guayaquil-based Partido Social Cristiano (PSC) as well as the Quito-based Democracia Popular (DP). In addition, parties that traditionally represented popular-sector interests, such as the Partido Roldosista Ecuatoriano (PRE) and Izquierda Democrática (ID), moved toward adopting a (neo)liberal, increasingly market-oriented discourse as well.[25] The articulation of business interests by political parties was certainly facilitated by the close connection and, indeed, significant overlaps between political and economic elites, as is most obvious in the case of the PSC in Guayas/Guayaquil (Eaton 2011).

Third, economic experts or technocrats with close relations to the business community and/or with (neo)liberal academic credentials came to play an important role within the different governments. As Catherine Conaghan has summarized, economic policy making after 1978 became increasingly shaped by "technocrats or businessmen without formal ties to parties," who supposedly had the professional expertise to devise appropriate reforms and negotiate with the international financial institutions (1995a, 454; see also Conaghan et al. 1990). Fourth, semi-autonomous state institutions and "councils" in which business representatives participated became an additional conduit for business influence. Examples include the Consejo Nacional de Modernización (CONAM), established in 1992 to promote

Durán-Ballén's "modernization" plans, and the Consejo de Comercio Exterior e Inversiones (COMEXI), created in 1997 to define trade policy and promote international trade agreements.[26] Another example is the Junta Monetaria, an entity within the Central Bank that played an important role in devising economic policy during the 1980s and 1990s. In 1996, business representatives accounted for three of its five board members (Coronel et al. 2019, 152-53). In this sense, we can identify "islands" of state capture—that is, specific areas and agencies involved in economic policy making that were largely controlled by business interests.

Business groups and associations, however, used their instrumental power only in part to push for some kind of overarching neoliberal politico-economic change. In contrast to Peru, business elites failed to develop a strong peak association that could transcend sectorial and regional differences and, in particular, the cleavage between the coast and the Andean highlands.[27] While national associations or federations existed for different sectors (industry, commerce, agriculture), the regional chambers in Guayaquil and Quito remained the most powerful and influential actors (Chiasson-LeBel 2020, 124; Thoumi and Grindle 1992, 20). As Felipe Burbano de Lara (2006, 295) has emphasized, business elites' relationships with the Ecuadorian state were not characterized by a Gramscian logic of "political hegemony" but, rather, by the "corporatist pursuit of economic advantages." This orientation toward the achievement of particular benefits for individual economic groups or sectors was reinforced by the close relationship of individual business leaders and representatives with different political parties, which similarly lacked a national agenda and fiercely competed with one another for political power and spoils (Conaghan 1995a).[28]

Throughout Ecuador's neoliberal era, this prevented the establishment of any lasting pro-business coalition, as can be seen in the cases of both the Febres-Cordero presidency and that of Durán-Ballén. The exception to this can be found at the local level, and most notably in Guayaquil. There the PSC under long-lasting mayors Febres-Cordero (1992-2000) and Jaime Nebot (2000-2019) managed to form a truly hegemonic "neoliberal policy regime" built upon a close alliance between the local government and the city's business elite (Eaton 2017, 107-16).

Furthermore, a particular feature of Ecuador's post-transition democracy systematically limited instrumental business power as well as the presidents' capacity to use informal mechanisms to build de facto coalitions around an agenda of economic reforms (Mejía

2009): the institution of mid-term elections for Congress, introduced in 1979 and abolished with the new constitution of 1998. In light of the persisting unpopularity of austerity measures and neoliberal structural adjustment, Febres-Cordero, Borja, and Durán-Ballén all lost significant parliamentary support after two years in office (Hey and Klak 1999, 73, 79; Thoumi and Grindle 1992, 75). The strategy to push through the reform agenda by means of a referendum hardly offered an alternative, as Durán-Ballén was to learn most emphatically. In November 1995 a majority of the population voted down all eleven governmental proposals, which encompassed key elements of Durán-Ballén's "modernization" agenda, including the partial privatization of social security (Hey and Klak 1999, 80).

These dynamics, on the one hand, also reflect the fact that popular sector organizations in Ecuador remained a relevant counterweight, much more so than in Peru and even Bolivia. Led by the FUT trade union federation in the 1980s and the indigenous movement organization, the Confederación de Nacionalidades Indígenas del Ecuador (CONAIE) in the 1990s, these "anti-neoliberal" forces frequently proved able to overcome their fragmentation and mobilize their followers in the face of harsh austerity measures and neoliberal structural adjustment (Silva 2009, ch. 6; Wolff 2007; Yashar 2005, ch. 4).[29] On the other hand, popular resistance against economic reforms points to the relative lack of discursive business power and, more generally, to the failure to establish a neoliberal hegemony at the discursive level.

According to Hey and Klak (1999, 67–68), during the 1980s neoliberalism "gained hegemonic status" in Ecuador in the sense that "the thinking and action with regard to economic policy among elites and state actors" converged around the set of policies usually associated with the neoliberal agenda. As far as the public debate is concerned, private media, most of which belonged to powerful economic groups (Pástor 2019, 105–33), certainly helped in propagating a pro-market and pro-business discourse, as did business associations and like-minded think tanks. With hindsight, however, the discursive success of these activities seems rather limited. In contrast to Peru, neoliberal hegemony remained limited to the elite, never really permeating popular thinking; and even among the elites it failed to gain the strength that characterized the heyday of "pacted democracy" in Bolivia.

In Ecuador, convergence around neoliberal recipes reflected a (perceived) lack of alternatives in a context of high levels of foreign debt, dependence on international loans, support from the IMF and United States, as well as the weakness of competing ideologies (Hey and Klak 1999).[30] Furthermore, the Ecuadorian armed forces never bought into neoliberal ideology and at times joined the critics of economic reforms. In addition to defending material interests (the privatization agenda also threatened the broad range of companies and holdings owned by the military), this reflects the persisting discursive power of nationalism and state sovereignty as well as the peculiar social and developmentalist identity of the Ecuadorian military (Isaacs 1996, 52; Rivera and Ramírez 2005, 133).

The Durán-Ballén government (1992-1996) nicely illustrates the key dynamics that set Ecuador apart from Bolivia and Peru when it comes to the interplay of business power and democratic politics in shaping the implementation of neoliberal reforms in the 1990s. Together with his vice president, Alberto Dahik (an orthodox economist who had already participated in the Febres-Cordero government), Durán-Ballén pushed for a far-reaching neoliberal agenda under the label of "modernization." This agenda included, inter alia, austerity measures; the (further) liberalization of financial markets, trade, and foreign investment; the reduction or elimination of price controls and subsidies; a market-oriented agrarian reform; decentralization and state reform, including through privatization (Bowen 2014, 100-101; Hey and Klak 1999, 77-81; Mejía 2009, 127-28). The Durán-Ballén government was indeed able to implement a series of market-oriented reforms, especially during its first two years in office. Such reforms as financial liberalization and land reform were promoted by, and significantly benefited, business elites (Coronel et al. 2019, 152). In addition, the implementation of neoliberal reforms was also facilitated by strong international support for Durán-Ballén's "modernization" agenda, which culminated, in 1994, in "the completion of crucial debt-restructuring agreements with the Paris Club and the IMF" (Hey and Klak 1999, 80).[31] Yet, over the years, both the persistent fragmentation of "the right" along regional and partisan-personalist lines and the failure to achieve broader popular support for the neoliberal agenda seriously weakened the Durán-Ballén government and effectively prevented a more thorough restructuring of the state and the development model.

Durán-Ballén, a conservative politician from Quito, had broken with Febres-Cordero's Guayaquil-dominated PSC and established his own party (Partido Unidad Republicana, PUR) just before the 1992 elections. After the elections, even though both parties essentially shared the same neoliberal agenda, the PSC rejected any kind of official support for Durán-Ballén—basically because PSC politician Jaime Nebot "did not want to be seen as collaborating with the government he was planning to run against in 1996" (Mejía 2006, 81). As a way out, as Andrés Mejía has shown, a clandestine informal agreement was struck that enabled the passage of market-oriented reforms in exchange for PSC access to state resources, government jobs, and control over key judicial institutions. Although initially successful, this "ghost coalition" proved unstable and quickly disintegrated as conflicts between the PSC and the government escalated (Mejía 2009, 127–28). As a result, in 1995, although Congress still approved Ecuador's entry into the World Trade Organization (WTO), it also passed a law that explicitly prohibited the sale of public enterprises in "strategic" sectors such as telecommunications and hydrocarbons (Hey and Klak 1999, 80).

At the same time, the "modernization" agenda was not precisely met with enthusiasm by the population. Led by CONAIE, the main indigenous movement organization, alongside a broad alliance of trade unions, leftist parties, and other urban movements, this coalition of interests mobilized against the reforms, in particular against privatizations (Rivera and Ramírez 2005, 127–28). The military "joined the chorus of voices objecting to the proposed reforms" (Isaacs 1996, 52). Consequently, the government lost both the 1994 mid-term elections and the 1995 referendum, and in late 1995, approval ratings of 16 percent made Durán-Ballén "the most unpopular Ecuadoran president" since 1979 (Hey and Klak 1999, 80).

In sum, throughout most of the 1980s and 1990s, business actors, interests, and ideas played a predominant role in Ecuadorian politics. Yet, the persisting fragmentation of both business elites and their political allies, as well as the primarily particularistic orientation characterizing both business representatives and political parties, prevented the emergence of a stable neoliberal policy coalition. Still less did they build a hegemonic project able to garner broad popular support. Pro-business ideas certainly shaped economic policy making, while business representatives and like-minded technocrats dominated decision making in key areas and individual business leaders and groups were frequently able to secure particularistic benefits. However, this does not resemble a configuration of state or political capture. On the one hand, business elites continuously lacked the unity to be able to (or even try to) steer policy making in the direction of a somewhat coherent pro-business agenda. On the other hand, the fragmentation and chronic instability of Ecuadorian politics made any sustained capture of "the state" or policy making on behalf of some specific group virtually impossible.

Finally, and in contrast to both Bolivia and Peru, Ecuador saw another wave of neoliberal reforms in the early 2000s in response to the dramatic financial crisis, which erupted in 1999 and culminated in the 2000 decision to adopt the US dollar as the country's official currency (Rivera and Ramírez 2005, 131-32; Beckerman and Solimano 2002). Consequently, President Jamil Mahuad, who had announced dollarization as a desperate means to bring an end to the internal and external devaluation of the sucre, was toppled by a protest movement led by the indigenous movement and later joined by parts of the military (Wolff 2009, 1008). Under pressure from the United States, this rebellion-turned-coup was quickly reversed and Mahuad's vice president Gustavo Noboa took over.

Based on a broad alliance of center-right parties around DP and the PSC and with support from the IMF, Noboa implemented dollarization and oversaw the adoption of a series of economic reforms. These included "significant labor markets, fiscal, monetary, financial and trade reforms" (Mejía 2009, 9). In this case, it was a sustained campaign initiated and led by business representatives—initially from the coast but later joined by key associations from Quito as well—that brought the issue of dollarization onto the agenda and succeeded in uniting a broad and, indeed, national alliance of business associations, center-right parties, and economic experts (Wolff 2003, 94-101). This exceptional episode, in which an explicitly business-led alliance succeeded in pushing through a strategic long-term decision against broad popular resistance, was certainly enabled by the extraordinary depth of the financial crisis. In any case, it proved only temporary. In fact, rather than inaugurating a period of business- and elite-dominated politics, the early 2000s were characterized by persistent political instability, the demise of Ecuador's traditional parties, a series of mass protests, and the rise of political outsiders (Rivera and Ramírez 2005). This prepared the ground for the election of Rafael Correa as president and the serious challenges to the neoliberal model and business interests that came with his "Citizens' Revolution."

CONCLUSIONS

Whereas Bolivia and, subsequently, Peru experienced processes of rapid, intense, and far-reaching neoliberal reforms, this was much less the case in Ecuador where the fractured sociopolitical conditions were less conducive to radical change. In Bolivia, the hyperinflation of the early 1980s—exacerbated by the decline in commodity exports and the onset of the debt crisis—produced political conditions that favored the dramatic about-turn of 1985. The state-led model of development was palpably exhausted. In Peru, Fujimori's neoliberal "revolution" was the product not only of hyperinflation but of what could be called "hyper-violence," a condition of internal warfare that, alongside the economic crisis, generated a collapse not just of a model of state-level development but of the state itself, effectively galvanizing business elites. No such conditions prevailed in Ecuador, and the political environment was not conducive to crisis-solving measures either. Although the country underwent processes of liberalizing economic reforms, these were erratic and partial and encountered societal resistances largely absent in the cases of Peru and Bolivia.

But as the period wore on, it was Peru, not Ecuador, that proved the outlier. The Fujimori regime broke with the prevailing constitutional order in 1992, whereas in both Ecuador and Bolivia the new neoliberal development model meshed more easily with democratic norms. In Ecuador, parties of the center-right and center-left succeeded one another, with some degree of policy continuity. In Bolivia, the system of party pacts produced an unusual degree of continuity that helped sustain neoliberal policies. Indeed, the 1990s saw attempts to extend political participation designed to foster legitimacy. The experience of Peru under Fujimori proved very different, with democratic institutions increasingly sidelined and power concentrated in a tight alliance between the executive, the business sector, and the security forces, arrangements forged in part by fears generated within elite circles by the scale of the internal conflict. Weakened by the crisis of the late 1980s, opponents of neoliberal reform, particularly unions, found themselves excluded from channels through which to negotiate policy. And unlike Bolivia and Ecuador, Peru did not see the same degree of "indigenization" of opposition politics and with it the emergence of a powerful critique of extractive development (Van Cott 2005; Yashar 2005). By the end of the 1990s, opposition movements had gained strength in Bolivia, but in Ecuador they continued unabated throughout much of the period, repeatedly forcing governments to backtrack on economic policy, a tendency exacerbated by the practice of mid-term elections. A key actor in Bolivia as well as in Ecuador was the rise of indigenous movements, which happened to make their first appearance on the national stage with the impressive marches of 1990.

The power of the business class was most in evidence in Peru, but business power in all three countries grew in response to neoliberal reforms, privatization in particular, investing business elites with both increased economic standing and greater political access to decision making. The structural power of business was probably most in evidence during the initial phases of stabilization and adjustment when attracting capital—from both foreign firms and domestic investors—as well as foreign credit formed a crucial element in rectifying macroeconomic imbalances. This was more the case in Bolivia and Peru than in Ecuador where the economic crisis was much less severe. The instrumental power of the business class was more in evidence in Peru than in the other two countries, given the extremely privileged position achieved by firms and business organizations under the Fujimori administration, a power that was to prove enduring under his immediate successors. The cohesive nature of business and the influence wielded by its peak organization, Confiep, set Peru apart, though the absence of business-backed parties (as in Ecuador) meant that this influence was largely conducted through informal, non-party channels. Likewise, the discursive power of business, which basked in what it liked to call "the Peruvian miracle," was much more marked in Peru where social acceptance of the new economic model became widespread. In Ecuador and Bolivia, such levels of discursive capture were most clearly in evidence at the regional level, especially in Guayaquil and Santa Cruz, cities that had long pursued regionalist agendas and in which business ideologies were widely shared. However, in all three countries the dissemination of neoliberal ideas was in evidence in the form of growing acceptance of ideas of private initiative, individualism, and entrepreneurialism.

Still, the degree and endurance of state capture at the highest level was more marked in Peru, where opposition to business influence was effectively marginalized. Such capture was to persist well beyond the end of the Fujimori regime and the return to democracy, thanks in part to the idea that growth had to continue under the leadership of the private sector, not the state. In Ecuador, we can identify "islands" of state capture, given the ability of business associations to control specific areas and agencies of decision making. The degree of capture under Sánchez de Lozada in Bolivia was markedly less, even though business influence increased. Yet the overall picture is one of fragmentation of elite interests and increasingly assertive indigenous movements within a political system in which instability made it difficult for any one group to gain systematic control of economic policy making. In Ecuador, opposition obliged even the more committed neoliberal presidents—León Febres-Cordero and Sixto Durán-Ballén—to retract on their respective agendas while the combined power of organized labor and indigenous organizations proved sufficiently powerful to unseat another neoliberal enthusiast, Jamil Mahuad, as president in January 2000. In Bolivia, too, there was a significant increase in business power (across the three different dimensions) but not to the point of state or political capture. Given the fragmentation of business elites, the political logic of elite-centered "pacted democracy," and the resilience of popular organizations, elites found it difficult to consolidate the influence they had gained in 1985, especially as opposition built up in the late 1990s and the cracks in the neoliberal edifice became increasingly evident. Peru thus stands out from its neighbors; opposition remained weak and fragmented, partly due to repression but also to the argument about the country's "economic success," while the alliance between government and business remained remarkably solid. Peru was not about to go down the road of the "pink tide."

CHAPTER 4

CHALLENGES TO BUSINESS POWER DURING THE "PINK TIDE"

The first decade of the new millennium saw a new wind blowing through public policy in many Latin American countries. Voters were tired with the shortcomings of the neoliberal policies initiated in the 1980s and opted for left-of-center presidents and parties espousing more state-centered and redistributive policies of a neo-developmentalist kind. A new preoccupation emerged with tackling the social ills such as poverty and inequality that appeared to have worsened as a result of neoliberal policies. Similarly, governments became more concerned with encouraging greater inclusion in public life, especially among indigenous peoples and other socioeconomically disadvantaged and politically marginalized social groups, and with deepening those democratic systems that had restricted effective participation and helped business elites sustain a privileged relationship with the state. Throughout the region, new political forces had emerged over the previous decade, dissatisfied with the shortcomings of liberal democracy and demanding a greater voice in decision making and in the redrawing of the frontiers between the private sector and the state. The early 2000s therefore represented a dividing line between what had gone before, a discernible shift in the strategic orientation of economic policy making and the development model at large, a change denominated in much of the literature as "post-neoliberalism" (see Burdick et al. 2009; Macdonald and Ruckert 2009; Ruckert et al. 2017).

The nature of the "pink tide," as it became known, varied greatly between one country and another. It is not our intention here to go into detail on this point, simply to say that the force, ideological direction, and the duration of such changes responded to specific political and economic conditions in each and every country (Levitsky and Roberts 2011; Weyland et al. 2010; Cameron and Hershberg 2010). The image of a "tide," pink or otherwise, washing over the whole region is thus somewhat misplaced, particularly since some countries remained closely aligned with neoliberalism. The chronology of the moments of change lasted a full decade, arguably beginning with the election of Hugo Chávez as president in Venezuela in 1998 and running through to that of Fernando Lugo in Paraguay in 2009. Left-of-center governments adopted very different ideological stances depending on the contexts in which they were elected and subsequently operated. The experience of Brazil was markedly less radical, for example, than that of Venezuela or Bolivia, while others, like Argentina under the Kirchners, were somewhere in between. Indeed, some countries—such as Colombia, Peru, Mexico, and to a lesser extent, Chile—brought little by way of change from what had gone before, at least in the economic sphere and in terms of their relations with the United States. Further, the duration of these (more or less) leftist governments varied greatly with some, such as Lugo's in Paraguay, proving short-lived, whereas other presidents such as Evo Morales in Bolivia managed to perpetuate themselves in office for well over a decade.

Academic work on the course, characteristics, and outcomes of the "pink tide" has been plentiful in recent years. Scholars have examined the reasons why the neoliberal development model broke down more in some countries than others (Madariaga 2020), why leftist governments adopted more (or less) radical programs (Levitsky and Roberts 2011; Weyland et al. 2010), the extent to which new social movements emerged with specific policy agendas (Van Cott 2005; Yashar 2005; Silva 2009), how the relationships between state and society were transformed (or not) (Cameron and Hershberg 2010; Cannon and Kirby 2012; North and Clark 2018; Silva and Rossi 2018), and in the more recent literature, why many of these governments faltered and gave way to a distinctly conservative reaction (Ellner 2020; Falleti and Parrado 2018). Our prime interest here is with the role of business elites and the extent to which the privileged position they occupied under the neoliberal model was effectively challenged by the "pink tide" and how they sought to respond to that challenge.

What is clear is that throughout the region new political actors emerged to challenge the privileged position that such elites had gained as a result of neoliberalism. Indeed, such challenges were often long in gestation, since the liberalizing tendency engendered contestation throughout the region as far back as the late 1970s and early 1980s. The forces that challenged neoliberalism grew in assertiveness throughout the 1990s, utilizing both the electoral spaces available to them and, at the same time, mobilizing beyond the confines of formally constituted democratic institutions. In some cases, as in Colombia, Central America, and Mexico, insurgent organizations included the anti-neoliberal discourse in their respective armed uprisings.

The emergence of leftist governments from 1998 onward, with agendas of greater state intervention, redistribution, and the inclusion of new groups in government, came as a shock to business elites, forcing them to adapt to the new reality and to reengineer the mechanisms used to protect their economic interests and wider privileges (Chiasson-LeBel and Larrabure 2019; Luna and Rovira Kaltwasser 2014; North and Clark 2018). Their success in doing so likewise varied a great deal from one country to another and between different conjunctures in time. In countries in which business groups were most strongly entrenched, they managed to ride out the challenges to their hegemony with relative ease. The situation in Mexico and Colombia stands out and, the business elite in Peru was strong enough to resist challenges to its primacy. The responses in countries such as Venezuela and Bolivia proved different, with elites resorting to much more assertive and even unconstitutional postures in their efforts to defend themselves. Most other countries found themselves in between these extremes, with business elites remaining accommodating until the opportunity to change the political direction arose, while working within established systems to protect themselves from perceived threats.

The various governments associated with the "pink tide" benefited from the unusually benign economic conditions produced by the commodity boom between 2002 and 2013. This had the effect of protecting those governments, affording them greater autonomy, and reducing their structural dependence on the business sector, whether domestic or international. The commodity boom likewise reduced government's dependence on the international financial institutions, enabling them to shake free from the economic policy conditionalities that had typified and helped reinforce the neoliberal development model. In the same vein, deepening ties with China gradually reduced the dependence on trade with—as well as investment, loans, and aid from—the United States (and Europe). This arguably increased the leeway enjoyed by Latin American governments (Stallings 2020; Wise 2020). Given the scale of inward investment to profit from buoyant market conditions, this was not a period in which capital was in short supply, nor was it a period in which governments, as previously, were fearful of the dangers of capital flight.

The structural power of business vis-à-vis the state varied considerably between one case and another given different economic structures as well as varying patterns of ownership in key commodity-exporting industries. In those countries in which both the economy and state income depended significantly on one specific export sector, controlled by the state itself and/or a small group of foreign companies (such as hydrocarbons in the case Venezuela, Ecuador, and Bolivia), governments were able to cream off the rents from high commodity prices and reinvest them, without challenging broader business interests. In cases where a range of companies controlled a rather diversified export economy, the private sector emerged in a much stronger position. This was the case in Peru.

As a consequence of the "pink tide," business elites found their ability to influence decision making through lobbying activities, collective action, and through support for conservative political parties restricted. New actors entered the political arena with links to previously underrepresented social groups that struggled to impose their own agendas on policy makers (Roberts 2018). In several countries, new or previously marginal parties took power, providing new forms of social mediation. Some of these had clearly popular roots, such as the Partido dos Trabalhadores (PT, the Workers Party) in Brazil, the Bolivian Movimiento al Socialismo (MAS) and the Frente Amplio in Uruguay (Anria 2019). In addition, the weakening of traditional parties—and in some cases, the entire breakdown of established party systems—undermined key vehicles of business power. Although these changes did not necessarily block business influence or seek to redistribute assets, the lines of communication between business interests and party representatives and state officials became a good deal less clear than they had been previously. There were countries in which radical change seriously interrupted patterns of business influence, Venezuela being a leading example. There, business opposition took on a more conspiratorial turn, as was shown by the active role of the Federación de Cámaras y Asociaciones de Comercio y Producción de Venezuela (Fedecamaras) in the attempted coup of 2002.

Beyond the narrow confines of policy making, this period also saw a distinct change in the wider parameters of public debate on social issues. Neoliberalism was no longer regarded as the only show in town to which, to echo the words of a Margaret Thatcher speech, "there is no alternative." Partly as a result of the growth in opposition to narrowly construed neoliberal policy recipes—on the streets, in the media, and in public debate—new horizons came into view, with the policies espoused by the Washington Consensus increasingly lambasted for their negative social impacts, the privileged positions of economic elites, and the arrogance at times shown by technocrats. Indeed, even among the international financial institutions themselves, such debate began to make itself felt even before the "pink tide" appeared: organizations such as the World Bank and the IDB began to focus their attention on matters such as poverty and inequality as potential challenges to the sustainability of neoliberal policies. The shift in discursive power was also echoed in the academic and related worlds where environmental as well as social issues and movements became increasingly matters of serious concern and study. The social mobilization that prepared and accompanied the "pink tide" also helped to propagate new ideas and ways of doing things. The extent and intensity of such mobilization varied a great deal between one country and another, with Bolivia arguably being the case in which social mobilization was strongest. Attempts to build new media conduits to challenge established interests had only limited effects in most countries, however (Artz 2017).

Overall, then, business found itself on the defensive in this new context, unable to monopolize political influence and forced to contend with competing sources of power. Where the "pink tide" took on a more radical hue, the ability to influence policy proved more limited; in those countries where more "social democratic" governments basically respected the institutional constraints of established political systems, as in Brazil, Argentina, or Chile, the scope for influence was much greater. What is clear, however, is that there is no case (with the possible exception of Venezuela) in which business power came close to being broken altogether. The initial shock of left-wing electoral victories quickly gave way to strategies of rebuilding business power with business organizations seeking new ways in which to regroup and restore their capacity to wield power, albeit more confrontational in some contexts than others. As well as navigating domestic politics, business groups sought to take advantage of more global changes to help themselves reassert that power.

As we turn to consider how this played out in the countries of the Central Andes, these contrasts become evident. We begin our survey in Bolivia, the country that went furthest down paths of change under the MAS. Then we consider Ecuador under Correa, an intermediate case, and finish up with Peru, a country where elites fended off the challenge of the "pink tide" with greatest success.

BOLIVIA

Bolivia's so-called *democracia pactada* was, by and large, an elite-centered affair.[1] Starting in the late 1990s, however, a wave of social protests and the rise of anti-system parties progressively undermined the viability of this specific politico-economic configuration, and the election of Evo Morales as president in December 2005 effectively brought this period to a close. In terms of mass protests, key events included the 2000 "water war" (*guerra del agua*), which forced the government of Hugo Bánzer to reverse the privatization of Cochabamba's water system; the protests over a tax reform proposal in February 2003; and the "gas war" (*guerra del gas*) in October 2003, which was provoked by the plan to export gas to the United States via a Chilean port and which culminated in the forced resignation of president Gonzalo Sánchez de Lozada. In the context of this cycle of contention, which has been studied extensively, the MAS and its leader, Evo Morales, succeeded in uniting a broad and diverse range of indigenous, peasant, and other social movements, including women's organizations linked to the popular sector and parts of the urban middle class.[2] Programmatically, this alliance combined the socialist and "national-popular" critique of neoliberalism, indigenous demands for a refoundation of the postcolonial state, and the anti-imperialist resistance to US interference in domestic politics (and to the "war on drugs" in particular). It also challenged the neoliberal concept of development by introducing indigenous values such as *vivir bien*.[3] In terms of electoral politics, this alliance scored a first symbolic success during the 2002 elections and, three years later, brought Morales into the presidential palace—with a historic victory on the first round.

Once in government, the MAS initiated a process of far-reaching reforms that brought changes to both the political system and the economic development model.[4] In terms of the former, a new constitution was written and adopted, which defined Bolivia as a "plurinational" state, introduced new mechanisms of direct democracy and civic participation, and established a broad range of political and civil, social and economic, as well as collective indigenous rights (IDEA Internacional 2010; Wolff 2012). The assembly in which the new constitution was devised was dominated by the MAS and presided over by Silvia Lazarte, a coca-producing *campesina* from the Chapare district of Cochabamba (Zuazo and Quiroga 2012).

Overall, the constitutional reform formed part of a process of politically incorporating Bolivia's indigenous peoples who, arguably, constitute a majority of the population in the country (Silva 2018; Wolff 2018c). In the realm of economic policy, the Morales government decidedly turned away from neoliberal recipes. The neo-developmentalist agenda pursued by the MAS included a significantly increased role for the state in the economy through state-owned companies, public investment, and political regulation. It also sought an expansion of social policies through cash transfer programs, a widened universal pension, state investment in basic infrastructure, as well as a revival of agrarian reform (Gray Molina 2010; Wolff 2019). In terms of funding, these policies relied primarily on state income generated from extractive industries and the gas sector in particular. The "nationalization of gas," symbolically declared by Morales on May 1, 2006, included increasing taxation, the renegotiation of the contracts with foreign gas companies, and the revitalization of the state-owned hydrocarbons company YPFB (Kaup 2010).

These changes challenged business interests on several fronts. In addition to the overall policy agenda with its emphasis on the state (as opposed to the market) and on social redistribution, the MAS government's rhetoric about "nationalization" and an "agrarian revolution" signaled potentially far-reaching threats to private property. The process of constitutional reform brought heightened uncertainty, precisely at a time when the traditional economic elites saw their political influence vanishing, as popular sector groups and representatives significantly gained in access to, and presence in, the political arena. Furthermore, the entire notion of "refounding" and "decolonizing" Bolivia, which found its direct manifestation in the actual presence of Bolivians of indigenous or *"cholo"* background in key political posts, also constituted a direct attack on the broader social privileges of an elite that was essentially made up of "white" people (Molina 2020).[5]

At the same time, foreign actors—diplomatic missions, financial entities, and NGOs—that had previously provided strong support to neoliberal reforms found themselves cut out of policy-making networks. As a consequence, business elites joined the traditional political elites in an attempt to resist as much as possible what was dubbed the "process of change." Although this oppositional alliance united the country's "old" political and economic elites during the first years of the MAS government in ways that extended throughout the national territory, support was increasingly concentrated in the lowland departments often referred to as the *media luna* or "half-moon." There, and in Santa Cruz in particular, "conservative autonomy movements" led by an alliance of business associations, elite-centered civic committees, and local political forces openly defied the MAS-led central government (Eaton 2011). These elitist regional autonomy movements tried systematically to obstruct the process of constitutional reform, both via their official political representatives in the Constituent Assembly and through extra-institutional protests and blockades that included the use of physical violence (Bowen 2014, 104; Romero et al. 2009). In Santa Cruz the regional movement against the central government had also quite explicit racist undertones, juxtaposing the supposedly hardworking, entrepreneurial, and predominantly "white" *cambas* of the lowlands against the lazy, state-oriented, and indigenous *collas* of the highlands (Espinoza 2015; Peña 2010).

The confrontation between the MAS and these opposition movements came to a head in 2008, bringing the country to the brink of a violent regional rift. Finally, however, negotiations led to an agreement in Congress. Based on a detailed revision of the draft constitution originally adopted by the Constituent Assembly, a two-thirds majority in parliament voted in favor of convoking a constitutional referendum (Romero et al. 2009). As far as key business interests were concerned, the modifications to the constitutional draft included dropping references to "social control" by the country's social movements; the removal of a clause that would have allowed expropriation of private property that does not fulfil a "social function"; and, most important to large landholders in Santa Cruz, the introduction of a non-retroactivity clause that exempted existing agrarian property from the new limit on the maximum permitted size of landholdings. Still, overall, the regional opposition movements failed to prevent the adoption of a new constitution, which would receive overwhelming approval from the population in February 2009, paving the way for the triumphant reelection of Morales later that year.

The far-reaching transformations, which combined a redistribution of political power and significant policy changes, were enabled by the relative diminution of business power—with reductions at the discursive, the instrumental, and the structural levels reinforcing one another.[6] At the same time, however, the sort of "revolution" pursued by the MAS government was very different from traditional social revolutions in that it was not accompanied by any sustained effort at expropriating and replacing the domestic economic elite. As a result, we can identify a certain "post-neoliberal equilibrium" (Wolff 2016, 2019), in which significantly reduced but persistent business power corresponds to significantly reduced but persistent business influence on policy making. A series of identifiable key factors have facilitated and sustained this equilibrium.

In the dimension of instrumental power, the support and mobilization of popular sector organizations constituted a counterweight to business power that both facilitated the rise of the MAS and helped sustain the Morales government, in particular during the first years in which it faced fierce resistance. Previously privileged sectors found themselves excluded from circuits of decision making. This shift in societal power relations was accompanied by an emerging discursive hegemony of the MAS, which enabled it to enjoy a series of electoral successes between 2005 and 2014. These successes, in turn, allowed the MAS to overcome the veto power of the (pro-business) opposition parties and endowed the Morales government with uncontested democratic legitimacy. At the same time, the commodities boom—reinforced by changes in the gas sector, international support from like-minded governments, and an increasing macroeconomic relevance of public investment and public enterprises—brought about a relative decline in the structural power of the domestic business elite.[7] Finally, after the united attempt by the political opposition, business elites, and conservative autonomy movements in the *media luna* failed to thwart the constitutional reform process, internal divisions within the "old" elite came to a head, in particular between the political opposition and business elites in Santa Cruz.[8] On the one hand, these splits further reduced instrumental business power. On the other hand, however, the deliberate disassociation from the opposition and the turn toward a nonpartisan business agenda encouraged cooperative relations between business associations and the MAS government, which also meant a certain recuperation of instrumental business power.

During the years of pacted democracy, the political parties had constituted a crucial vehicle of instrumental business power. Starting in the early 2000s, business elites saw this vehicle being gradually dismantled with the demise of the traditional political parties and the simultaneous rise of the MAS, underpinned by a powerful alliance of popular sector organizations. During the first years of the MAS government, opposition parties still held a veto position in Congress as well as in the Constituent Assembly of 2006-2008.[9] But this ended with the 2009 elections, which enabled the MAS to achieve a two-thirds majority in the new Plurinational Legislative Assembly. In addition, at the level of the executive, business elites lost the usual business representatives and/or like-minded technocrats who had greatly facilitated influence over policy making. This far-reaching shift in power relations within the political institutions brought a dramatic reduction in direct business influence and a corresponding incorporation of popular sector organizations (Anria 2019; Silva 2018; Wolff 2018c; Zegada and Komadina 2014).

Even before the MAS came to power, the most powerful business elites—situated in the *media luna* and in Santa Cruz in particular—had responded to the gradual loss in instrumental business power at the national level by putting emphasis on the subnational level (Bowen 2014; Eaton 2011; Peña 2010). The key aim of these regional autonomy movements was to limit the power of the central state by demanding far-reaching autonomy for the country's departments. In the most important case of Santa Cruz, this elite-centered alliance included not only the departmental government and the Civic Committee (Comité Pro Santa Cruz) but also the FEPSC, which unites regional business associations such as the Cámara Agropecuaria del Oriente (CAO) and the Cámara de Industria, Comercio, Servicios y Turismo de Santa Cruz (CAINCO). After the strategy of unified elite resistance failed against the MAS government, the economic elites reconsidered their strategy. Starting in 2009, business representatives from both regional associations from Santa Cruz and national business chambers signaled an increasing willingness to engage in dialogue with the government.

This move included a deliberate distancing from openly "political"—that is, partisan—positions and led to increasing splits between economic elites and the political opposition, most notably in Santa Cruz.[10] At the same time, the MAS government similarly signaled an interest in a rapprochement, as long as the business elites would refrain from "meddling" in politics. Between 2009 and 2012, a process of negotiations and dialogue unfolded that produced not only an increasingly cooperative relationship between business elites and the government but also a series of policy agreements, most notably with a view to promoting the expansion of agricultural production in the lowlands (Colque et al. 2016; Ormachea and Ramírez 2013; Webber 2017; Wolff 2016). In this way business associations became, once again, regular interlocutors of the government, which meant a partial recuperation of their instrumental power.

This shift from confrontation to negotiation and cooperation was most pronounced in the case of Santa Cruz, but it was generally in line with the evolution of state-business relations at the national level. In

September 2009, for instance, CAINCO invited Morales to the opening ceremony of the International Fair of Santa Cruz (ExpoCruz)—in and of itself a remarkable step. In Santa Cruz, this invitation met with severe criticism on the part of the Comité Pro Santa Cruz but explicit support among the wider business community, including the CNI. Given the controversy, Morales refrained from participating, but a year later he opened the ExpoCruz together with the president of CAINCO, inaugurating "a new phase in the relationship between the private sector and the state, between orient and occident, between the traditional and the emerging elites" (quoted in Wolff 2019, 118).

In December 2011 and January 2012, when the Morales government invited all kinds of social organizations to a two-step national debate (Encuentro Plurinacional para Profundizar el Cambio), a whole series of business representatives participated, including key associations from Santa Cruz but also CEPB at the national level. In the country this was read as the ultimate sign that the government had managed "to incorporate the private sector" (quoted in Wolff 2016, 131). Generally speaking, during that time, meetings between the MAS government and both regional and national business associations became the norm. At the national level, this overall shift in the economic elites' attitude vis-à-vis the MAS government arguably also reflected changes within the business community.

During the economic boom years between 2004 and 2014, many Bolivian industries were bought by foreign investors (Molina 2019, 35, 106). And, although transnational companies certainly lobby for their specific interests as well, they have been much less entangled with Bolivia's traditional elites and tended to stay out of domestic politics and partisan disputes (Wolff 2020a, 156). A case in point is SOBOCE. Over decades the cement firm was owned by the family of Samuel Doria Medina, the founder of the party Unidad Nacional (UN) and a prominent leader of the opposition to the MAS. In late 2014 SOBOCE would become Bolivia's last major national industry to be taken over by a foreign investor, in this case by a transnational cement company owned by the Peruvian economic group Gloria (Molina 2019, 43, 96).[11] The largest corporations that have remained under the control of local businesspersons or economic groups are in the financial sector (Molina 2019, 35, 49-74). And again, this sector, as represented by the Asociación de Bancos Privados de Bolivia (Asoban) (Molina 2017), has been quite cautious in not adopting explicitly political or partisan positions.[12]

Finally, changes within the regional business elite from Santa Cruz also facilitated the latter's "de-radicalization." Important in this regard was a supposed "terrorist" plot uncovered in early 2009 in Santa Cruz, which massively weakened the radical faction of the regional autonomy movement. Most notably, it forced Branko Marinkovic, a large landowner from the economically and politically powerful Marinkovic family, into exile (see Crabtree and Chaplin 2013, 135-36; Espinoza 2015, 318-19; Wolff 2019, 117). As president of the Comité Pro Santa Cruz, Marinkovic had played a key role in the (violent) resistance waged against the MAS government in September and October 2008 (Eaton 2017, 40).[13]

These shifts in instrumental power and toward a more accommodating business attitude vis-à-vis the MAS government were closely linked to corresponding changes at the level of discursive power. If neoliberal hegemony in Bolivia throughout the 1990s had remained mostly limited to the elite level, it was openly contested and eventually replaced by a "national-popular" discourse during the early 2000s. The persisting ideological legacies of the 1952 revolution and a widely shared state-centered nationalism that cuts across partisan divides have certainly been important in this regard (Mayorga 2006), as have the socioeconomic consequences of neoliberal policies themselves (Arze 2008).[14] By combining a decidedly anti-neoliberal discourse with indigenous, nationalist, socialist, and anti-imperialist elements, the MAS succeeded in constructing a hegemonic agenda. This agenda was, of course, fiercely attacked by a vocal minority, including an important part of the middle class. But, at the national level, it remained without serious competitors throughout the first decade of the MAS government. In enabling a whole series of electoral victories—including the 2005 presidential election, the approval of the constitution, and the 2009 reelection of Morales (with 64 percent of the vote), which also brought the MAS a two-thirds majority in parliament—as well as consistently high popular approval ratings, this discursive hegemony also contributed to lending important democratic legitimacy to the "process of change."

The other way round, the MAS discourse, with its strong and self-conscious references to "the indigenous" and "the popular," arguably reduced the capacity of the business elites to speak plausibly on behalf of "the country" or "the common interest." As Molina has suggested, this had also an important socio-ethnic dimension, given that the class of large property owners as well as the top management of large- and medium-sized companies remained essentially "white," with surnames of distinctly European origin (Molina 2019). In this sense, one can perhaps read the election of Demetrio Pérez as the new president of the Asociación de Productores de Oleaginosas y

Trigo (ANAPO) in early 2009 as an indicator that the predominantly elitist composition of the economic hierarchy was also perceived as problematic within key business associations. Pérez, the first ANAPO president who did not come from the local elite of Santa Cruz (but from a rural Quechua family from Potosí), reportedly played a crucial role in the initiation of the business dialogue with the MAS government (Wolff 2019, 117).

Finally, the consolidation of the MAS government once in power and the largely successful implementation of its agenda can only be understood against the background of a relative decline in structural business power that was caused by the international commodity boom. Rising state income from the gas sector significantly increased the relative autonomy of the government vis-à-vis the domestic private sector, which does not play a role in this area. This autonomy was further enhanced by the winding up of earlier agreements with the international financial institutions that had brought with them policy conditionalities. In this context, the Morales government also benefited from significant international debt relief as implemented before 2006 under the Highly Indebted Poor Country Initiative (HIPC) and, later, from foreign aid and loans from countries such as Brazil, Venezuela, and China (Agramont and Bonifaz 2018, 68-73).

These changes were not merely the result of positive external shocks, however, but were also actively promoted by the MAS. Already, before Morales was elected for the first time in 2005, the MAS and its allies had successfully pushed for a referendum on reforming gas legislation, which had led to the introduction of a hydrocarbons tax (Impuesto Directo a los Hidrocarburos, IDH) of 32 percent in 2005. Reinforced by additional reforms of the sector in the context of the subsequent "nationalization," the government's share of the overall income generated by gas exploitation and export increased dramatically. All this meant that the government challenged vital interests of those foreign companies that, after the de facto privatization of the 1990s, had come to dominate the Bolivian gas sector, most notably Brazil's Petrobras and the Spanish Argentine Repsol-YPF. In this regard, the regional nature of the "pink tide" proved helpful to the MAS government, as both Brazil's president Lula da Silva and Argentina's Néstor Kirchner were much more supportive of the Bolivian attempt to increase its role and share of the gas sector than could have been expected in other historical contexts. Furthermore, an additional type of international "rent," which increased the relative autonomy of the MAS government during its initial stage, was the direct support provided by the Venezuelan government under Hugo Chávez.

Over the course of the first years of the MAS government, the economic boom and the increasing role of public investment and public enterprises in the Bolivian economy meant that structural business power shrank further. But this reduction remained only relative. Generally speaking, the Bolivian "economic miracle" also depended on thriving private business, an issue that became increasingly tangible as external economic conditions worsened (first temporarily, in the context of the global financial crisis of 2008, and second, and in a more sustained way, with the ending of the commodity boom in 2014). More specifically, as Kent Eaton (2017, 163-66) has argued, large-scale agricultural and livestock producers (from Santa Cruz, in particular), in addition to making important contributions to Bolivian exports, continued to play a crucial role as providers of essential foodstuffs for the domestic market, which de facto turned them into key players for the government's food security and sovereignty agenda.

When the MAS government responded to rising international food prices by imposing export restrictions for key agricultural goods, producers from Santa Cruz deliberately withheld their production. Food shortages, in the end, forced Morales "to lift both the price controls and the export restrictions" (Eaton 2017, 165). Although business elites shifted from confrontation to cooperation mainly in response to their loss of instrumental power, the willingness of the MAS to do the same was, therefore, primarily driven by the persisting structural power of key business sectors.[15]

In sum, following the first years of confrontation (2006-2009), the relationship between the government and the business elites was characterized by the emergence of a sort of post-neoliberal equilibrium, "in which domestic private business retains much of its traditional structural power and has recuperated some of its instrumental power, but without fully regaining its previous capacity to influence policymaking" (Wolff 2016, 125). In terms of economic policy, this equilibrium was sustained through a joint interest in upgrading the country's material infrastructure, the expansion of agricultural production, and the promotion of Bolivian exports. This, in particular, concerned agribusiness, but increasing public investment benefited many private businesses (Gray Molina 2010, 67). In addition to all those companies (in construction and commerce) that directly profited from state contracts, private business across the board—including banks, importers, services, transportation, and agribusiness but also in the informal sector—gained from the impressive growth of the domestic market as well as from improvements in the physical infrastructure of the country.

In macroeconomic terms, this peculiar type of class compromise relied on the excess revenues generated by the (restructured) hydrocarbon sector—a problem that would become more tangible as the commodity boom gave way to a sharp decline. At the same time, from 2009 onward, the resource-based, neo-developmentalist agenda of the MAS led to increasing tensions and conflicts between the government and important popular sector organizations that, originally, were core constituencies of the MAS. This increasing distance between the MAS government and parts of its support base was further reinforced by the decreasing official emphasis on redistributive structural reforms that, at the beginning of the Morales presidency, represented an open threat to vital private business interests. This, again, is most notable in the area of land and agriculture, where the "second agrarian reform" initiated in 2006 lost much of its steam after 2010 (Webber 2017). This configuration—a merely tactical alliance between the MAS and the business elites that was vulnerable to shifting correlations of forces on the one hand and a deterioration of the alliance of popular forces on the other—contributed to the debilitation and eventual demise of the Morales government.

ECUADOR

Whereas the "pink tide" in Bolivia was the result of a clear-cut cycle of contention that had gradually undermined a surprisingly stable configuration of power in this historically unsettled country, the election of Rafael Correa as president in Ecuador in late 2006 followed ten years of almost continuous political crises (Pachano 2012, 45–52). Reflecting the failure to construct viable governing coalitions, no elected president since 1996 had managed to reach the end of his term. In 1996, Abdalá Bucaram was removed from office by parliament, after trying to impose a program of severe neoliberal reforms including the establishment of an Argentine-style currency board; the official justification for his removal was his alleged "mental incapacity." Four years later, in the context of a financial crisis, Jamil Mahuad was deposed as president by a coalition led by the indigenous movement and middle-ranking military officers. In 2002, one of the rebellious colonels who led the 2000 revolt, Lucio Gutiérrez, was elected president, running on an anti-neoliberal platform with the support of the indigenous movement.

Once in office Gutiérrez quickly switched course, however, and thus lost the support of the left-to-center parties, including the indigenous party Pachakutik. The alliance with Gutiérrez and its brief interlude in government left the indigenous movement both weakened and divided; in the end, it was not Gutiérrez's "turn to the right" that led to his downfall but the controversial, and arguably unconstitutional, attempt to remain in power by taking control of key judicial institutions (Wolff 2009). This led to a new wave of mass protests, this time led by urban middle classes and the "traditional" political parties (Navas 2012). In April 2005, parliament unseated Gutiérrez, handing over power to his vice president Alfredo Palacio. During the interim presidency of Palacio, the heterodox economist Rafael Correa made his first political appearance, temporarily serving as minister of economy and finance until his differences with Palacio over economic and social policies and Ecuador's relationship with the IMF and the World Bank made him quit the job.

The election of Correa in 2006 was thus not the result of a progressive power accumulation and increasing coordination among leftist forces in the country (Conaghan 2011, 261). In fact, the end of the Palacio government saw Ecuador's center-left as divided as usual and the indigenous movement much weaker than it had been in 2000 (Silva 2018, 50). Also, even if Correa had earned some anti-neoliberal credentials during his few months in the Ministry of Economy and Finance, he was far from the obvious leader of a future leftist government. His political movement, Alianza Patria Altiva I Soberana (Alianza PAIS), was established with a view to the 2006 elections only and was essentially made up of a small group of leftist academics. So, whereas Evo Morales won the first round of the 2005 elections in Bolivia with an absolute majority of votes, a year later Correa initially received a mere 23 percent of the vote, making it to the second round only because of the high degree of political fragmentation.

In this second round it was the widely shared rejection of his competitor—the banana tycoon Álvaro Noboa—that helped Correa to achieve an impressive victory (57 percent of the vote). In the end, most popular and/or leftist organizations, including the indigenous movement organization CONAIE and its "political arm" Pachakutik, supported Correa in the second round as well as in his first years in government. But this relationship was neither reliable nor institutionalized. In fact, Alianza PAIS deliberately refrained from building (institutionalized) alliances either with other parties or social (movement) organizations, while Correa's anti-corporatist agenda and his confrontational discourse targeted not only business associations but also indigenous and trade union organizations (Becker 2013; Lalander et al. 2019; Ospina 2013, 246-53). Reflecting the fragmentation and overall weakness of organized leftist forces in Ecuador, the central pillar of Correa's government from the very beginning was the direct appeal to the popular sectors. In fact, as Eduardo Silva (2018, 50-56) has argued, the broad support that Correa gained and maintained among the general population in both urban and rural areas was based on direct links between individual citizens and the state through public policies, on ties with local barrio organizations and rural (indigenous) communities, as well as on the use of clientelist networks (in particular, in the coastal area). National-level organizations such as CONAIE were deliberately bypassed and, thereby, further weakened.

The electoral campaign that brought Correa to power was characterized by a twofold promise: to break with the political dominance of a group of political parties that were broadly viewed as opportunistic and corrupt (the so-called *partidocracia*), and to turn away from neoliberalism and, thus, from economic policies that were widely seen as benefiting only a tiny group of national crony capitalists as well as international investors and creditors (see Conaghan 2011, 264-66).[16] In terms of the former, Correa skillfully took advantage of the ongoing decay and loss of reputation of the country's entire party system to push through elections to a constituent assembly. As Alianza PAIS won more than 60 percent of the seats in the Constituent Assembly, which would later also replace Congress, the right-wing opposition lost any veto capacity—a situation that would be confirmed by the 2009 elections to the new parliament, the Asamblea Nacional.[17] Just as in the Bolivian case, the center-right opposition had little option but to retreat to the subnational level, most notably to the coastal city of Guayaquil, which continued to be governed by the conservative PSC (see Bowen 2014; Eaton 2011).

The dramatic weakening of the country's traditional political elite at the national level also brought significant shifts in terms of personnel in influential positions. In contrast to previous governments, the incoming Correa administration was characterized by "a majoritarian presence of academics, in return for an almost complete absence of persons linked to the country's productive sectors (banks, trade, industry, etc.)" (Almeida 2007). To be sure, in his attempt to build a hegemonic political force, Correa also deliberately included a series of individuals with ties to the old *partidocracia* (Ramírez 2012, 127). Still, the incorporation of a "young and well-prepared techno-bureaucracy," made up of professionals (including many women) "that did neither come from the old parties nor from the oligarchic business sectors" (Paz y Miño 2012, 29) brought about an important change. At the same time, Correa cut the usual ties between the government and Ecuador's business chambers. In fact, during the first months of the government, there was reportedly not a single meeting of the business associations with the newly elected president. In line with his overall anticorporatist strategy, Correa also reduced the direct business influence within state institutions, such as in COMEXI (Wolff 2016, 133).[18]

In terms of economic policies, the Correa government adopted a set of post-neoliberal policies that combined an emphasis on the economic and developmental role of the state with a focus on the domestic market, public investment, and social policy.[19] As in the Bolivian case, Correa significantly increased the government's share of oil profits, extended state control over the sector, and forced foreign companies into renegotiating their contracts (Rosales 2020). In addition, the government also significantly increased fiscal revenues by strengthening the tax administration, thereby reducing tax evasion, and implementing some progressive measures of tax reform (Schützhofer 2016). Increased fiscal revenues were then used both to boost investment in public infrastructure and to expand social programs, with the dual aim of promoting state-led productive development (to change the "productive matrix") and improving social welfare. The Correa government also opposed free trade negotiations with both the United States and the European Union and—in response to the repercussions from the 2008 global financial crisis—introduced temporary tariffs and import restrictions (Wolff 2016, 133).[20] With a view to consolidating this post-neoliberal turn, the new constitution of 2008, in addition to introducing important changes to the political system (ILDIS and La Tendencia 2008; Wolff 2012), "prohibits land concentration, eliminates autonomy of the central bank, gives priority to local investors over foreign investors, and provides for a larger state role in strategic sectors such as oil, mining, telecommunications, and water" (Madrid et al. 2010, 168).[21]

As in Bolivia, the loss of business influence on policy making and the turning away from market-centered and outward-oriented economic policies challenged domestic business interests in significant ways. Yet, in contrast to Morales, Correa never openly confronted "the economic elite" as such or its vital interests. In a nutshell Correa's "revolution" was in many ways a "state-building project" (Clark and García 2018), aimed at (re)constructing a viable state apparatus with relative autonomy and administrative capacity (Ramírez 2016). With a view to the economy, Correa's discourse aimed at a "modern," less oligarchical, and more productive capitalism. His rhetoric was, therefore, not anti-private sector or anti-capitalist but, rather, involved targeted attacks against the financial and banking sector (as opposed to the productive sector).

His discourse also took up cudgels against those economic conglomerates that Correa depicted as concentrating too much economic power and manipulating public opinion (usually involving banks that also owned private media outlets). He criticized "speculative" and "corrupt" practices, again usually characterizing these as typifying the banking sector. His actual economic policies were not anti-business per se, but state intervention and increasing regulation was aimed primarily at the banking sector and private media (see Bowen 2014, 108; Conaghan 2011, 275-77; Kitzberger 2016). His opposition to free trade agreements and the turn toward protectionist import restrictions, however, also went against the broader interests, respectively, of export-oriented businesses and importing sectors. Finally, in addition to private banks and the private media, Correa also directly attacked specific *grupos económicos*—especially those whose owners were openly aligned with opposition parties—while, however, maintaining good relations with most other groups and owners (see Acosta and Cajas 2020a; Chiasson-LeBel 2019).[22] Overall, the challenge to business interests in Ecuador was less clear-cut and comprehensive and much more explicitly political than was (at least initially) the case with Morales in Bolivia. In particular, absent any serious agenda of agrarian reform, the economic elites from coastal Ecuador never felt as directly threatened by the Correa government as did their counterparts in lowland Bolivia.

This more variegated picture is also reflected in the business response to Correa. Generally speaking, the "citizens' revolution" proclaimed by Correa met with opposition from both the "old" political and economic elites.[23] At the national level, during the first years of the Correa government, the country's main business associations were clearly associated with the opposition (Bowen 2014, 108-9; Ramírez 2012, 126). Business chambers in Guayaquil lent direct support to the conservative autonomy movement in Guayas whose leader, Jaime Nebot, also happened to be a key opposition figure at the national level (Eaton 2011, 303; 2017, 104-38).[24]

In January 2008, when 130 business leaders representing 30 national associations met to voice their rejection of key government decisions, the pro-business daily *El Comercio* commented that, given the current weakness of the opposition parties, the business elite had become the "face" of the opposition (quoted in Wolff 2016, 129). Yet, conflict between business representatives and the government remained, for the most part, issue- and sector-specific and took much less of a partisan turn. In Ecuador, therefore, there was never the kind of unified and regionally concentrated opposition as was the case with Bolivia's autonomy movements. Although specific sectors, such as the exporters, adopted a relatively hard-line response, most other elite sectors refrained from taking an openly confrontational stance, preferring instead to pursue a rather pragmatic wait-and-see approach (Bowen 2014; Wolff 2016). Such conduct was also because many business representatives soon recognized, as did their Bolivian counterparts, that they were doing quite well economically, benefiting from political stability, the boom in public investment, improvements in the country's physical infrastructure, and the growth in domestic demand (see Acosta and Cajas 2020a; Ospina 2015).

How does a focus on business power help explain this trajectory and pattern in Ecuador, particularly when compared to the Bolivian case? In Ecuador, as in Bolivia, the loss of instrumental business power was a key element that enabled the far-reaching political changes. Yet, unlike Morales, Correa could count on much less of a counterweight of organized popular sectors and relied more on his personal charisma and grip on power. He took advantage of the fragmentation of both political parties and economic elites—that is, of the already relatively low degree of instrumental business power, as well as (at the discursive level) of the far-reaching delegitimization of the "old" elites, the established political system, and the preexisting economic development model—by immediately pushing for the Constituent Assembly, which would be elected during his first year in office and that would eventually replace Congress,[25]

Correa was able to overcome the usual checks and balances and quickly disempower institutional veto players. As a result, whereas veto positions in Bolivia's Congress and Constituent Assembly triggered three years of fierce elite resistance to the Morales government (2006-2008), within less than a year of Correa taking office Ecuador's business elites found themselves bereft of strong political allies at the national level. In addition, economic elites' capacity to resist was also lower in Ecuador's coastal region when compared with the situation in the Bolivian lowlands. Business associations in Guayas lacked such comparably strong vehicles as the FEPSC or the Comité Pro Santa Cruz that could unify business elites across sectoral differences and rival *grupos económicos* (Eaton 2011, 303-4). Elite power suffered also from persistent fragmentation in Guayas, where Guayaquil Mayor Nebot had to compete with two important businessmen (Álvaro Noboa and Guillermo Lasso) who were running their own political projects.

In sum, instrumental business power in Ecuador was already

rather limited at the outset, and then it diminished rapidly. This helps explain why Ecuadorian business associations never adopted the openly confrontational stance that characterized their Bolivian counterparts. As soon as Correa signaled his interest to improve relations, or at least engage in dialogue, most business elites were willing to play ball.[26]

The episodes of mass protest that preceded the Correa government had not led to the formation of an effective counterweight in terms of organized popular sector support and mobilization. Yet these episodes and the movements that shaped them were clearly important at the discursive level. As a political outsider without the backing of a political party or of organized social forces, Correa could only manage to establish a discursive hegemony by skillfully drawing on the criticisms, the demands, and policy proposals that had emerged prior to him taking office. These had been developed and brought onto the national agenda by the indigenous movement-led anti-neoliberal alliance of the 1990s and early 2000s, as well as by the urban middle-class movement that had toppled Gutiérrez in 2005 (Lalander and Ospina 2012; Navas 2012; Yashar 2005, ch. 4). Years, or even decades of resistance to the neoliberal agenda and the overall delegitimization of both the political system and the development model thus prepared the discursive ground for Correa to work on (Becker 2013, 50; Silva 2009, ch. 6).[27]

In addition, Correa managed to use opposition to his agenda on the part of the "old" elites as a further discursive tool: elite resistance to the "citizens revolution," in the end, only proved that he was indeed the embodiment of the will of "the people" (Conaghan and De la Torre 2008, 278). At the material level, the structure of the Ecuadorian media sector presented a key obstacle to this strategy. Given their entanglement with private business groups, the private media, which dominated the scene, acted as key voices of, and vehicles for, these "old" elites (Kitzberger 2016).[28] In response, Correa engaged in an almost continuous public campaign—especially through his (in)famous *sabatinas* (Saturday morning radio/TV shows)—and established a whole series of state-owned media outlets. At the same time, opposition-leaning private media, as well as individual journalists, saw themselves confronted with harsh rhetorical attacks, judicial prosecution, and significant increases in state regulation (Burbano de Lara 2020; Conaghan and De la Torre 2008; Kitzberger 2016).

When it comes to structural business power, the pattern in Ecuador is quite similar to the Bolivian one. The commodity boom was again crucial as an enabling condition (De la Torre et al. 2020).

High oil prices meant increasing state income, which was further boosted through an additional tax on the windfall profits of foreign oil companies (Madrid et al. 2010, 168). Overall, it was only in the context of the oil boom that the Correa government could adjust and renegotiate the terms of oil production in ways that significantly increased fiscal revenue while still assuring relatively stable profits for the foreign companies (Rosales 2020). These changes, in turn, enabled the significant expansion of public investment and the scope of public enterprise, which further reduced the economic importance of domestic private business.[29] More so than in the case of Bolivia, Chinese loans played an additional role in facilitating the funding of the Correa government's investment projects.[30]

Still, as in Bolivia, the shrinking of structural business power was only relative. Private business remained an important source of economic growth, both with a view to exports and in terms of domestic economic activity. And the oligarchical structure of Ecuador's private economy remained largely untouched.[31] The persisting structural power of private business groups became obvious in the context of the global financial crisis of 2008 and 2009, which had direct consequences for Ecuador because of the sharp drop in oil prices and the constraints on monetary policies imposed by the official dollarization of the local economy (Wolff 2016, 138).

In substantive terms, the response to this external shock was far from pro-business. During 2009, the government introduced temporary protective tariffs and import restrictions, increased the currency export tax, and regulated certain food prices. The way in which this was done signaled a first step toward a more cooperative relationship. In fact, as Bowen has put it, "several of the country's largest importers (many with long-standing links to right-wing political parties and the leading chambers of commerce and industry) signed an agreement with the president in 2009 to restrict imports as a way to protect the government's balance of payments and stimulate domestic production" (Bowen 2014, 108). In early 2009, Correa also—for the first time since his election—met with representatives of the private banks, and these meetings similarly led to a couple of agreements on anti-crisis measures (Wolff 2018b, 100–101).

The effects of the global financial crisis in the end proved temporary, but the next external shock came in 2011, when decisions by the EU threatened Ecuador with the loss of trade preferences in the context of the Generalized System of Trade Preferences (GSP). Throughout Correa's first years in office, his opposition to bilateral trade agreements had been a major issue of contention with the country's exporters. But in response to the immediate threat of losing preferential access to the EU market, the government changed course. It increased access to business representatives and started to dialogue regularly with the country's main business associations. In terms of substantive policies, the promotion of foreign trade took center stage, with the reaching of an agreement with the European Union an important item on the agenda.[32] Institutionally, in June 2013, Correa reestablished the Ministry of Foreign Trade (which he had abolished upon coming to office) and appointed a new minister, a move much welcomed by the business community (Wolff 2016, 134).

In sum, the overall shift in business-government relations in Ecuador—from confrontation to cooperation—roughly corresponds to the Bolivian case, as do the underlying power dynamics. Persisting structural business power, activated through external shocks, pushed the government to approach the business elites. Given their loss in instrumental power, the latter were more than happy to reengage with the Correa government, more so than was the case in Bolivia. However, just as the period of confrontation was less severe in Ecuador, the process of rapprochement was also less uniform and more sector specific. The government's relationship with the export sector evolved from an initial situation of confrontation and pronounced policy difference to a pattern of cooperation and policy convergence.

As regards other sectors, however, most notably the private banks, conflicts continued to erupt throughout the entire ten-year Correa presidency (Wolff 2018b, 101-2). The constraints of dollarization arguably played a role here: just as the lack of a domestic currency implied an immediate dependency on access to US dollars, which enhanced the structural power of the export sector, the limited range of available policy responses to a current account deficit pushed the government to anti-crisis measures that restricted and/or taxed imports and international bank transfers. In addition, attacks on private banks were part and parcel of Correa's confrontational discourse, which he used to present himself as the "president of the people" standing up against the old, "neoliberal" elite that was only waiting its opportunity to take back political power.

Business elites, however, not only cooperated with the government and, in doing so, reestablished some of their lost instrumental power (Wolff 2016), but as Thomas Chiasson-LeBel (2019) has shown, they started working on improving their instrumental and discursive power. They did this in a number of ways: making their associations more inclusive by opening up to small- and medium-sized businesses; strengthening their national-level organizations such as the CEE; and by adapting their discourse to make it both more unifying (vis-à-vis the country's business community) and more appealing to the general public. The fruit of this strategy became apparent in 2015 when the Correa government was confronted with major protests against its proposed inheritance tax. During these protests, which ultimately led Correa to withdraw the proposal, business leaders re-emerged as "leading opposition voices" (Chiasson-LeBel 2019, 162). This reconstruction of business power would come to full fruition under Correa's successor, Lenín Moreno, after 2017.

PERU

At much the same time as Morales and then Correa won their first elections in Bolivia and Ecuador respectively, radical alternatives also emerged in Peru, voiced by Ollanta Humala, founder of the Partido Nacionalista Peruano (PNP). His presidential candidacy in 2006 was inspired and encouraged by Venezuela, and his later bid in 2011 was supported by Brazil. Yet (unlike Morales and the MAS in Bolivia), Humala and the PNP lacked a strong social base of support and (unlike Correa in Ecuador), the charismatic leadership qualities to enable him to rule from above. When he finally won the presidency in 2011, the economy was still booming, while social discontent was gaining some ground regionally, limited mostly to episodic conflicts in provincial Peru but with the potential of becoming more intense. In spite of the initial "red scare," his government saw a quick accommodation to business interests in this notably anemic expression of the "pink tide." Humala was soon surrounded or "captured" by big business, who had a close, special relationship with the presidency through Nadine Heredia, the first lady who promoted mega projects, and the finance ministry MEF, which continued to operate basically as a state within the state.

Throughout the first dozen years of the new millennium, the overall correlation of forces continued to favor the kind of elite strategies that had first been adopted under the Fujimori administration in the 1990s and then successfully adjusted for the post-Fujimori period. Under Humala, the structural power of business continued, and its instrumental power was able to adapt and retain strong influence over policy making. At the ideological level, pro-business sentiments prevailed; thanks to booming private investment, Peru was portrayed as a global success story; growth was seen to be significantly reducing poverty and generating a more prosperous "new middle class."[33]

What seemed to be needed was more effective social policies geared toward reducing levels of inequality without jettisoning the economic model.

Back in 2006 Humala managed to craft an electoral alternative that had, rhetorically at least, challenged the dominance of the neoliberal right.[34] Appearing as something of an outsider, he was initially backed by a new generation of leftist and social organizations. He did well in that election and was only narrowly defeated by Alan García on the second round of voting by 52.6 percent to 47.4 percent. García won by courting the right and the business elites, successfully casting aside his "populist" past and arguing for the need to continue with and deepen pro-business economic policies. At the same time, he managed to portray Humala as a dangerous pawn of Venezuela's President Hugo Chávez.

Five years later, in 2011, Humala won the presidential election by a similarly narrow second-round margin, beating Keiko Fujimori (daughter of the former president) by 51.5 percent to 48.5 percent. This was achieved by toning down the more radical elements of his former agenda, in particular moderating his economic program. The new government proffered new social policies like Pensión 65 for older people without access to contributory pensions, Beca 18 to provide university scholarships for those from non-elite backgrounds, and the Kali Warma program to provide daycare for low-income families. However, confronted by Peru's powerful business elite, Humala refrained from challenging the neoliberal model as such, seeking accommodation with more conservative forces. While the three new social programs proved innovative, they were eventually constrained by the conservative fiscal policy of the MEF, the "super-ministry" that controlled the government's purse strings.

Once in office, Humala showed a disposition to dialogue with investors and even to "deepen" some of the liberalizing economic policies initiated by Fujimori and continued under his successors Alejandro Toledo (2001–2006) and García (2006–2011). In order to calm international markets, Humala appointed technocrats to head up the MEF, the Central Bank (BCRP) and other regulatory agencies (Dargent 2015, 110). As Humala's presidential advisor for a short period of time after his electoral victory, Sinesio López (2012), has put it: "Humala threw in the towel even before the fight [had begun]." If there was any consideration about incorporating more "progressive" elements into his administration, it was largely limited to appointments to the ministries in charge of social policy (Durand 2012).

This, arguably, was not surprising. In a context of a weak and atomized party system (not least on the left) and a prevalent discourse about the "economic success" of the neoliberal model in achieving macroeconomic stability, in restoring growth, and in reducing levels of poverty, the accommodation of elite power to democratic norms seemed politically viable. Political alternatives on the far right had been eclipsed by the ousting of Fujimori in 2000 and the discrediting of his authoritarian and corrupt modes of government. In this new context, business elites did their best to uphold democratic values as long as elections and elected governments did not threaten the stability of the economy and their place within it. Yet, they maintained links with *fujimorismo*, visible again once it began to reorganize itself as a congressional force under the leadership of Keiko Fujimori.

Apart from Humala and his leftist allies prior to the 2011 elections, most of Peru's political leaders accepted the economic model and shared the view that what the country needed above all else was the promotion of large-scale private investment. As soon as the democratic transition of 2000 took place, the first two presidents—Interim President Valentín Paniagua (2000-2001) and then Toledo—limited institutional changes to dismantling the system of judicial cooptation established by Vladimiro Montesinos by appointing anticorruption judges and introducing systems of plea bargaining to convict those involved. They also introduced some constitutional changes—for example, rescinding those clauses in the 1993 constitution that permitted consecutive presidential reelection. The economic model, by contrast, remained largely untouched. In fact, it was deepened with the enactment of trade agreements and an aggressive policy of concessions (airports, roads, mining) and through agro-exporting subsidies that further enhanced the structural power of business. Business elites were able to continue as influential players within the ruling coalition, post-Fujimori. In the absence of major popular demands for a change in the economic model, the dominant parties could persist with "successful" neoliberal policies without the risk of losing voter support.

Although Toledo included some leftist demands in his 2001 election agenda, his basic orientation was to avoid any change in economic policy but to focus on the agenda of (re)building democracy. The first democratically elected president of the twenty-first century Toledo (like Humala, later), initially included some leftist leaders in cabinet positions (for example, Nicolás Lynch as minister of education), but a subsequent shift to the right saw the confirmation of technocrats and businessmen to key posts. The international financial investor and banker Pedro Pablo Kuczynski became the leading cabinet figure during Toledo's administration and fully supported his negotiations with then President Lula da Silva of Brazil to develop a mega public works program. The special relationship between Brazilian construction firms (notably Odebrecht), initiated during the Fujimori administration, continued without interruption under successive governments until the eruption of the Lava Jato bribery scandal in 2016, right at the end of Humala's term in office (Durand 2018b, 183–84).

Confiep and the major corporations and economic groups quickly accommodated themselves to the various parties that competed for the presidency from 2001 onward, a new one winning in every election. Within Congress, business organizations maintained close ties with conservative parties, including the Fujimoristas, targeting members of key congressional committees. They used the instrumental levers at their disposal, both legal and not so legal. As the Lava Jato scandal was to show, leading companies vied with one another in bribing presidents (Toledo and García) or in enticing primary cabinet figures with lucrative contracts (Kuczynski) (Durand 2018b, 284). Tolerance toward corruption thus became the norm. In the case of the construction industry, which received large public sector funding, the use of bribery, it later transpired, had become almost institutionalized. An example was the formation of a cartel named the Club de la Construcción, led by Odebrecht, and its most significant local counterpart, the Graña y Montero construction group (Villena 2020).

At the same time, the more legal mechanisms of influence also worked well. These included the funding of the election campaign expenses for leading parties and candidates for the presidency and Congress; intense lobbying focused on the various regulatory bodies (Távara 2006); maintenance of close and privileged relations with officials at the BCRP, the MEF, and other key ministries (notably mining, energy, commerce, and agriculture); and the use of the "revolving door" to place managers, corporate lawyers, and pro-business technocrats in key executive positions. These varied mechanisms of instrumental power proved effective, and together with the support of the pro-business media (notably the El Comercio group, with its family links to Graña y Montero), they helped guarantee the continuation of state capture and the defense of the economic model (Crabtree and Durand 2017, 104–29).

As under Fujimori, policy making was insulated from democratic oversight. Key legislation was frequently enacted through executive fiat. The use of legislative decrees had originated under Fujimori, and the practice continued after 2000 under Toledo, García, and Humala.

Under the 1993 constitution, the executive can ask Congress (with the support of the majority party or parties) to grant it special powers in order to legislate on economic matters subject to retroactive congressional approval. The MEF's list of legislative proposals was usually rubber stamped by the legislature, with the president then signing them summarily into law. Rule by decree, even if it was designed for urgent or extraordinary circumstances, became a regular normalized mechanism to approve economic legislation in ways that bypassed democratic oversight (Durand 2018a).[35]

The model was further reinforced during this period by an array of free trade agreements that helped reinforce adherence to the economic model: first with the United States (initiated by Toledo and then signed by García), followed by bilateral and multilateral treaties with Chile, the European Union, China, India, and other countries. Among other things, these offered important degrees of legal protection to the multinational companies investing in Peru. With Bolivia and Ecuador shifting to the left in 2006 and 2007 respectively, distancing themselves from business elites, and renegotiating contracts with multinationals, Peru was going in the other direction, priding itself on becoming one of the most open and welcoming economies to foreign investors. Local investors even claimed that the liberalization of the capital account meant that foreign investors received even more favorable treatment than they did (Arce 2010, 192).

Support for private investment continued as the MEF and BCRP acted to guarantee "sound" macroeconomic policies: monetary stability, low inflation, fiscal conservatism, and investment promotion. The export bonanza (2002–2014) brought a huge stimulus to private investment in mining (mainly in copper, gold, and silver), gas, agricultural exports (fruit, vegetables, and sugar, with a new generation of powerful agribusiness enterprises dominating the subsector), and fishmeal. In this context, increasing capital inflows and the conditions that gave rise to them significantly increased the structural power of business elites.

The consolidation of business groups had been greatly assisted by the Fujimori regime, but the extractives boom that began in the early 2000s greatly increased the power of those involved in the export sector, primarily in mining. Many of the world's largest mining companies, including Glencore, Rio Tinto, Anglo-American, Newmont, Freeport MacMoRan, MMG, and Chinalco, invested in Peru during these years, bringing with them large inflows of investment income. The boom in demand for minerals, mainly copper, from China underpinned this pattern of export-led growth, while Chinese companies also became major investors in the industry. The growth in mining exports reinforced their structural power in the Peruvian economy, and many took advantage of the permissive legislation passed under Fujimori to negotiate favorable contracts that protected their tax position. By 2014 mining companies and foreign banks, either on their own or through joint ventures, had come to occupy a key position in the Peruvian economy, a much larger presence than in other Andean countries (Peru Top Publications 2014).[36]

These years also saw expansion, much of it relatively labor intensive, in informal and illegal activities, including unregulated mining (chiefly for gold), contraband, illegal timber extraction, and the production and trafficking of coca and cocaine (DESCO 2013). The urban economy also experienced remarkable growth. Shopping malls mushroomed in every city, and consumption grew rapidly with the "democratization" of credit provided by banks and department stores, which encouraged the use of credit cards. Urban growth and construction boomed, both in Lima and all major intermediate cities (Dietz 2019). Tourism also took off, thanks to private investment in the hospitality industry and the prevalence of political and economic stability.[37] Finally, the energy sector also developed with major investments in gas exploitation and distribution for home and industrial use (from the Camisea field in Cuzco), as well as new hydroelectric plants (Cerro del Aguila in the central highlands) operating in a nationally integrated grid.

Peru, according to Elmer Cuba, a leading neoliberal economist who later became a director of the BCRP, was indeed "taking off" (Cuba 2008). It came to be widely regarded as "the star of the South" given its high growth rates, positive international credit ratings, and the praise lavished upon it by the international financial institutions associated with the Washington Consensus. Although the global crisis of 2008 generated a one-year dip in growth in 2009, the economy recovered rapidly thereafter, in great part thanks to massive Chinese investment in copper, Peru's main export commodity.[38]

Some clouds, however, appeared in this otherwise sunny panorama. Availing themselves of democratic conditions and notwithstanding organizational weaknesses and a lack of governmental support, civil society organizations and NGOs started to regroup. They began not only to demand better wages but also to defend indigenous and gender rights. They began to push for better environmental policies as a reaction to the negative impacts caused by extractive industries and as a response to growing concern about the effects of climate change. Sporadic episodes of social conflict became part of the new political landscape. High-profile protests in the mining sector included the cases of Yanacocha in Cajamarca in 2000 and environmentally questionable new projects like Tambogrande in Piura in 2001, followed by several others.[39] There was also regional protests, such as the so-called Arequipazo in 2001-2002, which was directed against water privatization and deregulation in Peru's second city. Further, indigenous protests erupted in the Amazon basin, most notably the 2009 "Baguazo" in defense of indigenous land rights threatened by legislation approved in the wake of the US-Peru free trade agreement. Finally, occasional strikes took place in the state sector, organized mostly by the teachers and health workers. But it was protest against big formal mining, coinciding with the start of the commodity boom, that became the focus of greatest contention, in some cases resulting in the suspension of major investment projects (Bebbington 2007). Two particularly contentious projects, Conga and Tía María, represented investments worth US$6.2 billion (US$ 4.8 and $1.4 billion respectively) (Gestión 2020). More generally, annual editions of the Latinobarómetro, which measures public attitudes throughout Latin America, pointed to the very low levels of public faith in democratic institutions in Peru and to the perceived self-serving nature of political and economic elites.

Unlike the intense union activity of the 1980s and the relative labor "peace" of the Fujimori decade (Arce 2014), a decentralized pattern of regional social conflicts characterized the early years of the twenty-first century. In contrast to Bolivia and Ecuador, indigenous, peasant, and other social organizations in Peru were much less able to forge horizontal linkages and to build broader alliances, which arguably reflected the legacies of the authoritarianism and the violence of the 1990s (Silva 2009, 231-78; Yashar 2005, 240-50). This persisting weakness of social movements notwithstanding, big business and Confiep increasingly complained about the "political noise" generated by protest. They demanded a more robust government response to protect private property rights and to guarantee the unruffled development of investment projects. Slowly but steadily, and to deter opposition, legislation was introduced to prevent the blocking of highways (a common form of protest) and to afford greater police protection of mining enclaves.[40] Anti-terrorist legislation was used to confront the leaders of social movements. Many such movements were organized by regional "defense fronts" (*frentes de defensa*), a form of organization employed by a new generation of regional leftist leaders that exploited the useful but limited space for political mobilization beyond the capital. A key component of these *frentes* were unionized teachers. Unable to launch national protests, the left began to regroup through such regional mobilizations.

Depending on the circumstances and the interests involved, governments responded with a mix of repression and (where this proved ineffective) negotiation through dialogue forums (*mesas de diálogo*). As conflicts built up, the central government became more engaged in information gathering and follow-up, attempting thereby to preempt outbursts of protest and creating specialized mechanisms to deal with them, often outside the usual ministerial structure (Caballero 2012). Such tactics proved useful in preventing the transformation of regional movements into national ones by isolating and containing individual bouts of protest. Still, issues such as the demand for prior consultation (*consulta previa*) in the case of extractive projects became commonplace, particularly among indigenous communities in Amazonian Peru.

Legislation to introduce such consultation was only enacted in September 2011 under Humala, although its implementation remained deficient. Outright repression, however, was not as intense or as abusive as under Fujimori. The intelligence services created by Montesinos lost much of their power after 2000, and the use of extrajudicial violence became less common. The Servicio de Inteligencia Nacional (SIN), which had been developed by Vladimiro Montesinos was closed by Paniagua in 2000 and most of those who masterminded its activities were prosecuted. The new intelligence service created by Toledo had much more limited powers and was led by civilians. Repression became more a matter for the police (Rospigliosi 2006). The military also lost influence as a de facto power when Peru's armed forces abolished compulsory military service.

On becoming president in 2011, Humala inherited these political conditions, which he did relatively little to alter. At the beginning of his administration his government introduced a number of new social programs designed to alleviate poverty. These achieved some success and attracted considerable government funding. However, they in no way represented a rejection of the neoliberal policies that had typified Peru during the period since 1990. Lacking a congressional majority, Humala found himself having to moderate any initial leftist proposals. The "Great Transformation" that he had promised during his 2011 election campaign quickly downgraded to a much more prosaic "Route Map," or what DESCO, a leading Lima NGO, called "the Great Continuity" (2012).

The shift to the right became clear only months after his taking office with a bruising conflict in December 2011 over the expansion of Yanacocha's mining operations at Conga in Cajamarca. This led to the sacking of his center-left prime minister who was replaced by a retired army officer and businessman, Oscar Valdés. Humala's swift abandonment of the platforms on which he was elected bore some resemblance to that of President Lucio Gutiérrez in Ecuador: a nationalist military leader who allied with leftist forces and campaigned on a popular, anti-neoliberal platform but who, on reaching office, quickly turned to the right and toward the economic elites. As in the case of Gutiérrez, Humala's initial cabinet appointments included some notable figures from the left, but the key economic positions remained in the hands of neoliberal technocrats, as Confiep had demanded, to reassure investors (Cameron 2009; Dargent 2015, 110). The presidential couple, Humala and his wife Nadine Heredia, established a close personal relationship with ministers in charge of the MEF and with major investors, Odebrecht and Graña y Montero in particular.

Thus, confronted by regional social movements around mining, not just Conga in 2011 but also Tintaya in Cuzco (2012) and Tía María in Arequipa (2015), Humala found himself on the horns of a dilemma: to support business and investors, "unblock" major investment projects, and alienate his electoral supporters, on the one hand, or to side with popular demands in defiance of the private sector on the other. In the event, he opted for continuity, broke with the left, and sided with the mining companies and business sector more broadly. Not only was business pressure effective, but the temptations of public works and the flows of corrupt resources that came with them proved irresistible. Odebrecht ended up surreptitiously funding both Humala and his adversaries in the 2011 election.

The left, by contrast, was weak and disorganized, having no real leverage inside Humala's inner circle. It was thus possible for the president to switch direction because the immediate political costs were not high. Yet, lacking an organized social support basis of his own, politically Humala became increasingly isolated. Confiep and the business-supporting media remained distrustful, pushing the government to adopt their preferred agenda, especially in the promotion of mining, which, until 2014 at least, continued to benefit from high commodity prices. Business elites were thus able to maneuver and, through allies in government, steer the course of economic policy, benefiting meanwhile from the opportunities created by the export bonanza and the country's diversified export portfolio.

By 2014 new forms of urban social mobilizations had emerged: demonstrations against the incorporation of independent workers in the private pension fund (AFP) system and opposition to a labor law for the youth with reduced employment benefits. By then, both the president and Congress began to yield to popular demands, repealing the laws that had caused the most unrest. Business influence was beginning to find its limits. Another sign of this trend was changes in legislation governing theAFPs. Although Congress and Humala in 2011 had approved reforms proposed in the legislature to expand the role of private pension plans, in June 2016, at the end of his term and with his parliamentary alliance weakened, Congress prompted a "populist" turn, approving legislation to allow pensioners to withdraw up to 25 percent of their funds for house purchase and, in the case of retirees, up to 95.5 percent for their personal use. The Association of AFPs, for the first time since its foundation in 1994, found itself unable to block a reform that prejudiced the interests of its members (Durand et al. 2022).

The end of the export bonanza in 2015 further accentuated Humala's isolation. It was in this context that new alternatives on the left began to emerge. Verónika Mendoza, who had originally supported Humala, split to join Marco Arana, a leader of the anti-mining protests in Cajamarca, in forming the Frente Amplio for the 2016 presidential elections. In the end, Mendoza came third in the presidential contest, only narrowly surpassed by Kuczynski, whose lead was attributable, at least in part, to a negative campaign orchestrated by the corporate media (Tuesta 2017). In Congress, the Frente Amplio obtained the largest number of seats the left had won since the 1980s. While the left thus gained ground, *humalismo* waned. New actors, including women's and indigenous leaders won representation for the first time. Yet internal splits between Arana and Mendoza supporters divided the left within a few months of the election, causing a serious loss of momentum. As political analyst Alberto Adrianzén has argued, the Peruvian left remained one of the most "parochial" (i.e. regionally delimited) in Latin America (2018, 44).

Overall, the legitimacy of the neoliberal model was losing its luster as Humala's term drew to an end, driven in part by increasing criticism of social and environmental policies and revelations about the corrupt ties between business and government. Still, business elites managed to uphold their political and ideological influence, sustained partly by the role played by Confiep, by effusive media support, and by the strength of conservative opposition in Congress due to the alliance forged between *fujimorismo* and APRA. As subsequent revelations about the 2016 elections were to show, corporations continued to use their donations to sympathetic parties in elections to ensure that the suitable candidates were elected (Durand and Salcedo 2020). They also deployed well-honed lobbying techniques to secure favorable policy decisions from those elected, on such matters as taxation and deregulation, and continued to exercise a surreptitious influence over the various regulatory bodies (Crabtree and Durand 2017, 117).

At the discursive level, business organizations and the media continued to play an influential role in cultivating an ideological climate that was favorable to their interests. Their message meshed with a world in which consumerism had increased greatly, along with an individualism that came at the expense of collective identities. From the beginning of the Humala administration onward, this message took the form of a discourse about the importance of entrepreneurialism, with the focus on the significance of *emprendedores* of poor origin, resonant of the earlier work of Hernando de Soto (1989). It was also argued that Peru was witnessing, for the first time, the emergence of a dynamic middle class, coupled with news about the decline in poverty rates (from 50 percent in 1994 to 25 percent in 2014). Despite its social conflicts, Peru was seen as being on the cusp of becoming a developed nation, a view reinforced by discussions for it to join the Organization for Economic Cooperation and Development (OECD), the "club" of developed economies.[41] In its 2015 annual meeting of governors, held in Lima, the IMF lauded Peru as offering a model for the rest of Latin America. Recognizing that the end of the bonanza period generated demands for economic change in Peru and the region more generally, the IMF echoed the arguments of Confiep and the business sector more broadly in publishing a book that urged countries to copy Peru and to "maintain the direction of economic policy" ("Peru: Staying the Course of Economic Success") (IMF 2015).

The elites and the mass media played a critical role in disseminating an anti-statist message during the Humala years, pointing to what was termed excessive *tramitología*. Red tape, it was argued, was suffocating individual initiative and blocking the major investment projects on which Peru's future success would depend. Parallel to the demand for less government intervention was the demand for lower taxation, approved in 2014 (Durand 2017b). At the same time, prompted by criticisms of their negative environmental impacts, Peru's large-scale mining companies launched campaigns designed to improve their image and show their willingness to enter into dialogue with other stakeholders, notably the communities that surround mining operations.[42]

In sum, despite the export boom, the growth of private investment, the expansion of urbanization and domestic consumption, and government claims about improved living conditions, episodic social instability persisted in the extractive sector and began to spread to the urban environment. As the economic bonanza period ended in 2013-2014, public confidence began to recede. The capital-intensive extractive sector had contributed little to increasing employment. The boom had also done little to reduce informality, which, at around 70 percent of the workforce, was one of the highest in Latin America (Romero 2021). Labor conditions for most workers were precarious at best, and business organizations continued to campaign for the "flexibilization" of work contracts. Informal and illegal extractive industries (coca, gold, and timber) employed more workers than those in the formal extractive sector, generating a parallel, uncontrolled economy, tolerated in part because of corruption and the absence of national policies to regularize such economies (De Echave 2016; CIUP 2022). The triumphant claims of the mid-2000s that Peru was undergoing a dynamic "capitalist revolution" (Althaus 2007) and that through entrepreneurialism (*haciendo negocios*) poverty would fade (Córdova 2010) began to carry ever less conviction.

CONCLUSIONS

In the era of the "pink tide" it was Peru that emerged the outlier. Whereas Bolivia and Ecuador experienced a marked shift away from their previous trajectory following the elections of 2005 and 2006 respectively, Peru demonstrated continuity with the economic legacies of the "successful" model of the Fujimori years. However, the policies adopted in both Bolivia and Ecuador demonstrated the variability between those countries that followed the "pink tide," even in those cases that adopted some of the more radical policies under this overall rubric. Although business interests and power were challenged in both countries and their privileged access to decision making interrupted, the power of business was by no means broken. Bolivia went further than Ecuador in challenging the veto power of elites and bringing new actors to the fore in arenas of decision making. Comparison of the three dimensions of business power in our three Central Andean republics throws up telling contrasts that reflect on the differing domestic and international situations in each case.

That Peru differs markedly from the other two is clear. The large degree of policy continuity through the three post-Fujimori administrations of Toledo (2001-2006), García (2006-2011), and Humala (2011-2016) is striking. The country was one of the few in South America that kept to the "straight and narrow" of the policy prescriptions laid down under the Washington Consensus. The nearest Peru came to following others into the "pink tide" was the election of Ollanta Humala as president in 2011 on the back of a nationalist discourse that fed on widespread disillusion with the achievements of preceding governments. But the hiatus brought about by the 2011 election was short-lived at best. Business elites played a conspicuous role in ensuring continuity, in particular through the instrumental power of Confiep and other business lobby organizations.

Business power in Peru, fortified structurally by the commodity boom of the first decade of the new millennium, emerged far stronger and more influential than was the case in either Bolivia or Ecuador. In part this was due to the rise of China as an economic superpower and the role of Peru as a key supplier of strategically important minerals. At the same time, and in contrast to these two countries, the influence of alternative narratives and approaches to policy making proved much weaker. Although Peru saw bouts of protest throughout this period, social movements were far more fragmented than in either Bolivia or Ecuador, and their linkages to the policy-making world through left-wing political parties much more tenuous. Once he broke with the left, Humala faced no organized countervailing pressure to the direct influence exerted by business groups. He could switch tack relatively easily without paying a high political price. Unlike his successors, he lasted his full term.

Peru's relative success in sustaining growth, the scale of its capital inflows since 2000, and the seemingly dramatic reduction in poverty levels all contributed to a narrative that justified sticking with neoliberal policies. Internationally, the Peruvian "miracle" appeared a validation of the idea that neoliberalism could yield the social benefits needed to sustain itself politically over the long run. Domestically, this message was reinforced by reference to Peru's troubled past, particularly the economic debacle of the first García government and the lessons learned from its pursuit of economic heterodoxy. In this context, Peru's middle class remained a reliable supporter of the pro-business agenda—in contrast to Bolivia and Ecuador, where the crisis-ridden years that preceded the election of Morales and Correa had contributed to a certain radicalization of at least parts of the urban middle class.

The examples of Ecuador and Bolivia, while a far cry from that of Peru in these years, also reveal important differences between them in the relationship of business communities with the state. Of the "pink tide" countries (with the exception of Venezuela), the rupture between business and government in Bolivia under Morales stands out. Starting with the election of Evo Morales in 2005 and over the years that followed, the MAS effectively severed the links that had developed over the previous neoliberal period. The veto power of business was broken, and new "subaltern" forces emerged in powerful positions within what was referred to at the time as the "refoundation" of the state. It is the strength, the articulation, and the effective political incorporation of the country's social movements that make the Bolivian case stand out. The Correa government in Ecuador was not a direct product of the country's social movements in the same way as in Bolivia. Indeed, Correa sought to avoid entering any institutionalized alliances with social movements. And although Alianza PAIS drew on the agenda established by social movements, and that of Ecuador's indigenous movement in particular, the Correa government was not the result of a resurgent left. It was more the product of a power vacuum that Correa was skillfully able to exploit.

Still, in terms of the actual economic policies pursued by the Alianza PAIS government, Ecuador's "Citizens' Revolution" mirrored the Bolivian experience in important ways. A common feature was that they were more political than economic "revolutions." Old political elites were replaced by new actors, the privileged access of elites to decision making spheres was reduced, and the institutions of the state were restructured. In purely economic terms, although some important changes were made in policy, these were hardly "revolutionary." It is in this sense that the term "post-neoliberalism" implies something less than a clear break with the previous model of development. To be sure, in both Bolivia and Ecuador, the processes of political change and constitutional reform have been accompanied by important public debates over the capitalist and extractivist nature of the development model, with parts of the indigenous movements, environmentalist NGOs, and progressive intellectuals questioning also the very idea of development that has been guiding economic policy making throughout the postcolonial era (see, for instance, Escobar 2010; Grupo Permanente de Trabajo sobre Alternativas al Desarrollo 2011). Still, even if alternative principles such as the *buen vivir* or *vivir bien* were included in the new constitutions and came to officially guide national development strategies, the post-neoliberal development model that was pursued by both the Morales and the Correa governments remained essentially growth-oriented and extractivist (Artaraz et al. 2021).

The disempowerment of established political elites, the agenda of far-reaching constitutional change, and the adoption of post-neoliberal policies constituted significant threats to business interests in both countries. Business elites in Ecuador, however, did not feel the threat of rejection in the same way as they did in Bolivia. Although Correa sought to ramp up the role of the state in development, this did not necessarily prejudice the interests of the business community. His relationship with business was essentially pragmatic, seeking to focus criticism against specific sectors or groups within the business class such as the banking community and the owners of the country's media. There were no direct threats to agricultural interests through such distributive measures as agrarian reform as in Bolivia. The violent reaction of business groups toward Morales and the MAS, made manifest in 2008 when they supported what came close to armed rebellion in Santa Cruz, was far more challenging than anything witnessed in Ecuador. The strength of regional politics in both countries—largely absent in Peru—made for similarities between the two cases, but the rift between Santa Cruz and La Paz was more profound and potentially destabilizing than that between Guayaquil and Quito.

In both Ecuador and Bolivia, Correa and Morales were fortunate in taking office at a time of buoyant commodity prices. These prices greatly facilitated the economic expansion that helped underwrite an unusually long period of political stability in both cases. Dependence on hydrocarbons—over which the public sector exercised an increasing degree of control, benefiting directly from the tax revenues generated—fostered a return to a more state-oriented model of development. With oil and gas prices remaining high, resources for social and infrastructural spending were abundant. Of the two countries, due to its dollarized exchange rate, Ecuador proved more vulnerable both to the temporary effects of the global financial crisis of 2008 and to the eventual downturn in oil prices after 2013. In Peru, by contrast, with the much more diversified export sector almost wholly in the hands of a wide range of private sector companies, the state was less well structurally placed to reap the rewards of the commodity boom. Fiscal income as a proportion of GDP remained very low by Latin American standards, let alone those of the OECD.

Business groups in both Bolivia and Ecuador sought ways to come to terms with the new development model. In Ecuador this amounted to a wait-and-see policy that, with some exceptions, avoided open conflict. In Bolivia, following the failure of the 2008 rebellion in the *media luna*, leading business groups in Santa Cruz entered into a more transactional phase, seeking to engage with government and regain influence over state decision making. Deficient in discursive power, but drawing on persistent structural power, they sought to rebuild their instrumental influence. In both cases, the commodity-induced growth spurt provided for ample profitability, which helped reduce frictions and enable firms to pay workers higher wages. The fact that both the Morales and the Correa governments proved much more revolutionary in their rhetoric than in actual practice was also key in enabling the rapprochement between the business elites and government in each case.

The ending of the commodity boom reduced the relative autonomy enjoyed by the governments in these two countries. In the case of Peru, likewise, the ending of a long period of growth brought with it increasing social and political tensions that would spill over into the political arena, creating new sources of instability. The difference was that this would begin to challenge business hegemony, while in Bolivia and Ecuador it would herald a shift to the right.

CHAPTER 5

THE (PARTIAL) REVIVAL OF BUSINESS POWER AFTER THE COMMODITY BOOM

The second decade of the new millennium, especially the last five years of it, saw a notable reversal of what we have identified as the "pink tide." Throughout much of Latin America, but especially in South America, governments of a decidedly right-wing complexion replaced those of a leftist orientation. At the same time, the supranational organizations such as ALBA, UNASUR, and the CELAC that grew up with the "pink tide" atrophied and, in some cases, died. These new rightist governments, different as they were in many regards, shared some important qualities, among them the desire to reverse policies adopted over the previous decade that sought to bolster the role of the state and to use it to engineer a degree of social redistribution of income and political power. This "new" orientation, in most cases, involved a return to neoliberal precepts of privatization, encouragement of foreign investment, and trade liberalization. Unsurprisingly, this shift was enthusiastically supported, indeed engineered, by business elites that had increasingly opposed governments of the "pink tide," and which stood to benefit from the reorientation of policy.[1]

The rightward shift is often seen as beginning with the election of Mauricio Macri in Argentina in 2015, but political opposition from business elites to the "pink tide" began almost as soon as its implications came to be felt. In a few cases business resistance even took a violent form, as during the ultimately failed coup against Hugo Chávez in 2002, during which the Venezuelan business organization, Fedecamaras, played a key role. In other cases, such early resistance to the "pink tide" proved more successful. With the coup against "Mel" Zelaya in Honduras in 2009 and the controversial impeachment of Fernando Lugo in Paraguay in 2012, these two countries saw a shift (or rather a return) to the right well before Macri's victory in 2015. The period over which this reversal from left- to right-wing government took place was, indeed, lengthy, lasting at least until 2020 when voters in Uruguay voted out the Frente Amplio.

Just as the "pink tide" revealed major differences between one Latin American country and another (with some not experiencing the tide at all), so the types of right-wing governments that installed themselves in office during the second decade of the millennium also varied substantially, as did the methods that were used to attain political power. Such methods included opposition electoral victories (as in Argentina and Chile, with the election of businessmen Macri in 2015 in the former and Sebastián Piñera in 2009 and his reelection in 2017 in the latter); impeachments with coup-like features (as with Lugo in Paraguay in 2012 and Dilma Rousseff in Brazil in 2016); the electoral victory of an incumbent leftist party which, on taking office, switched its orientation to the right (as in Ecuador during the government of Lenín Moreno between 2017 and 2021); and the use of what many saw as a coup supported by the police and army (with the removal of Evo Morales in Bolivia in 2019). And, as with the "pink tide," there were significant exceptions to the rule, as was the case in Mexico with the election of Andrés Manuel López Obrador in 2018 and—arguably—the replacement of the arch-conservative Álvaro Uribe in Colombia with the more centrist Juan Manuel Santos in 2010. In Argentina (in 2019) and Bolivia (in 2020), leftist parties then managed to make a return through electoral means, having lost power to their right-wing opponents. Finally, the nature of rightist governments throughout the region also varied widely, not least in their respect for institutions, particularly those that the left sometimes continued to control. The most radical of all these right-wing presidents and arguably the least "liberal" was Jair Bolsonaro, elected president of Brazil in 2017.

There are unifying issues that affected most, if not all, "pink tide" countries and made it difficult for them to maintain their trajectory, revealing structural weaknesses that opened up avenues for right-wing opposition to wield power. Although Latin America survived, relatively unscathed from the 2008 global financial crisis, the ending of the commodity super-cycle in 2013 affected the whole region; it hit particularly hard those countries without a diversified export port-folio and those that had used the rents from extractive industries to engineer social change and redistribute income. The ending of the commodity boom thus created openings for the return of the right. But even here, the record was far from uniform: some commodities underwent a greater collapse in price than others, with those highly dependent on oil and minerals probably the worst affected.

From a regional perspective, the spread of right-wing govern-ments also had a self-reinforcing effect. At the height of the "pink tide," regional affairs were characterized by a relative hegemony of leftist governments, with the United States seeing its influence in Latin America reduced significantly. This was most obvious in the case of South America (as exemplified by the emergence of UNASUR) but also extended beyond this subregion (as in the case of the CELAC). With right-wing governments taking power in Argentina and Brazil, this pattern changed decisively. As a consequence, leftist govern-ments, and most notably that of Nicolás Maduro in Venezuela, saw themselves increasingly isolated within the OAS, while alternative regional organizations such as UNASUR and ALBA lost their power. In this context, even the US Trump administration's explicitly coer-cive strategy of regime change in Venezuela did not meet with broad regional resistance but, rather, met with acquiescence if not open support from the majority of Latin American governments.

Much of the literature on the shift to the right necessarily fo-cuses on the limitations of left-wing governments to achieve the transformation that they promised, leaving intact strongly consti-tuted areas of elite power (Ellner 2020; Chiasson-LeBel and Larrabure 2019; Correa Leite et al. 2018; López Segrera 2016). Although the "pink tide" produced substantive changes, the right proved more resilient than was widely perceived during its early years and more disposed to exercise its power in areas where it felt its interests were under attack (Luna and Rovira Kaltwasser 2014). As Barry Cannon (2016) has argued, elites could draw on a range of sources, not just instru-mental power. In many cases, left-wing governments found them-selves obliged to enter into deals with established elites because they failed to win the overall majorities required to act in an autonomous way, thus increasing the instrumental leverage of the latter. This was clearly the case in Brazil where from the outset Lula da Silva found himself obliged to do deals with the center-right in order to govern, as did his successor Dilma Rousseff whose center-right vice president participated directly in her overthrow. It was also the case in Chile. Even in those cases like Bolivia where the victory of the MAS in 2005 displaced them politically, the elites were able to draw on other sources of instrumental power to protect their interests. In most cases, left-wing governments found themselves obliged to negotiate with business elites to some degree, limiting the scope of change and enabling elites to retain influence over public policy. This was particularly evident in the rural sector where public ownership was more difficult to impose and where left-of-center governments failed significantly to transform the agribusiness model of development in favor of small-scale producers (Vergara-Camus and Kay 2017).

Although the ending of the commodities super-cycle created economic conditions that challenged the power of left-wing governments across the region structurally, the ways in which elites regained instrumental power depended greatly on local circumstances. Chiasson-LeBel and Larrabure (2019) stress the salience of domestic political factors, arguing that the left proved unable to disarm the right in a way that would prove lasting and sustainable, especially in those cases (like Chile) where business elites were well embedded within the state. They also hold that the "pink tide" governments failed to empower popular movements in such ways as to permanently challenge the power of elites.

These governments were thus forced to walk a tightrope between pursuing a transformative program while addressing challenges from the dominant class whose interests were thereby threatened (Nelson 2019). As left-wing governments had experienced previously (for example, in Chile under Popular Unity), pursuing transformation without first neutralizing the right could prove a short-lived experiment, but to negotiate with elites to facilitate that transformation would limit the changes possible and risk alienating those popular sectors that demanded them (Wolff 2016). In the same vein, Ellner (2019) argues that the inherently fraught nature of seeking to collaborate with sectors of the business class, as most "pink tide" leaders were obliged to do, involved, at the very least, the need for consummate political timing and an acute awareness as to the nature of the power balance and how far it could be pushed in specific conjunctures.

Whether the resurgence of the right represented a "new" right or, rather, a return to the old right relegated during the pink wave is also a relevant question here. Many of the new right-wing governments that took office in the 2015–2020 period seemed a throwback to the earlier period of neoliberal governance, with their insistence on reducing state intervention and defending private property. In a few cases, such as in Argentina and Ecuador, this agenda was reinforced by external conditionalities imposed by the IMF, but it is notable that the Washington-based financial institutions played a much reduced role at this time compared to that of the 1980s and 1990s.

The "new" right was most in evidence in Brazil where Bolsonaro rewrote the script, inspired more by earlier authoritarian (indeed, militaristic) leanings than economic liberalism. He followed the lead set by Donald Trump in the United States and by other "new" right populists in Eastern Europe (Mudde 2019). This opened up a schism between himself (and fellow authoritarians) and those backing an explicitly neoliberal agenda, personified by Finance Minister Paulo Guedes, a dedicated disciple of the Chicago School. Although elected with the enthusiastic support of much of the Brazilian business community, Bolsonaro succeeded in alienating broad swaths of the domestic and international business class. This divide was also present, but to a lesser extent, in other countries in which sectors of the right sought inspiration in an authoritarian past, indulging in populist methods to achieve and maintain political power.

This draws our attention to new elements emerging in political life that had been largely absent in the 1980s and 1990s. New sources of right-wing mass support had emerged alienated by the experience of the "pink tide." Conspicuous among them were the evangelical Christian groups that had increased markedly in number and voice throughout the region but whose support was courted not only by politicians like Bolsonaro in Brazil but by those in even relatively secular countries like Costa Rica. Politicians of the right could also appeal to public opinion on issues such as insecurity, which provided a useful distraction from left-wing appeals toward poverty relief and income redistribution. Law and order policies provided the right with a potent resource. In opinion polls in many countries, fear of insecurity came to greatly exceed issues such as unemployment in people's list of priorities. Meanwhile the extension of the Internet into ordinary people's lives provided new channels for political communication through which groups on the right usually proved more adept at influencing opinion than those on the left, changing ways of rallying ideological support. At the discursive level, therefore, conditions had changed in significant ways since the previous right-wing offensive of the 1980s. These, therefore, were some of the conditions that affected political developments in the Central Andes with the left experiencing significant reverses in two of its previous bastions—Ecuador and Bolivia—while in Peru the hegemony of the right began to show signs of weakness in the command it had over public opinion.

BOLIVIA

Initial confrontation between the MAS government and Bolivia's economic elites increasingly gave way after 2009 to relatively cooperative relations. This rapprochement characterized state-business relations in general, but it was particularly pronounced in the case of the economic elites from Santa Cruz. In terms of business power, this mutual turn toward greater cooperation reflected the dramatic loss in instrumental power (which created strong incentives for business elites to cooperate) as well as persisting structural power (which pushed the government toward cooperation). In terms of structural power, the end of the commodity boom, though not the initial cause of the rapprochement, proved important as it made the MAS government more dependent on economic sectors other than hydrocarbons and minerals (notably agriculture and food production).

Increasing cooperation between the government and Bolivia's key economic elites also meant that the latter could recover some of their previously lost instrumental power. At the same time, government-business cooperation was enabled by—and further contributed to—a retreat from the agenda of redistributive structural reforms pursued by the MAS government. This shift was most visible in the area of agricultural policy and land reform, where the initial attempt to improve land distribution in favor of indigenous and peasant communities as well as small property holders lost momentum, with land titling again increasingly benefiting agricultural enterprises (Ormachea and Ramírez 2013; Crabtree and Chaplin 2013, 31-32; Webber 2017). More broadly, the latter period of the Morales government was characterized by a lack of structural reform initiatives that would have challenged business interests (Arze and Gómez 2013; Webber 2016; Wolff 2019). On the one hand, this meant that structural business power was not further reduced; on the other, it contributed to increasing criticism and outright protest from significant sectors of the popular forces that had brought the MAS to power in the first place.

Here we look at how these dynamics shaped the final years of the Morales government up to its surprising downfall in late 2019. We also look at the brief period of Jeanine Áñez's interim presidency (2019-2020), during which the old elites, including traditional business elites, temporarily retook political power at the national level (Wolff 2020a). Before zooming in on how government-business relations evolved in this context, we will briefly summarize the main events that led from the triumphant reelection of Evo Morales in 2014 (with more than 60 percent of the vote) to his forced resignation in November 2019, to the dramatic shift to a right-wing interim government, and finally, to the new elections of October 2020 that brought the MAS back to power.[2]

Cracks in the broad alliance of popular forces that sustained the MAS governments had already temporarily erupted before the 2014 elections (Mayorga 2020b, 22). During the so-called *gasolinazo* in late 2010, massive social protests forced the government to withdraw a decree that would have cut fuel subsidies. In 2011 the plan to build a highway from Villa Tunari (Cochabamba) to San Ignacio de Mojos (Beni) through the Territorio Indígena y Parque Nacional Isiboro-Sécure (known by its acronym, TIPNIS) also provoked major protests, including a large indigenous march on La Paz. The march was spearheaded by the organization of indigenous peoples from Bolivia's lowland region, the Confederación de Indígenas de Bolivia (CIDOB) but also received the support of its highland counterpart, the Consejo de Ayllus y Marcas del Qullasuyu (CONAMAQ). Initially, the MAS government refused to negotiate, and the protest even met with instances of violent repression by the national police, but later Morales signed an agreement declaring the TIPNIS an "untouchable" area.

Still, the conflict over the TIPNIS would continue, as would the conflicted relationship between the Morales government and some key indigenous organizations (Postero 2017, 122-32).[3] As the 2014 vote would show, in and of themselves these conflicts did not constitute significant threats to the MAS hegemony at the national level. Yet, by fragmenting and partially demobilizing the powerful alliance of popular forces that had sustained the Morales government during its first years, they increased the government's vulnerability vis-à-vis an eventually reconstituted opposition (Moldiz 2020, 31-32, 70-80). In fact, the development model pursued by the MAS, the government's cooperation with agribusiness in the lowlands, and the consequences of all this for the environment and local populations would arguably resurface with the dramatic wildfires that affected important parts of the Bolivian lowlands in the weeks before the 2019 elections. In this context, critics not only condemned what they claimed was the timid response of the MAS government but also attributed the extent of the wildfires, at least partially, to the MAS's policy of expanding the agricultural frontier (see Brockmann 2020, 39-40).

The issue that would trigger the weakening and eventual downfall of Morales, however, was the question of his reelection, with the referendum of February 2016 being the key event in this regard (Mayorga 2020b, 16–22; Wolff 2020c, 164–65). He had already been reelected twice (in 2009 and 2014), and the term limits established by the 2009 constitution clearly prohibited Morales from running again for the 2019 presidential elections. Early on in the presidential term, the government therefore decided to convene a referendum with a view to changing this aspect of the constitution so as to allow Morales and Vice President Álvaro García Linera to present themselves for yet another election. The referendum helped unite and mobilize the fragmented opposition behind a common objective, but it was also met with significant criticism, or at least apathy, among some MAS constituencies. In the context of an alleged corruption scandal involving a former partner of Morales (Gabriela Zapata), a narrow majority of the voters finally rejected the government's proposal (Driscoll 2017).

Although recognizing the electoral defeat, the MAS decided to ignore the substance of the popular vote and decided to push through a constitutional reinterpretation by the Constitutional Court. In 2017, the Tribunal Constitucional Plurinacional (TCP) ruled that the term limits contained in the constitution were in breach of the universal right to political participation enshrined in the American Convention on Human Rights and, thus, unconstitutional. This very controversial move not only dealt an important blow to the legitimacy of Morales and his government in the eyes of important sectors of the population, including within (previous) MAS constituencies. It also led to a sustained protest movement "in defense of democracy" that united the political opposition and mobilized parts of the urban middle classes (Tórrez 2020, 111–16; Zegada 2019, 150–52). Combined with an increasingly difficult macroeconomic situation that limited the MAS government's capacity to respond to societal demands by fiscal means, this set the stage for the elections of October 2019.[4]

According to the official results (which were later annulled), Morales won the first round of the presidential elections on October 20, 2019, with 47.08 percent, surpassing the necessary 10 percent lead over opposition candidate Carlos Mesa (36.51 percent) only by 0.57 percentage points.[5] Already before the final results were announced by the Tribunal Supremo Electoral (TSE), protests erupted across the country in order to prevent what the opposition viewed as an ongoing electoral fraud. Supported by reports that purported serious electoral irregularities, including controversial statements by the OAS mission in the country, these postelection protests only continued to escalate once the final results were announced. The uprising, which mainly mobilized the urban middle classes, affected all major cities and included violent incidents such as the burning of regional election offices and attacks on MAS supporters and their property.

During these postelection protests, the oppositional right-wing elites from the Bolivian lowlands recovered the role they had gradually lost after 2008, once again becoming the protagonists of anti-MAS resistance. The rise of the radical leader of the Comité Pro Santa Cruz, Luis Fernando Camacho, who rapidly replaced presidential candidate Carlos Mesa as the leading voice of the anti-Morales campaign, is a case in point, as was that of Jeanine Áñez, an opposition senator from Beni who eventually succeeded Morales in the presidency (Tórrez 2020; Zegada 2020). After the General Secretariat of the OAS, based on contested preliminary results of an election audit, called for annulment of the results, Morales accepted the holding of new elections. In the meantime, however, protests had radicalized to the point of accepting only Morales's immediate resignation. As the national police had joined the protests and, finally, as the head of the armed forces publicly "suggested" that the president should step down, Morales was eventually forced to do so. On November 10, 2019, Morales and García Linera announced their resignation and, on the following day, were forced to flee the country.

Given that the MAS leadership of both chambers of the Legislative Assembly had similarly stepped down, opposition senator Áñez claimed that the presidential succession, as provided for by the constitution, fell to her. Under heavy criticism from the MAS, but with the endorsement of the Constitutional Court, Áñez thus assumed the presidency and formed a transition government to lead the country toward fresh elections.[6] This political about-turn—from the MAS to a government led by a very conservative politician from the Bolivian lowlands, which had at least coup-like features—provoked massive and, in part, violent protests from MAS supporters.[7] The military and the police, which then jointly moved into the streets to "pacify" the country, responded with violent repression. In the end, however, the Áñez government and the MAS majority in parliament struck an agreement that enabled the calling of new elections and brought an end to the violent conflict escalation.

It is striking that Bolivia's business elites assumed a cautious position and ostensibly played only a marginal role in the mobilization against Morales's renewed candidacy between 2016 and 2019, as well as in the postelection protests of October and November 2019 (see Wolff 2020a). Despite the obvious politico-ideological and sociocultural affinities between the economic elites and the emerging anti-MAS movement, business representatives and associations joined the protests in a very gradual, hesitant, and inconsistent manner.[8] For instance, in February 2018 the CEPB refrained from explicitly supporting the protests on the second anniversary of the referendum. By contrast, key associations from Santa Cruz (such as ANAPO, CAO, and FEPSC) but also the National Chamber of Commerce (CNC) joined the call for a "civic strike." Similarly, in response to yet another call for mass protests in December 2018, CEPB president Ronald Nostas emphasized that the role of his organization was to represent the specific business interests of the country's entrepreneurs. At the same time, those business associations that more or less openly supported the anti-MAS protests generally maintained cooperative relations with the Morales government.

Although the economic elites were certainly sympathetic to the protests and felt significant social pressure to join them, they refrained from openly confronting the Morales government as long as an end of the MAS rule still seemed a distant possibility. This cautious but calculating business behavior is strikingly different from the pattern that characterized the end of the Siles Zuazo government in the early 1980s. On the one hand, this reflects the tactical alliance between the MAS administration and the country's business elites. On the other hand, crucial differences in economic context certainly also mattered: in stark contrast to the 1980s, the Bolivian economy continued to do quite well, with growth rates well over the regional Latin American average right up until the 2019 crisis. Although low commodity prices led to rising deficits in both the current account and the fiscal budget, the large stock of foreign reserves accumulated during the commodity boom enabled the Morales government to maintain elevated levels of public investment (Wolff 2019, 120). The MAS, therefore, effectively bought time and refrained from making politically costly decisions, such as either turning to austerity measures or increasing the tax take from, for example, thriving business sectors and wealthy elites.

Throughout 2019 the main business associations would stick to their rather pragmatic approach vis-à-vis the MAS government—in contrast to the opposition movement, which brought together newly mobilized urban middle sectors, the political opposition and the resurgent civic committees. In February 2019 the Comité Pro Santa Cruz elected Camacho as its new president, a radical representative of the department's conservative autonomy movement. A month later, the president of the FEPSC, Luis Barbery, was elected as the new president of the CEPB. While also from Santa Cruz, Barbery represented the pragmatic mainstream of Bolivia's business elites that argued in favor of maintaining a "professional" or "apolitical" position vis-à-vis the increasingly polarized sociopolitical setting.[9] Throughout 2019 this pragmatic positioning of key business leaders and associations would attract increasingly harsh criticism from the anti-MAS movement, and from Camacho in particular. This criticism would culminate, in November 2019, in Camacho's calling for the resignation of the presidents of CEPB/FEPSC and CAINCO, Luis Barbery and Fernando Hurtado respectively (El Deber 2019).

Even during the mass protests against the supposed electoral fraud in late 2019, most important business associations held back from openly breaking with the government. While emphasizing the need to respect the will of the people as articulated in the elections, institutions like CEPB, CNI, CAINCO, and FEPSC called on the opposition movement to preserve the peace and refrain from upsetting normal economic activity. The CEPB, for instance, responded to the escalating anti-MAS protests by emphasizing that the country "should not enter into a process of confrontation between brothers, of division, of blockades and of a possible destruction of its productive sector," and even on the very day of Morales's resignation the organization merely called on the Legislative Assembly "to call for new elections." Other associations, in particular those from Santa Cruz, joined the anti-MAS protests much earlier. Almost immediately following the elections, a couple of associations from Santa Cruz such as the CAO voiced their support for the "civic" protests and for the Comité Pro Santa Cruz in particular.[10] It was only with Morales's forced resignation and Áñez's assumption of office as interim president that business elites finally closed ranks and openly joined the "new power bloc" that took over the control of the central state (Molina and Bejarano 2020, 172-78).

With Áñez, herself a politician from the Beni and member of the Santa Cruz-based conservative Demócratas party, Bolivia's previously disempowered politico-economic elite returned to power at the national level. In addition to Áñez, a range of cabinet members came from—or had close ties to—the business community and/or conservative political parties, with Santa Cruz-based elite sectors playing a key role.[11] In addition to the strong presence of business-friendly representatives within the new cabinet, the government also immediately restored mechanisms of business influence. These included the Consejo de Desarrollo Productivo, jointly established by the Áñez administration and the CEPB "as a consultative entity to propose economic policies" (quoted in Wolff 2020a, 154). Furthermore, the shift to the Áñez government was accompanied by a significant realignment of the media landscape. Quickly, all major media outlets, either private or public, converged around a pro-government and anti-MAS discourse (Molina and Bejarano 2020). In sum, the Áñez administration saw the restoration of the channels of business influence enjoyed by the traditional economic elites: like-minded individuals at the head of key economic ministries, a pro-business governing party with direct ties to economic elites, privileged political access granted to business associations, and a business-friendly media landscape. All this essentially meant a temporary return of the key features that had characterized economic policy making in the pre-Morales era.

Once in office, the Áñez administration initiated a swift political volte-face, leaving no doubt that the core aim was to take Bolivia back to the pre-MAS era. In the area of economic policy, this included steps toward dismantling the state-centered development model established by the MAS. Yet, given the continuing MAS majority in parliament and then the eruption of the COVID-19 pandemic in March 2020, actual changes in this area were gradual and limited only. In January 2020, for instance, the Áñez government issued a decree liberalizing agricultural and agro-industrial exports. Although it removed temporary export restrictions that the MAS government had imposed on a series of key products, the new government refrained from liberalizing all exports, maintaining restrictions on the export of rice and wheat (Wolff 2020a, 154). The COVID-19 pandemic and its socioeconomic consequences thus led to increasing tensions and disagreements between the interim government and the business elites. The criticism voiced by the different business associations in this context centered most overtly on disproportionate restrictions that impacted unduly on economic activities, on the lack of sufficient government support for companies harmed by the lockdown, as well as (on the part of the banking sector) the deferral of credit payments (Wolff 2020a, 160).

In the end, the short-lived Áñez government lacked the time and the power to reverse the development model in any decisive way. At the same time, Áñez's decision to present herself for the 2020 presidential elections divided the anti-MAS camp, prompting both Mesa and Camacho openly to criticize the interim administration. The government's poor management of COVID-19 and the corruption scandals linked to the pandemic further undermined popular support for Áñez who, in the end, decided to withdraw her candidacy. The MAS, in contrast, proved able to unite behind a new presidential ticket, made up of former minister of the economy Luis Arce and former minister of foreign affairs David Choquehuanca. The revanchist attitude and the openly racist rhetoric employed by some in the interim government and among its supporters, coupled with attempts to criminalize and repress members and (supposed) supporters of the MAS, helped the MAS to reestablish itself as the uncontested representative of the popular sectors. As a result, Arce scored a triumphant victory in the 2020 elections winning 55 percent of the vote on the first round. The elections finally took place in October, having been postponed twice, ostensibly on account of the pandemic. With 29 percent and 14 percent, respectively, Mesa and Camacho trailed far behind.

With the victory of Arce and the MAS, the return to power of the alliance of the traditional political, economic, and social elites proved but a brief and transient interlude. The attempt to build a new, anti-MAS hegemony was a spectacular failure. First, the personal rivalries of key figures such as Áñez, Camacho, and Mesa as well as the underlying politico-ideological differences that continued to divide the anti-MAS camps meant that the de facto alliance that had contributed to the toppling of Morales quickly disintegrated once the common enemy was ousted. Second, the continuing MAS majority in parliament and the capacity of the MAS and its allies to mobilize resistance severely limited the Áñez administration's room for maneuver. This made it more difficult for the government to use even more draconian policies to prevent a MAS return by, for instance, intensifying repression, outlawing the party altogether, or postponing the elections indefinitely or by enacting more far-reaching, and thus less easily reversible, policy changes.[12] Third, and perhaps most important, the Áñez government and its allies were guided by a dramatic misperception: while Morales's bid for yet another term, coupled with the serious allegations of fraud, did provoke widespread resistance among sectors of the Bolivian population, there was never a majority in favor of the kind of conservative volte-face that Áñez sought to pursue.

Ironically, by forcing the MAS eventually to look for an alternative to Morales, the interim government unwittingly facilitated a renewal of both the party and its ties with the popular sectors in general and the indigenous population in particular (Mayorga 2020c). Bolivia's business elites, in this context, played a notably passive role. Without having contributed significantly to the toppling of Morales, they clearly benefited from the change from the MAS to the Áñez administration. With the interim government and the corresponding changes in the positions adopted by media sector, their instrumental and discursive power increased significantly. Yet, as a social group, business elites were unable (nor did they seriously try) to use this regained power to contribute to the formation of a more sustainable governing coalition.

ECUADOR

In Ecuador significant cracks in the hegemony of the "Citizens' Revolution" first became manifest in 2015.[13] In contrast to Bolivia, the end of the commodity boom immediately plunged Ecuador into recession and pushed the Correa government into adopting controversial policy measures (Meléndez and Moncagatta 2017, 417–20). Among the series of anti-government protests that took place in 2015, two stand out (Ibarra 2015). In June 2015 plans to increase taxes on inheritance and real-estate capital gains provoked major protests among the urban middle class and business elites (Ramírez 2019, 16–18). In August 2015 the mobilization against constitutional reforms, centered on the government's plan to get rid of constitutional term limits, peaked in a "national strike." In both cases, protests forced the government to back down. The tax reforms were shelved in June.[14] And when the National Assembly approved the constitutional reforms in December 2015, they included the important caveat that the possibility of unlimited reelection would take effect only after the 2017 elections. By thus preventing Correa from standing for yet another presidential election, the Alianza PAIS government avoided the kind of sustained mobilization "in defense of democracy" that would later confront the MAS administration in Bolivia. Still, this concession meant that the governing party needed a new presidential candidate to succeed Correa, and this fell to Lenín Moreno who had served as vice president under Correa between 2007 and 2013 (Meléndez and Moncagatta 2017, 426–27).

For Alianza PAIS, the decision to shift power from Correa to Moreno was electorally successful but in the end proved politically fatal. Promising continuity in economic and social policies, but with a less confrontational and high-handed approach to government, Moreno narrowly won the 2017 runoff election over right-wing candidate and businessmen Guillermo Lasso.[15] After taking office, however, Moreno and his predecessor Correa rapidly fell out (Labarthe and Saint-Upéry 2017; Wolff 2018a). As a consequence, Alianza País split, Correa and his allies became Moreno's fiercest opponents, and Moreno gradually turned to the political right, toward the business elites and the IMF. As in Bolivia, Ecuador's experiment with post-neoliberalism was thus not voted out by the population but was effectively thwarted by nonelectoral political maneuvering. In the case of Ecuador, however, it was an elected president who oversaw the political about-turn. Ecuador under Moreno, in this sense, resembles the trajectory of "neoliberalism by surprise" (Ramírez 2019, 20), as coined by Susan Stokes (2004) to describe the postelection turn to neoliberal reforms by a number of Latin American presidents in the 1980s and 1990s.

Initially, Moreno proved quite successful in uniting the heterogeneous camp of anti-Correísta forces and in capitalizing on a widespread anti-Correa sentiment that was further fueled by corruption allegations against key representatives of the Correa administration. The formula that sustained political and popular support for Moreno during his first year in office was an agenda of politico-institutional reforms that, simultaneously, aimed at displacing Correístas from all key state institutions (Olivares and Medina 2020, 319; De la Torre 2020, 106-9). The "fight against corruption" played a crucial role in this regard. Since early 2017, partially triggered by the regional Odebrecht scandal, serious charges of corruption emerged against key figures of the Correa administrations (Acosta and Cajas 2018, 163-76). Moreno responded to these allegations by embracing an anticorruption agenda, and as a result, several (former) high officials were prosecuted, convicted, and imprisoned, including Moreno's vice president Jorge Glas, who had already served as vice president under Correa (De la Torre 2020, 106-7; Wolff 2018a, 286). Also Correa, who had left the country in July 2017, was convicted (in absentia), which has prevented him from running again for political office. A second policy change that facilitated Moreno's convergence with the broad range of anti-Correa forces concerned the lifting of legal and administrative restrictions on civic space and the public sphere that had been imposed during the Correa era.[16]

These policy changes were consolidated through a referendum in February 2018. Supported by virtually the entire range of Ecuador's social and political forces, governmental proposals met with overwhelming public support. The corresponding constitutional amendments, inter alia, allowed for a restructuring of the Consejo de Participación Ciudadana y Control Social (CPCCS). This enabled the Moreno government to replace, first, the members of the CPCCS and, then, all those authorities for whose appointment the council was responsible (e.g., the attorney general, the comptroller general, the judicial council, and the constitutional court). Also, by reinstating constitutional term limits for elected office and barring all those convicted of corruption from running for political office, Correa and key Correístas saw their possibilities to present themselves in future elections severely limited (Olivares and Medina 2020, 337-38; Ramírez 2019, 22; Wolff 2018a, 287).

In the area of economic policy, Moreno gradually moved toward an increasingly orthodox agenda of austerity policies and market-centered reforms. Early on, the new president emphasized that he had inherited much more serious economic difficulties than had ever been acknowledged by his predecessor. In particular, he pointed to a level of public debt—59 percent of GDP—that proved much higher than the Correa government had previously claimed (28 percent) and even surpassed the legal limit (40 percent) (Labarthe and Saint-Upéry 2017, 34-35). At the same time, however, he "promised that he would neither adopt neoliberal adjustment policies nor slash social spending" (De la Torre 2020, 109). Moreno's first cabinet included quite a few members with a business background, which was read as a sign of "opening up" toward the private sector and leading to "positive expectations" on the part of Ecuador's business chambers (El Comercio 2017a).[17] Notably, however, direct business influence on economic policy making had yet to extend to the Ministry of Economy and Finance. Generally speaking, the Moreno government in this early stage was still dominated by people with political trajectories established during the Correa government (El Comercio 2017b; Labarthe and Saint-Upéry 2017, 30).

In line with his promise to seek dialogue with all societal sectors, Moreno, almost immediately after taking office, initiated a national dialogue with representatives from a whole range of social and political organizations, including the country's key business associations but also the indigenous movement organization, CONAIE (Wolff 2018a, 283-84). In addition to having frequent meetings with business representatives, Moreno also established the Consultative Council on Production and Taxes (Consejo Consultivo Productivo y Tributario), which brought together key government officials and representatives of the private sector (Chiasson-LeBel 2019, 162-63; El Universo 2017a). As an immediate result of these contacts, the constitutional referendum of February 2018 included the key concession to business interests of abrogating the controversial tax on extraordinary capital gains (Ley de Plusvalía) (Criollo 2018).[18] Another policy change that directly responded to business demands included the resumption of trade negotiations with the United States—which had been aborted during the Correa government (El Comercio 2018).[19]

Over the course of Moreno's first year in power, the composition of his cabinet changed significantly, with individuals with a technocratic, apparently "nonpolitical" profile and close relations with the business community increasingly coming to dominate the government (Olivares and Medina 2020, 321-23). The key decision that consolidated this shift toward an openly pro-business (and anti-Correa) government was the appointment of Richard Martínez as minister of economy and finance in May 2018. As Thomas Chiasson-LeBel summarizes: "By inviting Martínez to join the government, Moreno integrated one of the main leaders and unifiers of the business class into his cabinet, the man who would ultimately implement the most recent neoliberal turn. The long-term strategy of some business chambers had proved effective: it mobilized at crucial political moments (inheritance tax reform) while also creating credible actors to fill state positions when the opportunity arose, and it recovered a great deal of control over state institutions even without winning elections" (Chiasson-LeBel 2019, 163; see also Ramírez 2019, 22).

In fact, as Chiasson-LeBel (2019) has shown, Martínez was one of those business representatives that had worked most assiduously toward reestablishing instrumental and discursive business power. Before becoming minister under Moreno, Martínez had served as president of the Cámara de Industrias y Producción (CIP) and the Comité Empresarial Ecuatoriano (CEE), working toward strengthening both institutions by broadening their membership, improving their technical capacity, adjusting their lobbying and public relations activities, and developing "a discourse designed to unify business leaders and chambers" (Chiasson-LeBel 2019, 161-62). The results of these efforts could be seen, first, in 2015 when key business chambers, acting collectively, became "leading opposition voices" in the protests against the Correa government's tax plans (Chiasson-LeBel 2019, 162).

Later, business associations proved well prepared to take the opportunity offered by Moreno's "opening up," the split in Alianza PAIS, and the president's search for new allies. It has to be emphasized as well, though, that this successful strategy on the part of Ecuador's business associations also greatly benefited from the increase in structural business power—an immediate consequence of the increasingly difficult economic context. As in Bolivia, but much more pronounced in Ecuador, given the dependence on oil and the dollarization of the economy, the end of the commodity boom meant that private sector activities significantly gained in importance: with a view to the trade balance (heavily affected by falling oil prices) as well as in terms of private investment, employment, and overall growth rates (in light of the decreasing role of the public sector) (see Acosta and Cajas 2018; Bayas-Erazo 2020).[20]

To be sure, these policy changes, reflecting the renewed business influence on economic policy making, did not come out of the blue (Acosta and Cajas 2020b). The Correa government had already responded to the increasingly difficult economic conditions by initiating a rapprochement with key business sectors and by embracing part of the business agenda (e.g., in trade policy). Also, since 2014, Ecuador had already "quietly returned to the fold of the World Bank and the International Monetary Fund" (Labarthe and Saint-Upéry 2017, 35).[21] Still, the Correa government had refrained from giving up on its redistributive agenda, as shown by the tax on extraordinary capital gains. It kept its distance from business associations and avoided officially returning to the IMF (Wolff 2016). Thus Moreno intensified the turning away from a more radical post-neoliberal course that had already been initiated under Correa to the point of actually reverting to the status quo that preceded Correa: a model of economic policy making in line with orthodox neoliberal thinking and predominantly shaped by pro-business people (Ponce et al. 2020, 11; Schützhofer 2019).[22] At the discursive level, this shift brought increased emphasis on the fiscal deficit, a supposedly oversized and inefficient state, and the need to attract and promote private investment in order to generate employment (see Ospina 2019; King and Samaniego 2019). This built on a discursive strategy promoted by business associations and "economic groups" that had, already during the Correa government, worked on improving their public outreach strategy in order to "sway public opinion to create a business-friendly environment, secure the public policies businesses want, and dispute the state's sphere of action" (Chiasson-LeBel 2019, 165).

In terms of actual economic policies, the first significant measure of the new minister of economy and finance Martínez was the Productive Development Law (Ley de Fomento Productivo), approved by parliament in August 2018 (see Bayas-Erazo 2020, 217; Ramírez 2021, 4; Chiasson-LeBel 2019, 154; Salgado 2018). As Franklin Ramírez Gallegos summarizes: "The law is the most aggressive instrument proposed in Ecuador in view of sustaining big business and restoring a market society: it imposed austerity, eroded labor rights, facilitated an enormous appropriation of rents to economic groups (pardoning the 50 largest tax debtors 55 percent of their outstanding taxes) and dismantled the main instruments of the developmentalist and distributive state" (Ramírez 2021, 4).[23]

In February 2019 the signing of an agreement with the IMF

consolidated the return to an orthodox reform agenda. In exchange for US$4.2 billion in loans, the Moreno government promised far-reaching austerity measures (through cuts in the public sector wage bill and public investment, reductions of fuel subsidies, and increases in indirect taxes), market-oriented institutional reforms (e.g., reestablishing the independence of the Central Bank), financial market and capital account deregulation, de facto privatization (through concessions), labor market "flexibilization," and the promotion of private sector investment (see Salgado 2019; Weisbrot and Arauz 2019). This time parliament was not even involved in the discussion of the agreement, which was "only discussed with the business community" (Ramírez 2021, 4). Failure to secure parliamentary agreement on such unpopular economic reforms quickly backfired on the government. Reportedly, Moreno had hoped to convince his de facto allies in the National Assembly to accept an increase in VAT as the key measure to fulfill the promises to the IMF. Key actors such as Guillermo Lasso's CREO had no intention of harming their future electoral prospects through support for such an unpopular measure. The government, therefore, had to turn to enacting its agenda by means of an executive decree—and the decision fell on the elimination of fuel subsidies (see Acosta and Cajas 2020b, 166-67; El Universo 2019).[24]

As previous experiences with major indigenous protests triggered precisely by cuts in energy subsidies might suggest, this decision provoked what came to be known as "the October rebellion." Massive protests, initiated by the transport sector but then quickly taken over by the CONAIE, culminated in a national strike, which shut down important parts of the country and the capital Quito in particular. The Moreno government and its de facto allies on the political right responded with aggressive rhetoric and the declaration of a state of emergency, but the repression only further fueled the protests, leading to some rioting and acts of vandalism. After eleven days of escalating protest, the government had to back down, initiating a dialogue with the indigenous movement and withdrawing the controversial decree.[25]

In a way, the failed attempt to push through unpopular reforms and the reemergence of the indigenous movement as the powerful protagonist within the camp of anti-neoliberal forces consolidated the return to the pattern of economic policy making that had characterized Ecuador during most of the 1980s and 1990s. Governments came under heavy influence from business leaders, parties of the political right, neoliberal technocrats and their international counterparts (such as the IMF), trying to implement market-, business-

and austerity-oriented economic reforms. However, given intra-elite tensions and popular resistance their success was partial at best.

The COVID-19 pandemic, which hit Ecuador with great force, only brought a temporary exemption from this pattern. The demobilizing effects of the pandemic, the severe restrictions imposed in response to it, and the sheer depth of the crisis it caused enabled the government to push through some controversial economic reforms without provoking major resistance. These included the elimination of fuel subsidies as well as the renovation of the agreement with the IMF (Ramírez 2021, 5, 9).[26] At the same time, the rescheduling of public debt with private creditors and international emergency loans, especially from the IMF, enabled the Moreno government to avoid overly drastic spending cuts and partially to mitigate the more dramatic socioeconomic consequences of the pandemic (ECLAC 2020). Still, the social and economic consequences of the pandemic were severe (Acosta 2020). Politically speaking, as in Bolivia and Peru, the poor management of the pandemic response and the eruption of corruption scandals further delegitimized the Moreno administration. They also harmed those on the right (like Guillermo Lasso) who, even if not officially participating in the government, were associated with it.[27] This was clearly reflected in the outcomes of the 2021 elections.

Even though Lasso eventually won the second round of the presidential elections in April 2021, the election results can hardly be considered a vote for the economically neoliberal and socially conservative banker from Guayaquil. Most unusually in Ecuador, Lasso had run as the joint candidate of both major right-wing parties, his own CREO movement and the more traditional PSC. Still, in the first round of the presidential elections in February 2021, he received only 19.74 percent of the vote.[28] So he was way behind the Correísta candidate, Andrés Arauz (32.72 percent), and only marginally ahead of Yaku Pérez of the indigenous Pachakutik party (19.39 percent), who managed to capitalize on the legacy of the October 2019 protests.[29] Even the political outsider Xavier Hervas, who ran as a centrist for the revived social democratic ID, did not fare much worse than Lasso (16.58 percent). In the newly elected parliament, PSC and CREO were to hold merely 31 out of 137 seats, with CREO winning only 12. Adding together the Correísta alliance Unión por la Esperanza (UNES, 49 seats), Pachakutik (27 seats), and ID (18 seats), these three center-to-left forces—theoretically—would have a two-thirds majority.[30]

Yet, in contrast to the political right and the business elites, the forces on the left remained deeply divided, in particular between

Correístas and anti-Correístas (Ramírez 2021, 7-10). This division proved crucial in the runoff elections. Confronted with the choice between Lasso and Arauz, Pérez, Pachakutik, and CONAIE decided to call for a null vote, and a large part of their supporters heeded this advice. In the end, the combination of an anti-Correísta vote and an extraordinarily high share of null votes (16 percent) led to Lasso's narrow victory (52 percent) over Arauz (48 percent).[31]

As in Bolivia, the results from Ecuador's 2021 vote reveal the failure to construct a (neo)liberal pro-business alliance capable of winning electoral majorities. To be sure, in both structural and instrumental terms, Ecuador's business elites and their political allies made a remarkable return during the Moreno government. Also, in terms of discursive power, under Moreno, public and private media, again closed ranks, converging around a (neo)liberal discourse, which tended to associate Correa's state-centered policies with a number of corruption scandals and the growing weight of the public debt (Ospina 2019; Ramírez 2019, 21). Yet, as the major protests of October 2019 showed, this discursive hegemony in the official public space failed to reach broader segments of the population. As Pablo Ospina (2019) has argued in the aftermath of the October 2019 protests, all those "television and radio talk shows among the same neoliberal opinion-makers who rant against the fiscal deficit and the 'obesity of the state' as the biggest problems of contemporary Ecuador" may have convinced "the government, the press and their friends in the business chambers that there was a consensus for the adjustment measures"—but this was clearly a misperception.

The victory of Lasso notwithstanding, the 2021 elections confirm this observation. Not even remotely was there a popular majority in favor of the kind of neoliberal recipes that had typified economic policy making in the decades before Correa. Still, in contrast to Bolivia, the persistent divide on the left of the political spectrum enabled the election of a right-wing president, who could certainly count on support from the business elites but who would lack broader support within both parliament and the wider society—and who, in addition, had to confront the still ongoing pandemic and extremely difficult economic circumstances (Cuvi 2021). To the extent that Lasso's political agenda and his power circle suggest the existence of a "plan to capture the state on the part of the economic and financial elites" (Pástor 2021), the new president would certainly have a hard time putting this into practice.[32] It is worth reflecting on what this might mean for Ecuadorian politics and the future trajectory of economic policy making.

PERU

At the end of the Humala administration, business elites seemed strongly entrenched and benefiting from the promotion of private investments in infrastructure and mining. The 2016 elections offered no direct threat. The two second-round candidates, Pedro Pablo Kuczynski and Keiko Fujimori, despite their differences of style, both advocated liberal economic policies, both benefited electorally from substantial private sector contributions (Durand and Salcedo 2020), and both enjoyed close ties to Confiep.[33] Moreover, Kuczynski, the eventual winner, had international financial kudos as a top Latin American financial investor (Kuczynski and Williamson 2003; Dammert 2009).

From a business perspective it seemed economic policy was going to be predictable and favorable. Like Mauricio Macri in Argentina and Sebastián Piñera in Chile, Kuczynski appeared to belong to a new generation of businessmen presidents (Adrianzén 2021; Nercesian 2020). His cabinet was headed by a top-ranking manager from the beer-producing monopoly Backus Corporation, Fernando Zavala, and the minister of economy and finance was Alfredo Thorne, previously director of global research at JPMorgan Chase. Politically, Zavala enjoyed close ties to the *fujimorista* camp and, on attaining power, he hoped to ease the tensions created by the election campaign (Sifuentes 2019). The Peruvian economy continued to grow at rates that compared favorably with elsewhere in Latin America. Perhaps the main concern was the surprising performance of the left in the 2016 elections with Verónika Mendoza of the Frente Amplio winning nearly 19 percent of the vote and eighteen seats in Congress, the left's best performance since the 1980s. Even so, Fujimori's Fuerza Popular (FP) won an absolute majority of seats (73 out of 130), and concerns about the left diminished as the Frente Amplio split in two shortly after the elections.

This heady confidence was soon to dissipate, however. The government became embroiled in scandals and judicial investigations, and Keiko Fujimori (who only narrowly lost in the second round) proved a bad loser, using her parliamentary weight to wreak vengeance against the executive.[34] As in the past—for example, with Velasco's coup in 1968 and Alberto Fujimori's 1992 *autogolpe*—executive loss of control over Congress proved thoroughly destabilizing. Eventually, Kuczynski was forced to resign in order not to be impeached over his earlier role in the Odebrecht affair.[35] Then his successor, Martín Vizcarra, sought to restore executive power by using his constitutional powers to dissolve Congress, before himself being the subject of impeachment by a new Congress in November 2019. During this period, governance was rendered particularly difficult by unusually high levels of political confrontation and the proliferation of ill-disciplined parties, a problem witnessed elsewhere in Latin America but nowhere more so than in Peru (Levitsky and Zavaleta 2016; Schneider 2010).

These political contortions, combined with the effects of corruption scandals, affected the business climate in serious ways, halting or delaying major investment projects, even though economic policies continued to support private initiatives and remained subject to market openness and fiscal conservatism. Although the structural power of business remained intact, political conditions prevented it from being further deepened. Corruption scandals damaged the image of business and its key political allies, and public concerns intensified concerning monopoly practices, labor policies, and the environmental and social impacts of extractive projects. Indeed, business capture of key areas of state activity became more visible, as did the question of "who rules?" in Peru's democracy (Crabtree and Durand 2017; Durand 2019; Cameron 2021).

Thus, it was that the dominant position occupied by business elites since the 1990s began to unravel. This dominance had begun under authoritarian conditions in the 1990s and survived intact following the political transition in 2000-2001. Business power deftly protected itself from the potential dangers mounted by Humala's election in 2011. By the latter years of the 2010s, however, while maintaining formidable economic and political force, business found itself having to operate in a hectic and unpredictable environment where it found itself losing legitimacy in fulfilling its claims to be the main creator of wealth and in defending its role as a "disinterested" economic agent.

The relationship between Kuczynski and Keiko Fujimori's Fuerza Popular (FP) was fraught from the start. Keiko had won in the first round of voting in 2016 as representative of a "popular right" across much of provincial Peru and with strong support from religious conservatives. In the second round of voting, Kuczynski won by the narrowest of margins (50.1 percent) on the back of a coalition of anti-*fujimoristas* and with the keen support of the *limeño* elite and the financial establishment. Fujimori felt her victory had been stolen. It was the beginning of an unnecessary "political war." Along with their allies in APRA, the *fujimoristas* in Congress embarked on a role of unrelenting opposition, exercising oversight on matters like the new airport in Cuzco, where they detected irregularities, and on issues of concern to religious conservatives like education policy. Equally important were the revelations arising at the time from the Lava Jato scandal and the role in it of Peruvian politicians and private contractors.

The salience of Lava Jato was hard to downplay given the evidence supplied directly by senior executives from Odebrecht. The giant Brazilian construction firm enjoyed close connections with a cartel of Peruvian construction firms known as the Club de la Construcción in which Graña y Montero (Peru's premier construction company) was a key player. The scale of corruption and abuse of power became common currency thanks to the work of independent journalists organized in international networks. The Lava Jato investigation uncovered not only cases of bribery but elaborate mechanisms used to conceal contributions to a range of political parties, directly affecting both APRA and FP, both of which came to be officially deemed as constituting "criminal organizations" (Durand and Salcedo 2020, 170-71). Outside of Brazil, the impact of the Lava Jato scandal was probably larger in Peru than elsewhere in Latin America.

The situation posed a serious challenge to the Peruvian business elite, many of whose senior members were caught up in the Lava Jato and connected scandals. At the same time, many of the ambitious investment projects that Kuczynski's campaign had promised to "unblock" were halted, and the plan supported by Confiep to boost productivity across the economy conspicuously failed to take root. So, while the structural power of business remained intact, it could not be expanded and further consolidated. At the same time, the instrumental power of business found itself diminished as the political situation deteriorated. Similarly, the ability of business to maintain any kind of moral high ground in the public realm was eroded by the avalanche of accusations of corrupt behavior.

As the scale of Odebrecht's operations became clearer, public works projects had to be halted, such as the politically sensitive pipeline to provide households in southern Peru with natural gas. The use of bribery and rigged contracts also came to light with the project to build the new international airport for Cuzco. This case highlighted the shortcomings involved in Private Public Partnerships (PPPs) and the avenues these provided for influence and lobbying to the detriment of the state (Dammert 2009).[36] Concerns about lobbying were closely connected with use of the "revolving door," a state capture feature where officials moved seamlessly between the public sector and private business.[37] The airport project provided an opportunity for the *fujimoristas* to corner the government at a time when they themselves were under attack for corruption, forcing the resignation in May 2017 of the then transport minister, Martín Vizcarra. Overall, the project helped reveal the reproduction of state capture practices under the new government.

The second line of attack by the *fujimoristas* was to attack the education minister, Jaime Saavedra, and his successor, Marilu Martens, over education policy. These moves were backed by religious conservatives and notably by the Opus Dei cardinal, Luis Cipriani, who had close ties to Alberto and Keiko Fujimori (Pásara and Indacochea 2014).[38] The conflict led the executive to demand a vote of confidence in the Zavala cabinet that, when denied, forced Kuczynski to dismiss it. This eventually paved the way to the dissolution of Congress in September 2019.[39]

Such relentless attacks took place as the head of the congressional committee looking into Lava Jato investigated the role played by Kuczynski in the adjudication of major construction projects—such as the Lima metro, the interoceanic highway (linking Peru to Brazil), the southern gas pipeline, and the Olmos irrigation project—to Odebrecht during the Toledo administration. Rosa Bartra, the committee's *fujimorista* chair, demanded that Kuczynski testify before Congress, a demand on which he stonewalled and refused to acknowledge any responsibility.[40] The committee proceeded to investigate the role played by two of his companies, First Capital and Westfield Capital (Dammert 2009; Durand 2018b, 190-91). Marcelo Odebrecht added fuel to the fire by telling Bartra directly how these firms had been involved in the financing of various projects (Durand 2018b, 284).

In December 2017 Kuczynski survived the attempt to impeach him by crafting a deal to release Alberto Fujimori from jail (León 2019, 76). However, the truce did not last long, and in March 2018 Kuczynski was obliged to resign the presidency to forestall a further impeachment attempt. This time FP, aided by APRA and the left, mustered sufficient support to mount a credible attack, on the basis that Kuczynski had lied about his dealings with Odebrecht.[41] Kuczynski was replaced as president by Vizcarra, hitherto his first vice president (Caballero 2019).

These skirmishes between the executive and legislature did not prevent Confiep from working out an agreement on the contentious issue of mergers and acquisitions. The issue had gained salience as a consequence of growing monopoly power in sectors such as banking, pension funds, foodstuffs, and pharmaceuticals. Abuse of market dominance had become notable over the decade. A bill was prepared by the congressional committee led by APRA's Jorge del Castillo that had the support of Confiep and its president, the mining tycoon Roque Benavides. However, the bill—designed to calm public disquiet over monopoly practices—eventually fell victim to the delays produced by the confrontation between executive and legislature.

The ongoing investigations into the Lava Jato scandal also posed a direct threat to Confiep. The scale of business support for Keiko's campaigns in 2011 and 2016 became known following the interrogation by prosecutors of Jorge Barata, Odebrecht's top manager for Peru and Latin America. Barata spoke about a meeting organized by Confiep for top businesspeople to contribute to a fund to "stop" Humala from reaching office and to defend the economic model. Lava Jato interrogated Confiep's then president, Ricardo Briceño, and obtained the list of donors that included the heads of Peru's largest companies. The case further damaged Confiep's public image.

These problems did not cease following Kuczynski's departure. Following a few weeks of détente with FP, Vizcarra realized that he was politically isolated, having no party of his own to back him up in Congress, and that the *fujimorista* cause was increasingly unpopular as the scale of its misdemeanors became clearer. With his popularity in rapid decline (León 2019, 150), he realized he had to take the initiative or become seen as a puppet of FP. Two judicial scandals enabled him to act.

The first concerned the Club de la Construcción on which further details became known as the Lava Jato inquiry proceeded. It became clear that the Club had paid bribes on a regular basis to win contracts and inflate budgets, and it had also placed one of its operatives within the Ministry of Transport (Villena 2020). Among its leading figures was José Graña Miró Quesada, head of Peru's largest construction firm, Graña y Montero. Graña had close ties to a dense network of investors and shareholders, as well as strong influence as one of the main shareholders in El Comercio, Peru's leading media organization.

The second corruption scandal started with the discovery of a judicial ring known as the "Cuellos Blancos del Puerto," the port being a reference to Callao through which cocaine was shipped with the complicity of judges backed up by top officials in the public prosecution service, the Fiscalia de la Nación (Guillén 2020).[42] As Pásara, a leading judicial expert has argued, the scandal confirmed the rising degree of institutional degeneration affecting the whole judicial system, lawyers and judges included, as well as parts of the public prosecution service (2019, 70).

The two cases were, indeed, linked, making the political entanglement even more complex—since the Cuellos Blancos del Puerto organization enjoyed political protection from FP and APRA, which together fought inside the judicial system and Congress to block the Lava Jato investigators. Vizcarra thus decided to seize the moment and lead the charge against a Congress whose members themselves faced corruption charges but were protected from prosecution by parliamentary immunity and supportive political networks. In response to such corruption, Vizcarra used his Independence Day speech to Congress on July 28, 2019, to announce reforms, including a reorganization of the party system, a ban on reelection by members of Congress, and changes in the procedures for appointing judges. The proposals, which were to be submitted to a referendum, enjoyed strong support (León 2019, 158, 161). The referendum, held in December, underscored public approval with 85 percent backing the reforms.

As he established himself in office, Vizcarra attracted interest from the business elite. Confiep sought to build ties, aware that the new president (unlike Kuczynski) was less of a known entity.[43] The hope was that he would be able to encourage renewed economic growth. Vizcarra's reappointment of neoliberal technocrats to key economic posts was reassuring, notably to head the all-important Ministry of Economy and Finance and Ministry of Energy and Mines. This underpinned the maintenance of a transmission belt between business and the state.

However, aware of his weakness in Congress, Vizcarra sought to use his attack on corruption as a way of garnering public support in the country. He quickly attracted high popularity ratings in opinion polls, which contrasted strongly with widespread criticism of Congress. By the end of 2019, he seized another opportunity to assert his leadership by backing the Lava Jato investigations, which had caused frictions with those elite interests in the firing line, including Confiep. On December 31, the Tribunal Fiscal Nacional voted three to two to remove the two prosecutors (Jorge Vela and José Domingo Pérez) in charge of the Lava Jato team, an indication of business influence over the judiciary. Vizcarra made clear his condemnation of this move, adding further impulse to moves to clamp down on corruption. Separately, Vizcarra also showed he was not a prisoner of business influence through his attempts to find a middle course between the interests of mining companies and the community protests that led to the paralysis of major mining projects. Conflict thus emerged in two spheres: in Lima over responses to Lava Jato and other corruption cases and in the provinces in response to mining disputes.

Emblematic of the more localized conflicts over mining were those that arose under Kuczynski and Vizcarra concerning the giant Las Bambas mine in Apurímac and the scheme to initiate mining operations at Tia María in Arequipa. The first of these conflicts involved MMG, a Chinese-owned company, and the second Southern Peru Copper Corporation (SPCC), a subsidiary of Mexican-owned Grupo México. The two cases exemplified problems of policy making under conditions of virtual corporate capture of the state in the face of strong protest movements.

The conflict at Las Bambas burst in February 2017 following MMG's decision to abandon a scheme for transporting mineral to port approved in its Environmental Impact Assessment (EIA).[44] MMG opted for trucking mineral by road to Matarani rather than building a costly conveyor belt. The communities along the route, which had originally supported the project, demanded compensation for the environmental distress caused. Kuczynski's government responded to protests and roadblocks with force, with police seconded to the mining camp. Vizcarra, then minister of transport and communications, was dispatched to deal with the protesters, but he used dialogue rather than force to achieve the lifting of roadblocks. This lack of firmness was much criticized within the mining community. Conflict broke out again in 2019 when Vizcarra was president. Prime Minister Salvador del Solar was sent to negotiate a settlement that upheld the agreements reached in 2017. This time the Catholic Church supported the negotiations; the retirement of Cardinal Luis Cipriani had deprived the mining companies of a strong spiritual ally.

Another major social conflict erupted in 2017, led by a radical faction of the teachers' union, SUTEP (Sindicato Unitario de Trabajadores en la Educación del Perú), with ties to the remnants of Sendero Luminoso, demanding that Kuczynski comply with campaign promises to increase salaries. The strike paralyzed the public school system. It continued for several weeks and eventually forced Kuczysnki to concede. Pedro Castillo, the leader of the union movement, became a national figure representing a new generation of union leaders. This was the first major union victory in decades, a sign that labor was back as a political actor. Castillo would go on to win the 2021 presidential elections.

The dispute over Tía Maria also revealed less than firm presidential commitment to mining development at any cost. The project was to build a copper mine in the Tambo valley, an area of relatively prosperous farming communities. SPCC already enjoyed a bad reputation in southern Peru, and the expansion of its activities ran into multiple sources of opposition, both rural and urban.[45] SPCC claimed that it had received a social license on the basis of dialogue with communities in the valley, and in 2019 Vizcarra approved the go-ahead. The ensuing protests led to prolonged disruption, in which locals managed to procure important support from social organizations elsewhere in Arequipa. Lobbied hard by local business interests in Arequipa, Vizcarra found himself in the crossfire. Attempts to straddle the issue eventually gave way to a decision that conditions did not permit the project to go ahead. Both the mining community and Confiep condemned Vizcarra's apparently vacillating position on the issue in view of the difficulties in achieving a social license. Given the lack of presidential support and both the scale and the scope of the conflict, the project was suspended indefinitely.

With tensions escalating between Vizcarra and the *fujimorista* majority in Congress and egged on by his popularity in the country, Vizcarra opted to use his prerogative to dissolve the legislature in September 2019. Prior to this, important sectors of the business elite saw an opportunity to get rid of Vizcarra through impeachment, aligning themselves with the FP-APRA majority in Congress. The process was backed by a previous vice president who had quarreled with Vizcarra, Mercedes Aráoz, and counted on the support of the then president of Congress, Pedro Olaechea Álvarez Calderón. Olaechea—a wine and pisco tycoon, originally elected on Kuczynski's ticket—was a prominent member of Lima's patrician elite.

The political crisis proved a difficult moment for Confiep, however. Although both Aráoz and Olaechea were figures who traveled in elite circles, Vizcarra clearly enjoyed majoritarian support in the country. Company leaders had to decide whether to remain neutral or to support either of the options of ditching or keeping the president. They opted to support the ousting of Vizcarra and the appointment of Aráoz in his place. A communiqué expressed the organization's "decided rejection of the violation of the constitution and democratic system perpetrated by the president of the republic Martín Vizcarra on the basis of an argument that is unconstitutional."[46] This proved to be a serious miscalculation. Noting her lack of any public support, Aráoz resigned her "presidency" in less than twenty-four hours. Vizcarra was able to dissolve Congress and call fresh legislative elections (Dargent and Rousseau 2022).[47] Confiep was obliged to retreat and then restart conversations with the president.

In the period between dissolution and the election of a new Congress, Vizcarra was able to rule by decree. Using his discretionary powers, he passed a number of measures that enjoyed the support of Confiep and the business community. Measures included the law governing mergers and acquisitions and the granting of special tax and labor rules to the benefit of agro-exporting companies. Company executives continued to demand more decided government support for mining investments, although the government continued to search for formulas that would satisfy both investors and communities. During this period some major public works projects were restarted, such as the Chincheros airport, but avoiding the PPP modality and adopting approaches that were less open to corruption.

The public reputation of business elites, however, was dealt another bitter blow in late 2019. The Lava Jato investigators raided the Confiep headquarters in Lima after new revelations emerged about the secret funding of Fujimori's FP by major corporate donors. The Romero group, led by Dionisio Romero Jr., admitted channeling US$3.6 million to FP for the 2011 elections, a sum matched by Juan Ramsus Echecopar, a tycoon with investments in the textile industry. In 2016 the Romero Group admitted donating US$450,000 to Fujimori and a further US$200,000 to Kuczynski. This mirrored the practice used by Odebrecht in spreading its bets on a variety of horses (Durand and Salcedo 2020, 188). Hit by such accusations of illicit funding, Confiep was forced to distance itself from such practices. At the November 2019 CADE, María Isabel León, Confiep's then president, openly criticized Romero's use of secret cash donations and called for his resignation. Romero found himself obliged to try and justify himself in an open letter entitled "Carta de Romero a su equipo," published in the newspaper *Perú 21* on November 11, 2019. A few months later he resigned as head of Credicorp and was replaced by his cousin.

The new Congress, elected in January 2000, took its seats in March. The election led to a sharp decline in representation for FP and APRA and a higher degree of party fragmentation than before. It did little, however, to resolve one way or another the standoff between the executive and legislature and to re-create the conditions to resume growth, a situation that exasperated private investors. The largest party to emerge was Acción Popular (AP), but this also suffered internal splits and divergences. Coalitions swiftly emerged, however, united by attempts to put a parliamentary stamp on legislation, producing serious departures (generally described as "populist") from the traditional economic policy preferences of the Ministry of Economy and Finance and the neoliberal rulebook.

The new Congress was no more amenable toward Vizcarra than its predecessor. In August 2020, Vizcarra appointed a pro-business cabinet with a well-known conservative, Pedro Cateriano, as prime minister. A business consultant, Rafael Belaúnde, became minister for energy and mines (Cateriano 2021). The idea was to promote what was termed "a private investment shock," a move supported by Confiep. But Congress forced Cateriano's resignation following a vote of no confidence and made new attempts to impeach Vizcarra. The opportunity to do so arose when a scandal burst about Vizcarra allegedly accepting bribes when he was governor of Moquegua between 2011 and 2014 (Paredes 2021, 190-91). Manuel Merino, the then president of Congress, replaced Vizcarra, but popular discontent across the country with this maneuver forced Merino to resign after less than a week. He was replaced, in turn, by Francisco Sagasti, whose mandate was to steer Peru toward elections in 2021 and deal with the devastating effects of the COVID-19 pandemic.

The rising tide of popular mobilization was revealed when protests broke out in December 2020 among workers in the agro-exporting sector of Peru's coastal valleys who demanded higher wages and improved working conditions. In Ica, as well as on the northern coast around Trujillo and Chiclayo, roads were blocked for several days, and two protestors were shot dead by police. Widespread support for the protests forced Congress to repeal a law, extended by Vizcarra, that provided employers with tax benefits for a further decade and perpetuation of a labor regime based on low wages and insecurity of employment. To the delight of business interests, the repeal was swiftly followed by a new and even more generous version that also introduced some minor changes in favor of labor. It was an instance of remarkable lobbying practice.

In sum, the period between 2016 and 2020 proved to be one in which business elites lost some of their instrumental ability to influence public policy decisions by the state. This was particularly the case after March 2018 when Vizcarra replaced Kuczynski in the presidency and attempts to tackle corruption took precedence over other priorities. The image of important business sectors was besmirched as a result of investigations into corporate wrongdoing, especially in the covert funding of business-friendly political parties. At the level of discursive business power, this deterioration in its public image made it hard for the business sector to occupy the moral high ground, while dwindling patterns of growth took the luster off Peru's previous claims to offer an "economic miracle." The instrumental power of business was also hampered by internal divisions within the elite, the gradual demise of pro-business parties, and the state's sometimes ambiguous response to popular protest, especially against the activities of large mining companies. Overall, however, although the ideological influence of business over public opinion diminished significantly in this period, its structural power remained strong and its ability to influence policy—although increasingly questioned by the public—continued to be quite effective.

This diminution of business control over political life was then suddenly magnified by the 2021 presidential elections with the unexpected victory of Pedro Castillo, a left-wing rural schoolteacher from Cajamarca, who became president of the republic on July 28, 2021. His victory owed much to a protest vote on the part of Peru's poorest and most marginalized sectors, in large part alienated by the unethical and oligopolistic practices of its business class and attracted by a more statist and nationalistic approach (OXFAM 2022). The business elite found itself plunged into defensive actions against what many came to see as a "communist" takeover. A new cycle of contention seemed about to begin. Within eighteen months Castillo was ousted by Congress.

CONCLUSIONS

Our analysis of business power in the three central Andean republics has stressed the ways in which it remained embedded despite the changes brought about by the "pink tide" in both Bolivia and Ecuador. There was much more continuity of business power in the case of Peru where the election of Pedro Pablo Kuczynski as president in 2016 was seen as a further assertion of the interests of the business class. To varying degrees, in all three countries, however, business interests managed to strike up a modus vivendi with elected governments of different stripes. This was evident in Bolivia after around 2011 when the Morales government moved toward a rapprochement with the country's business sector, and in particular to meeting the concerns of businessmen in Santa Cruz. Equally, there were signs of a retreat from some of the more radical propositions of the Correa administration in Ecuador although the gap between his government and the business sector was never as wide as in Bolivia.

Although these moves toward greater accommodation were notable in Ecuador and Bolivia, in Peru under Kuczynski, and even more so under Vizcarra after 2018, the degree of business capture began to be challenged. On the one hand, this was a consequence of the Lava Jato scandal, which broke at the end of 2017 not long after Kuczynski's accession. This scandal highlighted many of the illicit ties that had been forged between the private sector, both Peruvian and non-

Peruvian, over many preceding years, and involved some of the best-known figures in the Peruvian business community. It demonstrated to an already skeptical public how business interests, particularly Brazilian construction companies, had routinely bribed prominent politicians—including many past presidents—and funded their election campaigns. The discursive strength of the business community suffered as a consequence.

At the same time social movements showed signs of increased restiveness in pressing their claims against the government. Furthermore, while Morales and Correa had previously lost much of the backing they initially enjoyed among the urban middle class, the hitherto solid support for the status quo among Peru's middle class showed some signs of crumbling. So, as Bolivia and Ecuador moved in one direction, Peru seemingly moved in the opposite one with the once solid power of the business elite increasingly challenged.

The ending of the commodity super cycle increased the structural power of business, especially in Bolivia and Ecuador, by reducing the fiscal autonomy of the state and increasing its dependence on the private sector for a continuation in necessary investments. This was less the case in Peru whose economy was more diversified and which, in any case, managed to sustain relatively high levels of growth. Between them, however, Bolivia and Ecuador demonstrate significant differences. The collapse of oil prices in 2012 and its impact on Ecuador's balance of payments, coupled with the policy constraints imposed by the dollarization of its economy, forced the Correa government to change course, abandon policies that were antagonistic toward business interests, and shift back toward a policy stance more acceptable to the IMF and World Bank. This change in direction, much criticized by erstwhile supporters on the left, was pushed much further after Lenín Moreno took over from Correa in 2017. In Bolivia, by contrast, the impact of lower export earnings only seriously began to force a change of direction in 2019. This was because the government managed to maintain high levels of public investment, using the foreign reserves built up over previous years to finance it. Indeed, until 2018, Bolivia registered one of the highest growth rates anywhere in Latin America.

The importance of shifts in structural power were arguably less significant than changes in instrumental power. Again, perhaps the most dramatic shift was in Ecuador where the business sector swiftly availed itself of new opportunities to influence policy direction during Correa's last years in power. Under Moreno business gained further influence as the government opened itself up more explicitly to the private sector, creating new channels for communication and influence. The situation in Bolivia was more nuanced during Morales's last years with influence from the private sector balanced against that of popular movements of one kind or another. But this situation changed radically under Áñez when links with such movements were curtailed, and the government saw itself as actively promoting private sector interests and bringing business back into the heart of economic decision making. This proved unsustainable politically. The instrumental power of business that had shown its muscle in Peru under Humala weakened under his successors, particularly under Vizcarra. Policy making increasingly succumbed to the offensive waged by the Peruvian Congress against the executive, while the Ministry of Economy and Finance saw its supremacy diminished, and sectors of civil society became increasingly assertive. These cross currents ultimately led to the downfall of Vizcarra in 2020 and the election of Castillo in 2021 amid new and ever greater problems of governability. Organizations like Confiep could no longer orchestrate policy in quite the overt way they had done previously.

At the level of discursive power, the ability of the private sector to maintain a hegemonic narrative proved increasingly difficult to sustain. This was probably clearest in Peru where the image of business as a disinterested force promoting national development began to be questioned as evidence of systemic corruption became impossible to hide. The moral stance of the private sector was thus badly compromised. Similarly, in Bolivia, the excesses of the Áñez administration and its antidemocratic demeanor seriously detracted from the standing of business interests among the population as a whole, paving the way toward the landslide victory of Luis Arce in October 2020 and the return of the MAS to power.

Of our three countries, the discursive power of business probably remained strongest in Ecuador, not so much because of the achievements of the Moreno administration but because of the tainted memories of Correa's government, not least because of the accusations of corruption levelled against it. As elections in all three countries were to show, in the period between October 2020 and April 2021, voters shied away from pro-business models. Even in Ecuador, where Guillermo Lasso finally made it to the presidency, it was far from being a ringing endorsement of the pro-business policies that he advocated.

The restoration of business power in Ecuador and Bolivia in the second decade of the new millennium and its diminution in the case of Peru therefore reflect a mix of factors both exogenous and endogenous to the three countries. Although the end of the commodity boom represents part of the explanation, there were many other elements involved. In each of our three countries we can see a growing questioning within society of attempts to reenact the neoliberal transformation that took place in the 1980s and 1990s. Within a context of democratic politics, new actors had come to the fore drawing strength from unresolved problems of poverty and marginalization. This led, in turn, to a more precarious balance in which business organizations were no longer able simply to impose the economic model that best suited their strategic interests. Political contestation was in evidence in all three countries, even in Peru where for nearly quarter of a century social movements remained atomized and powerless at the national level. Institutional instability—or the "unsettling statecraft" to which Conaghan and Malloy (1994) referred three decades ago—was still very much a feature of the political scene in the Andean region. And the impact of the COVID-19 pandemic and its longer-term economic and social consequences may add a new element, constituting a new critical juncture that could further heighten political tensions and complicate economic management in the years ahead.

CONCLUSIONS AND OUTLOOK

In *Unsettling Statecraft*, Conaghan and Malloy analyzed how business groups, over the 1970s and 1980s, came to support democratization "as the means to escape from the uncertainty that reigned during the military governments of the 1970s." Based on what we have analyzed throughout this book as the three dimensions of business power, economic elites believed that formally democratic regimes would give them the opportunity to "occupy a 'privileged position' within the policy-making apparatus," enabling them to push through pro-business policies (Conaghan and Malloy 1994, 5-6). In the context of the regional (and indeed global) rise of the neoliberal paradigm, this expectation by and large bore out throughout the Central Andes. Yet, in neither of our three cases has the dual transformation of the political regime and the economic development model along (neo)liberal lines culminated in the consolidation of "neoliberal" or "market democracy." Unsettledness remained the overarching feature—with the temporary exception of Peru, in which, however, the return to semi-authoritarian rule under Alberto Fujimori played an important role in facilitating an unusually stable configuration of business capture that guaranteed the continuity of neoliberal policies well beyond the end of the Fujimori era.

The problem, from the perspective of business elites, is that formal democracy "tends to be real to some extent," as Dietrich

Rueschemeyer, Evelyne Huber Stephens, and John Stephens argued in their classic study on *Capitalist Development and Democracy* (1992, 10). After a certain lull in the mobilization of the popular sectors in most of Latin America's post-transition democracies, this proposition was confirmed by the wave of anti-neoliberal mass protests since the mid-1990s, which gave rise to the "pink tide" and a new phase of (contested) popular sector incorporation (Silva and Rossi 2018). Clearly, and in a very pronounced way in the particularly stratified postcolonial societies of the Central Andes—in which multiple, intersecting types of social inequality mutually reinforce each other—the fundamental contradictions between the logics of democracy and oligarchy (Foweraker 2018) or between democracy and private enterprise (Lindblom 1977) cannot be resolved but are almost constantly renegotiated. This (re)negotiation is a relational process, shaped by state-business relations on the one hand and state–popular sector relations on the other. Given the weakness of formal institutions in the Central Andean countries, these power dynamics and negotiations (and confrontations) are much less shaped and constrained by officially established rules of the game than in other contexts—indeed, they frequently lead to changes in the political regime as well. For the time being, "an unsettled regime type and an unsettling style of policy-making" (Conaghan and Malloy 1994, 6) will continue to characterize Bolivia, Ecuador, and Peru.

In the Central Andean countries, these processes of (re)negotiating and managing the tensions between capitalism and democracy continue to be shaped by the structural logics of a development model that has not seen fundamental and lasting change in the period under review. Despite major societal and demographic changes, the economies of Bolivia, Ecuador, and Peru remain marked by a dependence on primary exports, a pattern that tends to be self-reinforcing. Attempts to diversify on the back of redistribution of income and development of the internal market have proved fleeting and difficult to sustain. In conditions of marked social and ethnic inequality, capital-intensive extractive industries have done little to resolve deep structural inequalities. Indeed, many would argue that they have increased them. Further, the Central Andean region often lacks the technological expertise and experience in order to compete seriously on the world market in sectors that add value to production, thereby reinforcing the global division of labor. The existence of large sectors of the population effectively bypassed by the most dynamic areas of production—the great "left behind" who account for well over 70 percent of the workforce in Peru and Bolivia and not much less in

Ecuador—systematically perpetuates entrenched structures of socioeconomic, regional, and ethnic inequality and consequently further complicates the building of consent, exacerbates political tensions, and produces bouts of rejection against traditional patterns of domination by business.

COMPARATIVE FINDINGS ON THE CENTRAL ANDES

In Bolivia and a bit later in Peru, the economic crises of the 1980s and attempts by left-of-center governments to implement heterodox policies pushed business elites to strengthen their internal cohesion and expand their explicitly political role as protagonists of an anti-statist, pro-market agenda. In Bolivia, economic elites united to mobilize their structural, instrumental, and discursive power against the Siles Zuazo government. In Peru, a similar dynamic developed during the first Alan García government. The severe hyperinflation crises—in the case of Peru accompanied by the brutality of the internal armed conflict—brought about critical junctures that were used by business elites and their political allies to enact decisive structural changes in the model of economic development. The political path was different in the two cases, taking the shape of internationally supported elite realignments and pacts in the context of electoral politics in the case of Bolivia and a postelection volte-face followed by a "self-coup" designed to bring "order and progress" in the case of Peru. Still, business and political elite convergence around the aim to transform the state-centered development model along neoliberal lines was decisive in both countries, as was the shock therapy-like implementation of this transformation, justified as an inevitable response to hyperinflation.

Nothing of this kind occurred in Ecuador, which prevented the emergence of a similarly strong pro-business alliance. On the one hand, business elites and their political allies remained fragmented along regional, sectorial, and partisan lines; on the other, the capacity for resisting neoliberal reforms on the part of popular sector organizations and movements remained significant throughout the 1980s and 1990s. As a consequence, while would-be shock therapists were also elected in Ecuador, they were much less able to form viable governing coalitions and, thus, failed to implement similarly comprehensive neoliberal reforms. At the same time, tridimensional business power—supported by international actors and resources—was strong enough to move the country along a path of gradual pro-business reforms, while effectively blocking governments from

TABLE C.1. THE TURN TO THE NEOLIBERAL MODEL IN THE 1980S AND EARLY 1990S

Critical juncture	Breakdown of the ISI model
Outcome	Turn to neoliberal development model: radical change (Bolivia, Peru) versus gradual shift (Ecuador)
Power dynamics	Combination of democratization and debt crisis increases business power structurally, instrumentally, and discursively. Business power expanded through increasing role of IFIs, weakening of organized labor, and emerging global hegemony of neoliberalism. Threat by leftist/heterodox policies triggers organizational and discursive unification of business community (Bolivia, Peru). Failure of heterodox crisis response (hyperinflation) discursively and instrumentally facilitates pro-business agenda (Bolivia, Peru).

(re)turning to statist, developmentalist, or redistributionist policies (see table C.1).

In terms of social power relations, neoliberal reforms have a self-reinforcing effect as they tend to strengthen structural, instrumental, and discursive business power while undermining the collective action capacity of the popular sectors, organized labor in particular (Kurtz 2004; Oxhorn and Starr 1999; Wolff 2009, 2020b). This power dynamic, however, could at best mitigate but not solve the inherent tension between the promise and formal guarantee of political equality that came with democratization and the socioeconomic inequalities that tended to deepen with the transition from a statist-developmentalist to a neoliberal-corporate economic model. As a consequence, business power and the corresponding business influence on (economic) policy making consolidated in all three countries during the 1990s. Yet, while business representatives, like-minded politicians, and technocrats came to control crucial areas of economic policy making, neither Bolivia nor Ecuador saw the emergence of state capture in a broader sense.

The persisting fragmentation of elites along regional, sectorial, and partisan lines (pronounced in Ecuador but also observable in Bolivia) contributed to this. In contrast, the markedly different political context of the Fujimori years and the more cohesive business structure combined to set Peru on a diverging trajectory. Here, the authoritarian setting as well as the (legacies of the) internal conflict weakened the structural capacity of popular sector resistance against the neoliberal development model while forging intra-elite cohesion.

As a consequence, Peruvian business elites, which were characterized by less salient regional divisions and a stronger and more diversified economy, proved able to consolidate a unified peak organization and effectively make use of their three-dimensional power to the point of prolonged state—and indeed political—capture.

When the incipient "pink tide" in Latin America signaled the emergence of yet another critical juncture Bolivia and Ecuador (on the one hand) and Peru (on the other) found themselves facing very different domestic circumstances. In the former two countries, in the early 2000s, the fundamental "unsettledness" of the political regime and the economic development model became once again manifest, with social movements and mass protests openly challenging the discursive hegemony of elite-centered democracy and neoliberal economics. In Peru, by contrast, the end of the Fujimori era brought political democratization with far-reaching continuity in economic policies, which basically remained under the control of business elites and pro-market technocrats. Business quickly accommodated to parties and managed to influence the Congress whose decision-making role recovered with democratization.

In explaining these diverging outcomes, the successful mobilization of anti-neoliberal forces in Bolivia and Ecuador, and the lack thereof in Peru, is certainly a crucial variable. Yet, the strength of business power and the extent to which business elites succeeded in forging viable governing coalitions and constructing discursive hegemony also constitute important parts of the story. More specifically, in Bolivia and Ecuador, the gradual demise of traditional parties and the rise of alternative political movements or outsiders in the context of a persistently fragmented business community significantly reduced instrumental and discursive business power. It also revealed that the discursive hegemony of neoliberalism had failed to extend much beyond the countries' elites to begin with.

At roughly the same time, the international commodity boom enabled reforms of the hydrocarbon sector that reduced the dependence of the state on the private sector (and, thus, structural business power). In Peru, by contrast, the much more cohesive business community and its more consolidated role within both the political and policy arena and the public sphere meant that the commodity boom helped sustain the configuration of political capture. Under these conditions, business elites—through the instrumental and discursive power of key business associations such as Confiep and the use of party financing and lobbying to establish a privileged relationship with key branches of the state—contributed significantly to

TABLE C.2. THE "PINK TIDE" IN THE EARLY 2000S

Critical juncture	Contestation and crisis of the neoliberal model
Outcome	Turn to post-neoliberal development model (Bolivia, Ecuador) versus continuity of neoliberal model (Peru)
Power dynamics	Economic downturn of 1998–2002, wave of anti-neoliberal protests and demise of established political parties weakens business power instrumentally and discursively (Bolivia, Ecuador). "Pink tide" governments, supported by the incipient commodity boom, further weaken business power (Bolivia, Ecuador). Political capture based on strong instrumental and discursive business power contributes to preventing "pink tide" (Peru). In Peru's more diversified export economy, the commodity boom reinforces structural business power.

ensuring continuity in both the style and the substance of economic policy making, even as the political context, similarly to Bolivia and Ecuador, was characterized by a gradual demise of traditional political parties, the rise of political outsiders, and increasing social discontent with the political regime (see Table C.2).

Power, according to a famous dictum by Karl W. Deutsch, is "the ability to afford not to learn" (1963, 111). In Bolivia and Ecuador, with Morales and Correa, business elites had to respond to the gradual but significant loss in structural, instrumental, and discursive power and adapt to governments that turned from neoliberal recipes to statist, developmentalist, and in part, redistributive policies. They did so in fairly pragmatic ways until the end of the commodity boom and shifts in the domestic correlations of forces presented them with the opportunity, once again, to form part of politically forceful pro-business alliances. The result was a restoration of business power in both Bolivia and Ecuador, first gradually and partially (in the final years of the Morales and Correa governments), then markedly and openly so (under Jeanine Áñez and under Lenín Moreno). In Peru, by contrast, business elites could afford neither to adapt nor to learn until episodes of social-environmental conflict alongside major corruption scandals shook the political system (thereby undermining the usual channels and vehicles of business influence) and revealed the extent and forms of illicit business capture (thereby reducing the legitimacy of the business elite and its discursive hegemony).

The removal of Pedro Castillo as president in Peru in December 2022 and his replacement by a more conservative regime led by Dina Boluarte pointed toward the attempt of business elites, supported

TABLE C.3. THE RECENT RETURN TO A STATE OF OPEN UNSETTLEDNESS

Critical juncture	End of the commodity boom and COVID-19 pandemic
Outcome	Unsettledness of development model and ruling coalition (Ecuador, Peru) versus return to post-neoliberal model with unclear perspective (Bolivia)
Power dynamics	End of the commodity boom and weakening of "pink tide" Government re-increases business power and facilitates shifts to pro-business governments (Bolivia, Ecuador). Limited discursive business power and persistent strength of popular sector organizations prevent consistent (re)turn to market-oriented model (Bolivia, Ecuador). Division of leftist forces prevents return to post-neoliberal ruling coalition (Ecuador) Increase in popular sector mobilization and discursive and instrumental weakening of business elites (through corruption scandals, demise of established parties, and difficulties to pass legislation with a divided government) openly challenges neoliberal model (Peru). COVID-19 weakens pro-business agenda discursively but undermines fiscal basis for state-oriented development model.

by the military and right-wing parties in Congress, to regain control. But the widespread resistance her government encountered suggested that the new power block was far from consolidated. At the time of finalizing this manuscript (March 2023), the situation seemed more "unsettled" and indeed "unsettling" for Peruvian business elites than for their counterparts in Bolivia and Ecuador. In the case of Bolivia, although the MAS had returned to power, it did not present an immediate threat to vital business interests. In Ecuador, the conservative businessman Guillermo Lasso appeared unable to implement a coherent pro-business agenda but had already managed to implement some economic reforms and remained concerned to protect key business interests. Yet, arguably, the political changes brought about by the elections of 2020 and 2021 in the three countries, combined with the lasting and far-reaching consequences of the COVID-19 pandemic presented a new critical juncture for both the political regime and the economic development model across the Central Andes (see Table C.3).

With a view to the broader theoretical debate about business power and state-business relations, our comparative analysis makes three key contributions. First, our study confirms that the tridimensional framework of business power offers a useful theoretical lens with which to analyze the political role of business elites as well as state-business relations. Doing so offers important insights into the broader power dynamics that shape economic policy making as well as the contestation and evolution of models of economic development—in Latin America and beyond. More specifically, our comparative historical analysis has shown how the three types of business power (structural, instrumental, discursive) are important in and of themselves but also how, at the same time, it is really the complex interplay among the three that has to be studied. As seen in our cases, economic elites' capacity to ensure their privileged political role individually and collectively and protect their vital interests has depended on the three types of business power mutually reinforcing themselves.[1] As seen across our cases, limitations or losses of business power in one dimension can contribute to reductions in another dimension as well—for example, when limited discursive power leads to pro-business parties losing in elections, with negative consequences for instrumental business power. The other way round, the persistence of business power in one dimension can also be used to recuperate losses in other dimensions, such as when economic elites in Bolivia and Ecuador used their persisting structural power to reconstruct some of their instrumental power.

Second, this book has brought together the two, hitherto rather separate debates about business power on the one hand and state capture on the other. At the conceptual level, the simultaneous focus on business power and state capture forces us scholars to be more precise in delineating the point at which "normal" levels of privileged political access and influence become "undue" or "excessive" forms of effective control that benefit specific interests but sacrifice the common good. In addition, this distinction has also been shown to be empirically relevant, as demonstrated by the much higher resilience of the neoliberal model in the case of Peru as compared to Bolivia or Ecuador. Still, we also identified some "islands" of at least partial state capture in Bolivia and Ecuador, while even in Peru state capture was never all-encompassing. This suggests that, while it is useful analytically to distinguish between "normal" business power and a situation of state capture, empirically we will often be faced with shades of grey and differences in degree.

Third, our study shows the value of a power-based analysis that is both relational and dynamic. On the one hand, business power is not an absolute quantity that business elites somehow "possess." Rather, it can only be assessed in relation to and in comparison with the power resources held by other, potentially competing actors, groups, and institutions within and outside the state. According to our analysis, two factors are of particular relevance in this regard: the relative autonomy of the state, which is determined to an important extent by state access to resources that are not controlled by private business actors; and the power of non-elite groups, which is determined in particular by their ability to act collectively, be it in the form of mobilization or in the context of electoral politics. In addition, strong leaders and parties use discretionary powers and tend, based on their own political calculations, to act in ways that challenge or undermine business power.

On the other hand, business power—just as other types of power—is neither static nor given but dynamic. While rooted, in part, in structural features (the structure of the economy, fundamental societal cleavages, core institutional features characterizing a given political system and the organization of a given business community), we have seen how business power evolves and changes, at times quite rapidly. As concerns instrumental power, election results may significantly alter the chances of the business elite directly to access the political arena and influence policy making, just as external economic shocks directly impact on structural business power. At the discursive level, corruption scandals and monopolistic practices can quickly erode (or enhance, depending on the culprit) the prestige of business. In broader terms, business power as a factor that enables economic elites to shape policy making and political developments in general is, at the same time, shaped by the shifting politico-economic context in which it operates. Our argument throughout this book is, therefore, neither that business power somehow causes the continuity of unsettled regimes and unsettled forms of policy making in the Central Andes nor that an overall context of unsettledness leads business elites to respond in a particular way. Instead, what we hope our study has shown is the complex interplay between the two: how business power—and business behavior aimed at using, reinforcing, and/or rebuilding such power—has shaped change and continuity in the politico-institutional and politico-economic developments of the three Central Andean countries at hand, while being simultaneously shaped by these constantly evolving contextual conditions.

Finally, in line with Giddens's theory of structuration (1984), business power—as a capacity—is also dynamic in that it is shaped by the very agency of economic elites, which contributes to the reproduction or change in business power. This is most directly observable in the dimension of instrumental power, as deliberate efforts to unify the economic elite of a given country, if successful, directly foster a key source of business power. Political threats to vital business interests are the most common trigger that activates economic elites to better coordinate and unite. Still, whether business actors succeed in overcoming internal divisions between sectors or regions depends both on the structural setting and on the decisions by, and the interaction between, specific business groups and individual leaders. Once business elites succeed in creating a more cohesive organizational structure, however, this then can have quite long-term consequences for instrumental power, as can be seen in the case of Peru's Confiep. This is, again, in line with Giddens's general argument about structuration: business agency, in shaping the very social setting in which economic elites operate, creates institutional and discursive legacies that enable and constrain business agency and influence in the future.

THE CENTRAL ANDES AT A NEW CRITICAL JUNCTURE?

The writing of this book coincided with what may be construed as the most recent instance of a critical juncture, albeit one emanating more from the physical world of disease than from the global economy as such. The COVID-19 crisis broke upon an unsuspecting world in the first quarter of 2020. The longer-term impacts of this crisis are still difficult to evaluate. They will undoubtedly become clearer with the passage of time. Our tone in writing this epilogue is therefore necessarily speculative.

Latin America has been deeply affected by the coronavirus pandemic in sanitary, economic, and social conditions, perhaps more so than most other parts of the world (ECLAC 2022b). In proportion to population, the numbers of people suffering and dying from the virus were higher than elsewhere, at least in its first two waves. On the one hand this reflected the relative decline in the efficacy of public health services in the region over recent decades; on the other it showed how difficult it was to curb the spread of the virus in overcrowded communities where the lack of adequate employment meant that people had no alternative but to continue working to survive. Within Latin America, the situation in the Central Andean countries was particularly serious. Images of people dying in the streets of Guayaquil for lack of hospital facilities provided the world with an early but painful image of the sort of suffering that would become much more widespread. In the end, Bolivia and Peru competed for the unfortunate title as the country with the highest

COVID-19 mortality rate in the world. Although Peru had the highest number of reported COVID-19 deaths in proportion to its population, the estimated excess mortality rate for 2020 and 2021 was nowhere as high as in Bolivia (COVID-19 Excess Mortality Collaborators 2022).

The economic impact also proved severe: the Peruvian economy was particularly hard hit, with GDP contracting by over 11.0 percent in 2020. This was more than any other economy in Latin America and the country's worst economic downturn since the years of the debt crisis in the early 1980s. Ecuador and Bolivia did not fare much better, with their economies shrinking by 8.7 percent and 8.6 percent respectively (ECLAC 2022a). Because of the lockdown in all three countries, large numbers of people lost their jobs, further swelling the ranks of the unemployed and those seeking to survive in the informal sector. Consequently, poverty rates soared in all three countries. In Peru, those living in poverty are thought to have doubled as a consequence, with Bolivia and Ecuador also exhibiting marked increases. Similarly, indices of income inequality worsened as those with better access to jobs and health provision fared much better than those at the bottom of the heap. Besides job losses, income sharply declined in various groups, particularly affecting the informal sector but also the middle class. As a consequence, the improvement in social indices registered throughout much of Latin America during the first two decades of the millennium (which had already started to deteriorate in the years before 2020) were dramatically reversed by the effects of the pandemic, and the three countries in our study were by no means exceptions to the rule.

The response to this crisis included some significant shifts in public policy, with the state forced to step in as the private sector retracted. As in countries across the world, governments were obliged to abandon policies of fiscal austerity and state shrinking in favor of expanding state activities and bailing out companies affected by the pandemic.[2] Most countries also adopted policies to provide some sort of financial support to vulnerable populations, although such payments were often tardy and inadequate. The change in policy ethos was also underwritten by the discourse of international organizations; even the IMF urged countries to spend more, not less. Whether such advice would shift back to more time-honored policy preferences once the crisis passed is, of course, a matter of conjecture. However, the orthodoxies of the neoliberal school were clearly challenged, providing new arguments in the future for those advocating higher degrees of state intervention, and not just limited to public health. At the same time, the crisis put additional strain on public budgets, which had come under pressure anyway with the end of the commodity boom. This meant that the scope for responding to the crisis with massive fiscal stimulus, as could be observed in the richer parts of the world, was much smaller.

How will the private sector emerge from the COVID-19 crisis in the longer term? This is a topic that will undoubtedly be one for future research. However, the answer will probably be one that shows a varied picture, with those sectors producing for the global market recovering at a faster rate than those dependent on domestic demand, thereby further reinforcing the region's role as a provider of primary exports. The recovery in growth in both the United States and other developed countries in 2021 and the technological transition to new forms of energy had already pushed up the prices for key commodities to levels unseen since the commodity supercycle. Moreover, these were sectors in which the effects of lockdown proved only temporary, with production rates quickly recovering to pre-pandemic rates. In such relatively buoyant circumstances, continued private investment flows looked likely to continue, not least in sectors like mining. However, the war in Ukraine in 2022 produced further uncertainty, the most negative effects probably felt in Peru, a net oil importer.

The political impact of the crisis will probably dictate caution on the part of private investors. Throughout Latin America, deep discontent spilled over into the political sphere, not just in voting patterns but on the streets. Even in countries that had gained a reputation for relative stability and economic conservatism such as Colombia and Chile, citizens vented their anger and frustration against neoliberal policies and those politicians most closely associated with them. In both countries this was then reflected by the election of left-of-center politicians in presidential elections in 2022. The three Central Andean countries proved to be no exceptions in this regard. In 2021 and 2022, there were serious bouts of violent protests in all three.

In October 2020 voters in Bolivia endorsed the return of the left-wing MAS to government. They did so in wholehearted rejection of the Áñez administration, which had replaced that of Evo Morales a year earlier. Backed by the most conservative sectors of Bolivian society, Áñez had sought to reverse the statist and interventionist policies of the Morales era, moves designed to appeal to the business community, especially that of Santa Cruz. Her government had attracted strident criticism for its authoritarian leanings, its lack of respect for human rights, its poor handling of the COVID-19 crisis, and for some notorious instances of corruption. She also attracted criticism for seeking to outlive her initial status as "interim" president. It took mobilization by Bolivia's still powerful social movements to force the pace of holding elections. Replacing her in November 2020, Luis Arce, the MAS candidate who had won 55 percent of the vote the previous month, inaugurated a government that pledged itself to resuming the economic approach adopted by Morales. Arce, indeed, had been Morales's economy minister for most of the period since 2006 when Morales had assumed office.

The scale of Arce's victory provided an important degree of legitimacy that seemed set to protect the MAS administration from its critics on the right, at least for a time. For Bolivia's economic elites, the return of the MAS was certainly as unexpected as it was unwanted. Still, it offered the prospect of economic recovery from the disastrous downturn in 2020 as well as the possibility of returning to the sort of tactical alliance that had characterized the latter part of the Morales government. The response of the main business associations was in like manner, seeking to ensure their voice was heard in the formulation of policy on matters directly affecting business interests. Many business associations had been ill-disposed to supporting moves to subvert the Morales government, even though they enthusiastically welcomed its removal once this was accomplished.

Arce's government proved quite effective in speeding up the vaccination program against COVID-19, and during his first year, signs of economic recovery became manifest, helped by the recovery in commodity prices. At the same time, however, Arce largely refrained from responding to business calls for dialogue and avoided granting Bolivia's business representatives the space and recognition they had gained under Morales after 2009. Given the fragmented and weak opposition at the national level, the economic elites therefore had to largely rely on their persisting structural power. Politically, they found themselves wedged between, on the one hand, a central government that did not openly threaten their vital interests but denied them direct access to the political arena and, on the other, a radicalizing right-wing opposition in Santa Cruz that put increasing pressure on the business elites to openly join their resistance against the MAS but offered no viable alternative at the level of national politics (Wolff forthcoming).

In Ecuador, the Moreno administration's embrace of the liberalizing agenda had run into serious opposition on the streets in advance of the pandemic. Escalating mass protests in Quito and elsewhere forced Moreno into backtracking on fiscal reforms demanded by the IMF as a condition of its ongoing economic support package.

In the event, the government abandoned an adjustment package that involved sharp increases in fuel prices. Although the COVID-19 crisis, eventually, enabled both the passage of the corresponding adjustment measures and the unlocking of foreign loans, the political muscle deployed by social movements, which had contributed to bringing down three presidents in swift succession between 1996 and 2005, had reasserted itself. In the elections that followed in February 2021, in which Moreno was not a candidate, the majority of votes went to Correa's stand-in candidate Andrés Arauz but not by a sufficient enough margin to avert a second round. Guillermo Lasso's electoral victory in April 2021 offered few prospects of renewed political stability behind a business friendly program. Although the conservative Guayaquil banker who had unsuccessfully contested the presidency in 2013 and 2017 finally won, this was in large part because of abstention by the supporters of Pachakutik.

Business groups were gratified by Lasso's victory—with his agenda that basically meant consolidating the neoliberal turn in economic policies initiated by Moreno. This was also reflected in a cabinet characterized by a strong presence of business representatives and like-minded academics, invoking the image of state capture (Macaroff forthcoming). Yet, from the outset, it was clear that Lasso's plan to kickstart economic recovery by cutting taxes, reducing regulation, and attracting foreign investment into key sectors such as oil and mining would lead swiftly to opposition in both the National Assembly and on the streets. Within the legislature, Lasso's electoral alliance only held a minority of the seats, which were further reduced when the conservative PSC broke with the newly elected president early on during his mandate. As a consequence, Lasso was unable to implement the economic reforms most demanded by the business associations such as labor market reforms and an investment promotion law.

Still, given the weakness and fragmentation of the opposition parties in parliament, the president so far has been able to build temporary alliances, prevent the formation of majorities that could endanger his mandate, and use his executive powers to push through at least part of his economic agenda, including a tax reform (Macaroff forthcoming). In terms of popular support, Lasso initially benefited from broad approval in light of a successful vaccination program. But the lack of attention to socioeconomic grievances quickly provoked open resistance, most notably by the country's indigenous movement. In June 2022, a "national strike" led by CONAIE forced the government into a new round of negotiations over the indigenous movement's ten demands, which included a reduction in fuel prices, a credit moratorium, price controls for basic goods, and a moratorium on new oil and mining projects (Aguirre 2022). In this setting, the country's economic elites tried to distance themselves from an overly unpopular president while simultaneously using their instrumental and discursive power to counter the agenda of Lasso's leftist critics, in ways that included voicing support for a repressive response to protest.

Finally, in Peru, the April 2021 first-round elections revealed the depth of public animosity to perpetuation of the status quo. The second-round victory of Pedro Castillo, a little-known union leader from a far-left party, brought an immediate and extremely hostile response from Peru's business elite, and the more right-wing parties that emerged strengthened in Congress from the polarized electoral contest. The rise in Castillo's popularity had gone largely unnoticed in opinion polls prior to the election and was based emphatically in the poorest sectors of the Peruvian population (socioeconomic sectors "D" and "E") and in those parts of the country well beyond the confines of Metropolitan Lima.

Castillo effectively eclipsed the candidacy of Verónika Mendoza, hitherto the standard-bearer of much of the left. Advocating statist and redistributionist policies, his initial agenda was one of radical reforms including the nationalization of extractive industries and the rewriting of the pro-business 1993 constitution. This met with a menacing response from the political right, which, throughout the second-round contest, accused the left of being "Marxist," "communist," and sympathetic toward "terrorism." The business class appeared divided in its response, with some leading figures supporting campaigns to unseat Castillo and others adopting a more "wait and see" approach. Still, his election was met by considerable capital flight. The new government speedily ditched most of its more radical sounding policies, with the Ministry of Economy and Finance seeking to allay fears of nationalization and taking steps to promote continued foreign investment. The structural power of business appeared to be asserting itself while its instrumental power was much reduced.

Castillo faced unrelenting hostility from right-wing parties in Congress. A third impeachment bid in December 2022 proved successful following Castillo's frustrated attempt to close down the legislature and reorganize the judiciary. Dina Boluarte, hitherto vice president, succeeded him. She faced widespread resistance, however, with protests erupting across the country, especially in the south where people had voted massively for Castillo. With police and army repression leading to at least 60 deaths, her government appeared increasingly authoritarian in its demeanor, retreating from earlier promises to bring forward elections. Business elites were largely supportive of Castillo's abrupt removal, especially as the new minister for economy and finance appeared keen to pursue liberalizing economic reforms. Still, the economic and political future appeared far from assured under a government that, while claiming constitutional legality, lacked legitimacy in the eyes of the vast majority of voters.

Throughout the Central Andes, then, the effect of the pandemic and its longer-term sociopolitical consequences were to challenge the liberalizing consensus that business groups sought to generate—or regain—over the previous period. The "unsettledness" of the political climate appeared to have reasserted itself in all three countries. Important strands of business power had been weakened, most notably its capacity to shape public discourse and to craft broader alliances in this critical juncture. The "social question," aggravated by COVID-19, will most likely constitute a key theme on the political agenda across the region, as will be issues of (re)distribution in the face of fiscal deficits and rising debt levels. Yet, at the same time, the structural power of private business may well benefit from the consequences of the pandemic. Against this background, the extent to which business elites will be able to claw back their former primacy is but a matter of conjecture.

NOTES

INTRODUCTION

1. We discuss the relevant scholarship in the respective chapters of this book, but by way of broader overviews, see Etchemendy (2011), Oxhorn and Ducatenzeiler (1998), Oxhorn and Starr (1999), Remmer (1998), Smith et al. (1994), Stokes (2004), and Weyland (2002) on the regional turn to neoliberalism and its social and political consequences; Eckstein and Wickham-Crowley (2003), Johnston and Almeida (2006), Roberts (2008), and Silva (2009) on anti-neoliberal mobilization; Cameron and Hershberg (2010), Levitsky and Roberts (2011), Silva and Rossi (2018), and Weyland et al. (2010) on the "leftist turn"; as well as Burdick et al. (2009), Macdonald and Ruckert (2009), and Ruckert et al. (2017) on the debate about post-neoliberalism in Latin America. Most recently, scholars have also started tackling the end and legacy of the "pink tide" as well as the resurgence of the political right. See Balán and Montambeault (2020); Cannon (2016); Chiasson-LeBel and Larrabure (2019); Correa Leite et al. (2018); Ellner (2020); Falleti and Parrado (2018); Kapiszewski et al. (2021); López Segrera (2016); Luna and Rovira Kaltwasser (2014); and North and Clark (2018).

2. We follow Ruckert et al. in understanding post-neoliberalism "not as a complete break with neoliberalism, but rather as a tendency to break with certain aspects of neoliberal policy prescriptions, without representing a set of strict policies or a clearly identifiable policy regime." In terms of policies, key dimensions include "renationalisation of the economy; a new

approach to trade policy with the rise of new regional groupings; changes to revenue generation and taxation; social spending and labour market policy; land reform; and gender" (Ruckert et al. 2017, 1584).

3. Other studies that mostly focus on the role of social movements, trade unions, and other popular sector organizations on the one hand and political institutions, political parties, and party systems on the other include Balán and Montambeault (2020), Kapiszewski et al. (2021), and Silva and Rossi (2018).

4. On the more recent debate on Latin America's economic elites, business power, and state capture, see Bril-Mascarenhas and Maillet (2019), Bull et al. (2013), Cárdenas and Robles-Rivera (2020), Crabtree and Durand (2017), Durand (2019), Fairfield (2015a, 2015b), Karcher and Schneider (2012), Schneider (2004, 2010, 2013), and Wolff (2016).

CHAPTER 1: BUSINESS POWER, MODELS OF ECONOMIC DEVELOPMENT, AND THE STATE

1. Latin America is generally considered the region with the greatest inequality in the world, a trait that can be traced back to the colonial era and is so deeply rooted in the region's social, economic, and political structures that it has persisted throughout the two centuries since independence and even decades of democratic rule (Blofield 2011b; Burchardt 2012; Fairfield 2015a).

2. In this book, the terms *economic elites*, *business elites*, and *big business* are used interchangeably and refer to the upper stratum of local companies and business groups as well as foreign corporations and investors that, in any given country, control most of the economic wealth and generate most of the economic profit. In addition to this core group (the elite), a wide range of business actors encompasses medium-size companies, which may be important at the sectoral level or in a given region, as well as a vast array of small-sized companies and micro enterprises, including entrepreneurs in the informal economy. Unless stated otherwise, when talking about business power, we are focusing on the power held and exercised by the economic elite.

3. Throughout this book, when we refer to "(economic) development" and "models of (economic) development," we do not do so with our own substantive conception in mind of what development is or should be. Rather, we acknowledge that different models of development can also come with different notions of development. Empirically, however, the models that have come to shape economic policy making across the Central Andes and Latin America at large have generally converged around a modernization-type and growth-oriented conception of capitalist development.

4. Analytically, it is important to distinguish between the mere existence of power, in terms of power resources, and its actual use or enactment. But empirically, as Tasha Fairfield (among others) has argued, it would be misleading to associate "the exercise of power exclusively with overt actions." She goes on, "Influence may instead flow through anticipated reactions or act implicitly when policymakers share business's objectives" (Fairfield 2015b, 420n37). Throughout this book, we therefore take a broad look at the (re-)sources of business power, at the range of business activities that are enabled by, activate, and/or use such (re-)sources as well as at policy makers' perceptions of and responses to business power.

5. See, for instance, the classic study by Cardoso and Faletto (1968). For overviews of the structuralist research tradition in Latin America and the dependency school in particular, see Love (2005) as well as several chapters in Acharya et al. (2022).

6. In line with the overall qualitative and comparative-historical approach of this study, we do not pretend to measure structural (or instrumental or discursive) power in any strict sense. In the empirical chapters, we combine an analysis of quantitative indicators (wherever possible and useful) with qualitative assessments (based on primary and secondary sources) in a methodologically eclectic way so as to arrive at general assessments of the respective power structures and dynamics at play.

7. If such practices become the (informal) norm, we can talk of "crony capitalism" (Cave and Rowell 2015).

8. Studies on campaign contributions in developed countries that look at the long-term impact on the political system also consider money a potent mechanism of policy influence (Sachs 2011; Gilens 2012; Cagé 2018). Probably nowhere is this more the case than in US elections.

9. The institutional response to the challenges of the revolving door is the introduction of a "cooling off" period, where state officials must wait a period of time before moving to the private sector.

10. In Peru and Bolivia, *empresarios emergentes* are a relatively new phenomenon, visible in particular in Lima's Gamarra area, largely defined by its textile industry and stores, and in El Alto, the twin city of La Paz known for its huge open-air markets. Thriving entrepreneurs from these popular sector-areas, which are dominated by largely informal commerce, rarely interact with the traditional business representatives of the leading trade associations. In sum, the "fusion of elites" is incomplete, at least hitherto. Money is usually not enough to cross social bridges. For Peru, see Durand (2017b); for Bolivia, Espinoza (2015) and Molina (2019).

11. Focusing specifically on the discursive (or ideological) dimension of political capture, James Kwak (2014) has also introduced the concept of "cultural capture." Here, a given "industry" successfully shapes the broad-

er "understandings about the world" on the part of state regulators so that the latter effectively "serve the ends of industry" (Kwak 2014, 79).

12. A high concentration of economic resources (capital, land) in the hands of local and international corporations developed in a context where the private sector enhanced its role, with private property becoming the main and uncontested form of property. Privatization of state companies, easier access to natural resources, and the opening of new fields of private accumulation (such as pensions, infrastructure, public services) has heightened this trend since the 1990s.

13. See, among many others, Cardoso and Faletto (1968); Etchemendy (2011); O'Donnell (1973); Collier and Collier (2002); Conaghan and Malloy (1994); Domínguez (1998); Haggard and Kaufman (1992, 1995); Levitsky and Roberts (2011); Kingstone (2018); Oxhorn and Ducatenzeiler (1998); Oxhorn and Starr (1999); Pop-Eleches (2009); Remmer (1998); Smith et al. (1994); Stokes (2004); Weyland (2002); Weyland et al. (2010).

14. The significance of the interrelated changes in the economic development model and the political regime over the long term as a subject of analysis is particularly relevant during the first push for change that emerged in first decades of the twentieth century, a time when new leaders and parties, as well as popular organizations, effectively challenged traditional oligarchic rule. Some countries initiated the process of transformation (trend-setters) based on new economic policy precepts, and many others soon followed (demonstration effect). A smaller group remained attached to the old regime and were capable of resisting change for a long period of time (latecomers). The Central Andean region hosted a group of latecomers, partially because politico-economic transformations did not emerge out of a major crisis but out of a series of recurrent crises until the old tie was finally broken.

15. The opportunity for major changes—either for conservative elites or radical mass coalitions—comes in a point of crisis in which tensions increase among key players, business included. The critical juncture is thus a useful concept to help explain changes in both the political regime and the model of economic development.

16. A fifth, rather isolated type of statist model, has been represented by socialist Cuba since 1959. In contrast to the varieties of capitalist development models discussed in this book, here we are faced with a different economic regime that has remained defined by central planning, although the Cuban government allowed limited participation by the private sector in the 1990s (both international capital and small businesses).

17. This observation also holds for the post-neoliberal phase in Bolivia and Ecuador, even if it saw important public debates about alternative conceptions of development, including about alternatives to development,

as well as the constitutional recognition of principles like Buen Vivir or Vivir Bien that are hardly compatible with an extractivism-based and growth-oriented notion of development (see, e.g., Artaraz et al. 2021; Escobar 2010; Grupo Permanente de Trabajo sobre Alternativas al Desarrollo 2011).

18. For the overall debate about "post-neoliberalism" in Latin American, see Burdick et al. (2009), Macdonald and Ruckert (2009), and Ruckert et al. (2017).

19. Direct military interventions tended to wane after the late 1980s as democratization spread. Yet, in cases of high internal tension, the role of the military as a de facto power appeared from time to time as supporters of newly formed ruling coalitions. Two cases demonstrate the limited but important role played by the military in the formation of conservative pro-market coalitions: the Fujimori 1992 presidential coup (or *autogolpe*) that closed Congress and the forced resignation of Morales in the aftermath of the contested 2019 elections at the "suggestion" of the military.

20. There are some significant exceptions in the region in which more enduring political regimes combined with rather stable development models. The most notable cases include regimes that emerged from revolutions (Mexico in 1917, Costa Rica in 1948, Cuba in 1959), particularly bloody coups d'état (Brazil in 1964, Chile in 1973), and exceptionally, from a military invasion (Panama in 1989). Strong governments that were able to crush opposition enjoyed better chances of continuity but often lacked the ability to rule by consent.

CHAPTER 2: BUSINESS POWER IN THE ERA OF STATE-LED DEVELOPMENT

1. Kemmerer provided advice on new institutions for economic management, heading US missions to a variety of Latin American countries in the late 1920s and early 1930s, including Bolivia, Ecuador, and Peru.

2. ECLAC was established in 1948 in Santiago, Chile, originally as the UN Economic Commission for Latin America. It advocated a new approach, arguing that for structural reasons neoclassical policies were inadequate in helping Latin America (the periphery) to "catch up" with developed economies (the center). For an analysis of the origins and nature of structuralism, see Love (2005).

3. In 1960 manufacturing in Latin America (by no means all import substitutive) reached 20.8 percent of GDP, rising to 26.5 percent in 1977, a rate not dissimilar to that of developed countries.

4. Sanford Mosk (in 1950), quoted in Thorp (1998, 136).

5. Business elites found themselves pitted against the state in Argentina under Perón, especially in the agroindustrial sector, although in heavy

industries they benefited from state policies. In Chile, the early emergence of the left as a powerful political actor also meant that public policy was not always amenable to business interests. In both countries, class antagonisms eventually led to military coups in the 1970s.

6. In Mexico, the Confederación de Trabajadores de México (CTM) workers' confederation was an integral part of the long-standing ruling party, the Partido Revolucionario Institucional (PRI). In Brazil, during the Estado Novo, unions became highly subservient to government interests.

7. The civil war between La Paz and Sucre in 1899 represented a cleavage in the interests of different sectors of the mining elite, although it also involved popular mobilization on both sides (Klein 2003, 155–56).

8. There were some exceptions to this rule, as when, in 1923, President Bautista Saavedra introduced new taxes on mining, prompting Patiño to remove his mining headquarters from Bolivia to the United States.

9. According to the 1950 census, no less than 72 percent of the population was engaged in agriculture or related activities. Industry accounted for less than 4 percent of the economically active population, mainly in textile and food processing plants (Klein 2003, 211).

10. As finance minister in the left/nationalist Villaroel government (1943–1946), Víctor Paz Estenssoro adopted a conservative fiscal policy that left no money for social reforms (Klein 1971, 38). On the eve of the revolution, 65 percent of government income came from levies on foreign trade (Thorn 1971, 175).

11. The patterns of intervention by the United States in Bolivian politics are analyzed by Field (2014). For patterns of spending by the US Agency for International Development (USAID), see Heilman (2017).

12. This plan—endorsed by the US government, the newly created Inter-American Development Bank (IDB), and the government of West Germany—aimed at restructuring the tin mining industry and eliminating workers' control over the sector.

13. Moritz Hochschild moved his business operations to Peru and Chile; Aramayo and Patiño left the country; former landowners sought refuge in Peru.

14. Santa Cruz benefited from the system whereby 11 percent of the value of oil production went to the region in which it was produced. In 1955, 95 percent of the royalties thus went to Santa Cruz. Of the total agricultural credit made available between 1955 and 1964, 43 percent went to Santa Cruz, rising to 69 percent between 1970 and 1975. Of USAID loans made available to Bolivia between 1961 and 1971, 47 percent went to Santa Cruz (Barragán 2008).

15. Public sector investment and consumption rose from 20 percent of GDP to over 25 percent of GDP during the Banzer years, for most of this time a higher level than in either Peru or Ecuador.

16. By 1980 debt servicing accounted for around 30 percent of foreign exchange earnings.

17. On the role of the CEPB and the emergence of business as a strong political force, see Conaghan (1995b) and Conaghan and Malloy (1994, 121-29).

18. For a short history of Peru, see Klarén (2000). Also, Contreras and Cueto (2000) for a history of contemporary Peru.

19. In 1889, bankrupted by the War of the Pacific, Peru was forced into a renegotiation of its foreign debt, the so-called Grace Contract. The resultant Peruvian Corporation was given control of the country's railways and navigation rights on Lake Titicaca.

20. The short democratic interlude between 1945 and 1948 under President José Luis Bustamante y Rivero, in which APRA and the Communist Party shared power with other groups, was brought to an end by a military coup that restored oligarchic rule.

21. Manufacturing accounted for 13 percent of GDP in 1950, rising to 14 percent in 1960 and 17 percent in 1970 (Seminario 2015, 1115). However, unlike other Latin American countries, much of the growth in manufacturing during these years was not import substitutive but, rather, was dedicated to processing for export.

22. For an account of the Belaúnde government by an author closely associated to it, see Kuczynski (1977).

23. The standard works on the Velasco regime remains Lowenthal (1975) and its sequel by McClintock and Lowenthal (1983). For a more recent, and more culturally oriented work, see Aguirre and Drinot (2017).

24. The military had undergone a transformation in the 1950s and 1960s from rigidly defending oligarchical interests toward espousing a developmental agenda as a facet of national security (Klarén 2000, 337). The question of internal war, highlighted in the 1960s by land invasions, had become a major concern for the Peruvian military well before 1968 (Stepan 1978, 131).

25. It forced companies to share profits with workers and to include workers on management boards. Employers responded by underreporting profits to slow down the co-participation schemes,

26. Sinamos was an attempt to mobilize support for the government and its project among popular sectors, especially among shantytowns surrounding the larger cities, providing a route for controlled political participation in local affairs.

27. Debt service (amortization plus interest) rose from US$181.3 million in 1970 to US$484.9 million in 1976 and to US$1,280.9 million in 1980 (Banco Central de Reserva del Perú 1980, 158).

28. A tax reform introduced by Armando Zolezzi, who headed the government tax office, had only a very limited effect.

29. See Wise (2003) for an analysis of the growth of the state under Velasco and the reversal of this under Morales Bermúdez and Belaúnde.

30. The balance of payments deficit was US$576.7 million in 1975 and US$867.5 million in 1976. The public sector deficit for the same years was equivalent to 9.7 percent and 10.0 percent of GDP respectively.

31. Aware of the tough conditions likely to be demanded under an IMF stabilization program, Morales Bermúdez first approached a consortium of six US banks in 1976, led by Citibank. Only when the conditions proved impossible to honor was Peru forced into a formal agreement in 1977 with the IMF (Stallings 1983, 167–69).

32. The return of the news media to their original owners created an opportunity to address public opinion. Two newspapers in particular, *El Comercio* owned by the Miró Quesada group and *Expreso* owned by the future economy minister Manuel Ulloa, adopted a stridently anti-statist line.

33. Confiep emerged at this time with US support for peak business organizations in countries suffering problems of terrorism.

34. The growth of Sendero Luminoso from a regional irritant in Ayacucho to a full-blown threat to political stability is traced in (among others) Degregori (2012) and Stern (1998).

35. The Twelve Apostles constituted some of Peru's largest business groups, many of them family owned: the Romeros and Raffos (owners of Peru's largest bank, the Banco de Crédito), the Brescias, the Ferreyros, the Wieses, the Nicolinis, the Bentíns, the Lanata-Piaggio group, La Fabril (Bunge y Born), the Picassos, the Olaechea Alvarez Calderón group, and Cogorno. By building a direct relationship to these twelve economic groups, García sought to avoid intermediaries, specifically Confiep (Durand 2017a).

36. The GDP contracted by 8.3 percent in 1988, by 11.9 percent in 1989, and by 4.6 percent in 1990. Consumption fell 8.6 percent in 1988, 16 percent in 1999, and 1.3 percent in 1990. The average rate of inflation was 67 percent in 1988, 3,399 percent in 1989, and 7,482 percent in 1990. Reserves were –US$317.4 million in 1988, recovering to US$546 million in 1989, and US$692 million in 1990 (Banco Central de Reserva del Perú 1990, 145, 169).

37. For a detailed overview of these decades, see Quintero and Silva (1998b).

38. As in Peru at the same time, the 1979 constitution finally abolished literacy requirements, which had severly constrained suffrage before (Van Cott 2005, 113).

39. In Ecuador, "business interests crystallized into two powerful sets of regional associations organized by economic sectors. Coastal businessmen from the Guayas province organized into separate chambers of commerce, industry, and agriculture, as did businessmen from the interior

province of Pichincha where the capital of Quito is located" (Conaghan and Malloy 1994, 72). In addition to the regional fragmentation of the economic elites, it was (and still is) also the "diagonal integration of different businesses"—that is, the practice of organizing companies from different sectors in one "economic group"—that prevented even political decision makers that directly represented economic elites from governing in the specific interest of a particular sector (Chiasson-LeBel 2020, 102).

40. These years also saw a certain growth in industrial production, for instance in the textile industry (Acosta 2003, 104). However, the spread of capitalist relations, in the banana sector and beyond, was accompanied by the persistence of pre- or only partially capitalist economic sectors, such as cocoa production in the coastal region or the hacienda system and subsistence agriculture in the Sierra (Acosta 2003, 103-4; Ospina 2016, 44; Quintero and Silva 1998b, 7-74).

41. Ecuador's first agrarian reform from 1964 both followed from and further pushed these structural changes (Ibarra 2016).

42. With a view to the 1973 agrarian reform, Liisa North has argued that "the landowners from the coast and the highlands, with support from other elite sectors, managed to minimize the reformist content of the draft proposal presented by the military" (2006, 91).

43. For a brief summary of the evolution of Ecuador's economic elites as well as of key academic contributions, see Pástor (2019, 63-88).

44. Before the election of Roldós, the business chambers had lobbied hard to push through a gradual and controlled transition to democracy to ensure the persisting dominance of Ecuador's traditional parties. When this attempt failed, they campaigned—also unsuccessfully—against the constitutional referendum (Conaghan and Malloy 1994, 92-95).

CHAPTER 3: BUSINESS POWER IN THE ERA OF NEOLIBERALISM

1. To be sure, in quite a few countries the gradual dismantling of the state-led development model had already begun in the 1970s, mostly under authoritarian regimes. The most dramatic case is Chile, in which the neoliberal model was imposed by the military regime that took power with the 1973 coup. It was also the case in Peru, as we saw in the last chapter.

2. According to Susan Stokes (2004, 55), of the forty-four governments elected across the region between 1982 and 1995, only seventeen had sent clear campaign signals of their intention to liberalize. She finds that it was easier to "bait and switch" in this way when voters were confused about the effects of policy decision and when new parties took up the baton.

3. The Foncodes agency was established in 1992 to extend the radius of social assistance as part of a strategy to combat poverty in areas affected

by Sendero Luminoso and to build support for the regime. It was supported by the World Bank, which saw it as a way of mitigating the social costs of adjustment (Francke 2006, 95–97). Foncodes came under the umbrella of the all-powerful Ministry of the Presidency, which was tightly controlled by Fujimori himself.

4. Confiep led the opposition to García's bank nationalization and helped bankroll Fredemo in the 1990 elections. After 1990 it acted in close coordination with the MEF in the design and implementation of policy. Its remit did not extend to the world of small- and medium-sized business that accounted for the great numerical majority of firms in Peru.

5. This was a period in which there was considerable capital flight and currency speculation. Business profited from numerous state subsidies.

6. More than 65 percent of all economic legislation between 1990 and 2017, including all major reforms, were enacted by decree (Durand 2018a).

7. Of the sixteen largest privatizations, only one (Cementos Lima) was acquired by a domestic group (Rizo Patrón). By far the largest was the US$2 billion sale of the state telecommunications firm to Telefónica of Spain (Crabtree and Durand 2017, 81).

8. In the weeks that followed, Fujimori held meetings with several of García's onetime Twelve Apostles. Durand (2003, 360) quotes one business-man at the time saying "we were looking for a Pinochet and we found him."

9. On the role of technocrats within the MEF under Fujimori (and after-ward), see the study by Dargent (2015, 97–113).

10. The expansion of financial institutions during these years in-creased Confiep's membership and influence, turning it into a gremio ef-fectively controlled by banking and mining companies. The growth of min-ing during the Fujimori years (and afterward) reinforced the power of big business at the provincial level beyond Lima.

11. Roque Benavides, head of Peru's largest domestic mining company and subsequently president of Confiep, supported Fujimori in 2000. The slogan in the elections that year was the imperative need for continuity—el Perú no puede parar (Peru cannot be detained). Only a small number of dis-sident groups, notably supported by ADEX, worked to bring an end to the Fujimori regime (Durand 2003).

12. According to figures quoted by Tsolakis (2011, 181), public employ-ment in public companies shrank from 30.2 percent of the public sector payroll in 1985 to 19.5 percent in 1987.

13. It is important to note that this policy included the harsh repres-sion of organized labor, by means of a state of siege and the arrest of more than two hundred labor leaders (Conaghan and Malloy 1994, 149).

14. In 2004 the FEPSC formally split from the CEPB, arguing that it was not taking a firm enough stand against the government of the time.

15. After 1985 agricultural interests in Santa Cruz were well represented in the agricultural ministry (Eaton 2017, 151).

16. For instance, the governments of Jaime Paz, Sánchez de Lozada, and Hugo Banzer between 1989 and 2002 included at least four former presidents of the CEPB as ministers (Rojas 2009, 123).

17. Elections operated on a closed list system that gave party leaders greater control over those elected to the legislature.

18. In fact, the political reforms implemented during the first Sánchez de Lozada government unintentionally prepared the ground for the political rise of what would later become the MAS. This is demonstrated, most notably, by the success of MAS predecessor parties in municipal elections after 1995 as well as by the election of Evo Morales to Congress in 1997 with the highest share of votes among all winners of uninominal congressional seats (Van Cott 2005, ch. 3).

19. It is interesting to note that early electoral challenges to "pacted democracy" came, among others, from the Unión Cívica Solidaridad (UCS), a party founded and run by Max Fernández, a wealthy businessman of popular origin, who was the president and largest shareholder of Bolivia's national beer company CBN. Between 1989 and his death in 1995 and alongside another outsider's party (Conciencia de Patria [CONDEPA] of Carlos Palenque), Fernández appealed quite successfully to the popular sectors (Mayorga 2003).

20. For details on the gradual and inconsistent series of neoliberal reforms under Hurtado, Febres Cordero, Borja, and Durán-Ballén, see Acosta (2003, 157-237), Hey and Klak (1999), Mejía (2009), and Thoumi and Grindle (1992).

21. It was the Durán-Ballén government that most strongly pushed for privatization (under the name of "modernization"). Success remained limited, however.

22. As Thoumi and Grindle emphasize for the 1980s, the fact that the neoliberal reforms implemented in the first years of the Febres Cordero government mostly benefited the export-oriented economy (concentrated around Guayaquil), but harmed import-substitutive industries (situated mainly in the Sierra) meant that sectorial-cum-regional conflicts quickly emerged from within the sociopolitical alliance that had brought Febres Cordero to power (Thoumi and Grindle 1992, 59-60).

23. Between 1980 and 1985, crude oil accounted for 55-65 percent of overall exports, whereas the average share in the 1990s was 33 percent. This gradual diversification notwithstanding, income from the oil sector throughout the 1990s, still accounted for an average 41 percent of the state budget (Acosta 2003, 361, 374).

24. See Pástor (2019, 129-31) for an overview of the most important of these economic groups, based on Fierro's above-mentioned study.

25. As Simón Pachano (2006, 101) has noted, it is these four parties (DP, ID, PRE, and PSC) that dominated national elections between 1978 and 2002, together winning "about three-fourths of the vote" (see also Conaghan 1995a).

26. CONAM, which included representatives from both trade unions and business associations, "had the independent power to restructure and even eliminate entire government ministries" (Bowen 2014, 100). COMEXI, until it was reformed under Correa, was made up of six government and five business delegates (Wolff 2016, 133).

27. It was only in 2004 that the Comité Empresarial Ecuatoriano (CEE) was formed "to organize a collective business voice to influence the state in its free trade negotiations with the United States" (Chiasson-LeBel 2019, 162).

28. Ever since 1979 Ecuador's party system has been characterized by predominantly local or regional parties (Pachano 2006). The only temporary exception to this overall picture was Alianza PAIS during the government of Rafael Correa (2007-2017).

29. This is also reflected in the 1998 constitution. On the one hand, the Constituent Assembly that rewrote the new constitution was dominated by an explicitly neoliberal center-right alliance, based around the PSC and DP. It succeeded, for instance, in opening up "strategic" economic sectors to (partial) privatization. On the other hand, the indigenous movement, supported by other popular and leftist forces, also succeeded in securing a series of key demands, such as an inclusion of economic, social, and cultural rights (Andolina 2003; Rivera and Ramírez 2005, 130-31).

30. As Pablo Better, finance minister under President Borja, emphasized: "There is no consensus. There is apathy, not consensus" (Hey and Klak 1999, 87).

31. The fact that the World Bank later "suspended promised credits, arguing that the administration had failed to increase telephone charges and to privatize Emetel, as had been promised" (Hey and Klak 1999, 80), confirms the role of externally imposed conditionalities as well as their limited effect on domestic resistance against neoliberal reforms.

CHAPTER 4: CHALLENGES TO BUSINESS POWER DURING THE "PINK TIDE"

1. This section on Bolivia draws, in part, on Wolff (2016, 2018b).

2. For a small selection of accounts, see Crabtree (2005), Silva (2009, 103-46), Stefanoni and Do Alto (2006), Van Cott (2005, 49-98), and Yashar (2005, 152-223).

3. Although this concept, *vivir bien*, tends to mean different things to different people, it is usually taken to mean living in harmony with the

community and the environment. As such it represented a critique of development based on extractivism and capital accumulation. See, among many others, Artaraz et al. (2021), Escobar (2010), and Grupo Permanente de Trabajo sobre Alternativas al Desarrollo (2011).

4. For analyses of the first years of the MAS in power, see, among many others, Gray Molina (2010); Madrid (2011); Mayorga (2009); Pearce (2011); PNUD (2010).

5. The economic boom that characterized almost the entire first decade of MAS rule would also manifest in important changes in the social structure. In particular, Bolivia saw the emergence of a new "*cholo* elite," centered on the informal urban economy, most notably in El Alto. In general terms, this "sectoral *cholo* elite" has been supportive of the MAS and has benefited significantly from its policies, but this relationship has been based on mutual interests and a shared sociocultural identity rather than on a common politico-ideological agenda or institutionalized ties (Espinoza 2015, 213-60).

6. The Bolivian case in particular highlights the fact that business power is always relative. In a simplified tripartite structure comprising business elites, popular sectors, and the state, business power vis-à-vis the state can also decrease as a consequence of gains in popular sector power (see also Fairfield 2015a).

7. In addition to multilateral loans, which mainly came from regional development banks (IDB, Corporación Andina de Fomento [CAF]), Bolivia during the Morales government received important loans from Brazil, China, and Venezuela. In fact, increasing economic ties between Bolivia and China have come in the shape of loans in particular (Agramont and Bonifaz 2018, 68-73).

8. Traditionally, the economic elites from Santa Cruz have mostly preferred to act with relative autonomy from business associations at the national level, in order to use their particular economic weight (structural business power) and their privileged relationship with the well-organized social and political elites in the region (instrumental power) for their own particular purposes. Accordingly, in the context of the rise of the autonomy movement in Santa Cruz, the regional business association FEPSC in 2004 decided to leave the CEPB. With the increasing distancing of the *cruceño* business associations from the politico-civic opposition, regional- and national-level associations like the CEPB jointly engaged in a process of negotiation and dialogue with the MAS government.

9. Between 2005 and 2009, the remainders of the traditional center-right parties—largely, if loosely, organized in the electoral alliance Poder Democrático y Social (Podemos)—still held a majority in the Senate and, thereby, could force the MAS into negotiations, including over the process

of constitutional reform. In the Constituent Assembly, which was elected in July 2006, the MAS won an absolute majority, but the center-right opposition (with Podemos as by far the strongest player) at least held a one-third veto position, given that major decisions required a two-thirds majority. Escalating conflict enabled the MAS to override this veto position in the Constituent Assembly (the constitutional draft was adopted with a two-thirds majority achieved only by the absence of most of the opposition). In the end, still, a two-thirds majority in Congress was necessary to call for a constitutional referendum, which was possible only after the above-mentioned agreement with the opposition resulted in a substantive revision of the original constitutional draft.

10. The political opposition in Santa Cruz, and also other departments, had been significantly strengthened by the measure taken by the Mesa administration that turned the presidential appointment of departmental prefects into the popularly elected position of governors. As a result, the general elections of December 2005 also included elections at the departmental level, which saw the victory of a series of opposition candidates, including that of Rubén Costas in Santa Cruz who would become a leading force in the political opposition to the MAS administration.

11. According to a ranking compiled by economist Hugo Siles, the ten largest companies operating in Bolivia in 2017 were either state-owned or under the control of foreign investors. The former category includes the state oil and gas company YPFB and its affiliates as well as the renationalized telecommunications company ENTEL, the latter two private telecommunications companies (Tigo and VIVA), the biggest mine (San Cristóbal), the brewery CBN, the Coca-Cola bottling company EMBOL (Embotelladoras Bolivianas Unidas), and the cement firm SOBOCE (quoted in Molina 2019, 41–42).

12. Exceptions have included interventions into the public debate that directly concerned sectorial interests, such as when Asoban publicly criticized a new financial services law in 2013 (Wolff 2020a, 159).

13. The huge landholdings of Marinkovic were among the very few that were actually expropriated under the MAS government (Eaton 2017, 31).

14. The peculiar fusion of an explicitly indigenous and a broader "national-popular" agenda has certainly not been without tensions but was arguably key to the construction of a hegemonic political project (Mayorga 2006).

15. Even in those sectors where state-owned companies significantly gained in relevance under the MAS government (such as in extractive industries or telecommunications), private companies continued to play important roles. Most other sectors remained run by private businesses, with usually a small number of major (transnational) companies or economic groups dominating the scene (Molina 2019, 35, 41–42).

16. The following paragraphs draw on Wolff (2016, 2018b).

17. In line with Correa's promise to break with the established pattern of intra-congressional deal-making, Alianza PAIS had not presented candidates to the 2005 parliamentary elections.

18. In addition, Correa, early on in his first presidency, weakened business associations by initiating a judicial process to remove "the legal obligation for businesses to belong to a business chamber" (Chiasson-LeBel 2019, 158).

19. For overviews from different perspectives, see Clark and García (2018); Conaghan (2011, 275-78); De la Torre et al. (2020); Ospina (2013); Paz y Miño (2012, 27-31); and Ramírez (2016).

20. From the outset Correa had rejected a free trade agreement with the United States. In 2009 the government also suspended its participation in the ongoing trade negotiations between the Andean Community and the European Union (EU). When Ecuador and the EU "resumed talks in February 2010, the Correa government emphasized that it would not accept an agreement along the lines of the EU's bilateral treaties with Colombia and Peru" (Wolff 2016, 129).

21. The new constitution also undermined a crucial channel of business influence by prohibiting "banks, bankers, and all owners of bank assets from simultaneously holding assets in mass media" (Chiasson-LeBel 2019, 159). In fact, when Correa took office, "six of the eight television networks with a national reach were directly or indirectly linked to banking interests"—and these networks "dominated audiences and the advertising market" (Kitzberger 2016, 55). Business influence in Ecuador's media sector will be discussed below.

22. The most notable cases within the former group, which even faced judicial trials and expropriations, are the Grupo Isaías (centered on the banking sector) and the Grupo Noboa of the opposition politician Álvaro Noboa (centered on agri-food exports). The latter group, for instance, included the Grupo Eljuri and, ironically, the Grupo Nobis of Álvaro Noboa's sister Isabel (Acosta and Cajas 2020a; Pástor 2019).

23. For broader assessments of the "citizens' revolution," see Acosta and Cajas (2018), Sánchez and Pachano (2020), and for the first years of the Correa government, Álvarez et al. (2013), Mantilla and Mejía (2012), as well as Muñoz (2014).

24. It is important to note that the conservative autonomy movement in Guayas, while resembling key features of its counterpart in Santa Cruz, was much less radical in terms of both its demands and its tactics. The key instance of "resistance" against the Correa government constituted a mass protest in January 2008 with two hundred thousand supporters who called on the Constituent Assembly to grant autonomy rights to the provinces.

But, when Correa's party essentially ignored these demands, this provoked no major outrage that would be even remotely comparable to the Bolivian crisis of 2008 (Eaton 2011, 296-97).

25. On the political and legal struggle between Correa and later also the Constituent Assembly, on the one hand, and Congress, on the other, see Conaghan (2011, 271-73) and Ramírez (2016, 146-47).

26. With a particular view to the economic elites in Ecuador's highland region, James Bowen has also argued that the higher level of dependence on the state—a result of the limits of neoliberal reforms in Ecuador as compared, for instance, to Bolivia—created more incentives "to quietly cooperate" even with a leftist government (Bowen 2014, 96).

27. During the first years the Correa government also adopted the aspirations of the indigenous critique of extractive development. The 2008 constitution, for instance, established the *Buen Vivir* as an overarching principle and established "rights of nature." Also, under Alberto Acosta as Correa's minister of energy and mining (2007), the government made the innovative offer to refrain from exploiting oil reserves in the particularly vulnerable and biodiverse Yasuní National Park, if the "international community" would cover half of the revenue that could be earned otherwise. In the end, however, this initiative was abandoned (also because only a few international donors were willing to participate), and Correa pursued a course of expanding extractive projects in both the oil and the mining sectors (Acosta and Cajas 2018; Sacher 2017).

28. As Philip Kitzberger summarizes Ecuador's media sector at the time when Correa took office, the commercial sector clearly dominated radio, television, and newspapers, with private media ownership being characterized by an "overlapping of family networks and business conglomerates. Two newspapers represented approximately 65 percent of national circulation: the Pérez Group's *El Universo*, representing the political and economic elites of Guayaquil, and the traditional *El Comercio de Quito*, belonging to the Mantilla family" (Kitzberger 2016, 54; emphasis in the original). Still, although business influence was (and still is) also strong in the television and radio sectors, Ecuador has not seen the emergence of "multimedia groups with monopolistic tendencies such as *Globo* in Brazil or *Clarín* in Argentina [or *El Comercio* in Peru]" (Kitzberger 2016, 54). Instead, fragmentation and intra-elite competition have also shaped the country's private media sector.

29. In addition to rising oil income and the above-mentioned improvements in tax collections, the Correa government also initiated a "comprehensive audit of foreign debt," which culminated in the deliberate default on those government bonds that were found to be illegitimate (Ramírez 2016, 148).

30. During the Correa government Ecuador became one of the main recipients of Chinese loans to Latin America, which meant that in relative terms they played an exceptionally high macroeconomic role (Sacher 2017, 104–18; Stallings 2020, 49–51). Although this important influx of money initially facilitated the financing of government projects, it became an increasing liability later—in particular because the conditions proved far from concessional (Sacher 2017, 113–14).

31. For details on the small number of companies and *grupos económicos* that continue to control most of Ecuador's economic sectors, see Acosta and Cajas (2020a, 415–31) and Pástor (2019, 135–48).

32. The trade agreement between Ecuador and the EU was eventually signed in July 2014.

33. Between 2007 and 2013, annual GDP growth averaged 5.6 percent, peaking at 9.1 percent in 2008, despite a sharp dip in 2009. GDP per capita (in soles at constant 2007 prices) rose from US$11,224 to 15,000 over this period (Banco Central de Reserva del Peru 2015, 211). The rate of poverty fell from 30.8 percent in 2010 to 23.9 percent in 2013.

34. Humala had served as an officer in the army during the war with Sendero and subsequently in the brief war with Ecuador. He espoused many of the nationalist traditions of the Peruvian army, reminiscent of the Velasco era. In October 2000 he attempted to stage a rebellion against the Fujimori government in its dying days. He and his family were associated with the "etnocacerista" movement, an extreme nationalist organization (Alvarado Chávez 2022).

35. Once the MEF was authorized, a special team of legal experts—acting in close contact with Confiep, corporate law firms, and private tax consultants—would typically craft the legislation. This modus operandi was established in the early 1990s.

36. Between 2010 and 2013, Peru registered average annual net foreign investment of US$10.4 billion, compared with US$1.1 billion for Bolivia and US$526 million for Ecuador (ECLAC 2022a).

37. Tourist arrivals increased from 1.9 million in 2007 to 2.3 million in 2013.

38. Chinese economic influence in Peru stands out in these years, both in terms of trade (China became Peru's top trading partner) as well as in investment in mining.

39. Yanacocha was a joint venture between Newmont Mining, Peru's Buenaventura, and the World Bank's International Finance Corporation (IFC). The IFC has since withdrawn. Tambogrande was the attempt to initiate a gold mine involving the demolition of a medium-sized town. It was promoted by a Canadian firm, Manhattan Minerals. Other conflicts erupted at Tintaya in Cuzco, Rio Blanco in Piura, and Tía María in Arequipa.

40. The controversial policy of stationing police detachments within mining camps to protect private property from protests became widespread.

41. Of the Latin American countries, Chile, Mexico, and Colombia had been invited to join the OECD. Peru's membership remained in abeyance at the time of writing. The application to membership was seen as providing further external stimulus to maintain a pro-business agenda.

42. In 2004 Peru signed up for the Extractive Industries Transparency Initiative (EITI) designed to make more transparent the financial dealings between mining companies and the state. Peru has also seen the development of institutions designed to protect local communities from environmental degradation. However, matching such commitments to practice on the ground has proved problematic. In 2022 Peru faced the threat of being suspended from EITI.

CHAPTER 5: THE (PARTIAL) REVIVAL OF BUSINESS POWER AFTER THE COMMODITY BOOM

1. See Cannon (2016); Ellner (2020); Luna and Rovira Kaltwasser (2014); and North and Clark (2018).

2. On the following, see the analyses in Mayorga (2020a) as well as Souverein and Exeni (2020).

3. As regards the conflict over TIPNIS, a contested, government-controlled consultation process in the area led to the MAS majority in parliament in 2017 finally suspending the law that declared TIPNIS "untouchable." The TIPNIS conflict also pitted indigenous communities and organizations against each other, which enabled the MAS government to divide both the CIDOB and CONAMAQ.

4. A case in point was the conflict between the central government and a regional protest movement from Potosí over the distribution of (future) revenue from lithium extraction. Although centered on the city of Potosí and only partially extending to the rural areas of the department, during the 2019 election this conflict significantly reduced support for the MAS in this traditional stronghold and contributed to strong postelection protests in Potosí. The key figure here was Marco Pumari, the leader of the local civic committee, who would later join his counterpart from Santa Cruz, Luis Fernando Camacho, as his running mate for the 2020 presidential race (Tórrez 2020, 85–91).

5. According to the Bolivian constitution, in order to win the presidential race outright a candidate has to either surpass 50 percent of valid votes emitted or 40 percent plus a 10 percent lead over the second-placed candi-

date. For a detailed analysis of the 2019 elections, the controversy over the supposed electoral fraud, and the postelection political crisis, see Mayorga (2020b, 3-26) and Wolff (2020c, 166-78).

6. Eva Copa, who became president of the Senate, later claimed that MAS members of Congress were forcibly excluded from the session in which Áñez's succession was ratified, thereby questioning the legitimacy of the succession.

7. On the controversies over the alleged electoral fraud and the supposed coup d'état, see Wolff (2020c, 170-78).

8. As Molina has argued, during the MAS years, the marked differences in terms of social and ethnic status contributed to preventing the reconstitution of a status-based ruling coalition that would have united the business class and the political elite as in previous eras (Molina 2019, 194).

9. In an interview with the Cochabamba daily *Los Tiempos* in March 2019, right before his election as CEPB president, Barbery justified his distance vis-à-vis the opposition movement by emphasizing that politics was the job of other sectors and not of business associations, whose purpose was to focus directly on business-related issues (as quoted in Wolff 2020a, 142).

10. For the respective statements and press releases, see Wolff (2020a, 143-47).

11. A case in point is José Luis Parada, an economist from Santa Cruz. Before joining the Áñez administration as minister of economy and finance, Parada had made his career in both the private and the public sector of Santa Cruz (Wolff 2020a, 153). Initially, the Áñez administration was also characterized by the strong presence of people associated with Camacho, then leader of the Comité Pro Santa Cruz, who had gained in prominence as the radical face of the anti-MAS opposition during the 2019 postelection protests (Tórrez 2020, 81-85). The alliance between Áñez and Camacho didn't last long, however, as both eventually decided to run for the 2020 presidential elections (with Áñez stepping back from her candidacy only very late in the process) (Tórrez 2020; Zegada 2020).

12. Originally, new elections were scheduled for May 2020, but they were postponed to September because of the COVID-19 pandemic. When the TSE decided to further postpone the elections to October 2020, major protests erupted, which could only be tamed by the TSE's declaration and a corresponding law, approved by parliament, that the new date was now definitive and unpostponable (Mayorga 2020c, 21-26). Against this background, there was no way for Áñez to push for yet another extension of her interim presidency, even if this certainly would have been in her interest given plummeting opinion poll ratings. As a consequence, she withdrew her name from the race.

13. To be sure, criticism of Correa's government from former allies and members had emerged earlier. See, for instance, the collection of contributions in Álvarez et al. (2013) and Muñoz (2014).

14. The proposal for a tax on extraordinary capital gains (Ley de Plusvalía), however, was later reintroduced to parliament and approved in December 2016 (Criollo 2018).

15. Between 1993 and 2012 Lasso was executive president of the Banco de Guayaquil, the leading agency of an important financial conglomerate and also this bank's principal shareholder. In 2012 Lasso quit his position at the Banco de Guayaquil in order to run against Correa in the 2013 presidential elections, as leader of the political movement CREO (Creando Oportunidades), established and run basically by himself. Personally, he does not come from Ecuador's traditional coastal elite but has a middle-class background and, as a member of Opus Dei, represents orthodox conservative positions on religious and social matters. In terms of his (limited) political career, Lasso acted briefly as governor of Guayas (1998–1999) before being nominated by President Mahuad as his "super-minister" for the economy in the midst of Ecuador's escalating financial crisis—a position he held for one month (see Chiasson-LeBel 2019, 164–65; Pástor 2021; Plan V 2021).

16. The most important measures in this area included the reform of controversial regulations on civil society organizations and the media, the restitution of the legal status of an environmental NGO that had been closed in 2013, and the pardoning of indigenous activists who had been sentenced for engaging in protests (Wolff 2018a, 296).

17. A key example included the new minister of external trade, Pablo José Campana, a businessman with a trajectory in Isabel Noboa's Nobis group who also happens to have had family ties to this economic group (as Noboa's son-in-law). During the electoral campaign, Campana had led an initiative of 380 businesspersons (Proponle), which had supported Moreno's candidacy on the basis of a jointly agreed agenda to promote investment, production, and employment (see Acosta and Cajas 2020a, 428; El Comercio 2017a; El Universo 2017b). For more details on the personal relationships and overlaps between the Moreno government and Ecuador's economic elites, see Pástor (2019, ch. 7).

18. According to Gonzalo Criollo (2018), this concession was mainly meant to appease the construction and the real-estate sector as well as specific right-wing politicians such as Guayaquil mayor Jaime Nebot with his close ties to these sectors.

19. Also, beyond the issue of trade, improving Ecuador's relations with the US government was a key element in Moreno's about-turn in the area of foreign policy, which resembles the policy shift enacted by the Áñez administration in Bolivia (see Ramírez 2019, 23). In the area of trade, the

Moreno government also moved to join the free-trade-oriented Pacific Alliance.

20. In this context of deteriorating economic conditions, it is worth mentioning the increasingly hard-nosed position of China in shoring up credit to countries such as Ecuador.

21. For instance, in response to a major earthquake in 2016, Ecuador received US$364 million in financial support from the IMF (Meléndez and Moncagatta 2017, 420).

22. Opinion polls also reflected the way that Moreno both continued and significantly deepened a trend already initiated under Correa. According to Latinobarómetro data for Ecuador, for instance, the share of respondents who saw their country being governed "by a few powerful groups for their own benefit," which had fallen from more than 80 percent before the first election of Correa to a low point of 34 percent in 2013, increased during the final years of the Correa government (reaching 62 percent in 2016), but only under Moreno did it return to the pre-Correa levels (81 percent in 2018). Inversely, the share of those responding that their country was being governed "for the benefit of all the people," after increasing dramatically between 2006 (11 percent) and 2013 (62 percent), had already fallen significantly before Moreno's election (to 35 percent in 2016) and then fell sharply with Moreno's about-face (to 17 percent in 2018) (Latinobarómetro 2021).

23. Specific measures included a series of tax exemptions for private sector investments, restrictions on the government's ability to run a budget deficit, and the reintroduction of a fund for fiscal stabilization (to be funded through any income from nonrenewable natural resources) (Bayas-Erazo 2020, 217-81; Salgado 2018).

24. The de facto agreement in parliament between the pro-Moreno remainder of Alianza País and CREO remained fragile throughout the years. In general, the Moreno government never managed to build a reliable majority in the National Assembly and, correspondingly, mostly had a hard time getting parliamentary approval for its legal initiatives (Olivares and Medina 2020, 323-29).

25. On these protests, see the contributions in Martínez (2020) as well as Olivares and Medina (2020), Ospina (2019), Ponce et al. (2020), and Ramírez (2019).

26. As concerns fuel subsidies, the COVID-19-induced dramatic fall in the oil price (which temporarily turned negative!) provided a crucial window of opportunity. In this context, fuel prices were very cheap anyway (Acosta 2020, 13).

27. At the same time the pandemic, if anything, demonstrated the need for a functioning state that was capable of providing basic social services and a reliable social security system.

28. In the first round of the 2017 elections, Lasso had received 28 percent and Cynthia Viteri, the then-candidate of the PSC, received an additional 16 percent (Ramírez 2021, 10).

29. Pachakutik contested the electoral results, claiming electoral fraud, but ultimately failed to push through a recount of the vote (Ramírez 2021, 11). It is quite possible that such a recount would have led to Yaku Pérez making it into the runoff, instead of Lasso (Cuvi 2021).

30. Alianza PAIS won not a single seat, AP's presidential candidate Ximena Peña received a mere 1.5 percent of the vote.

31. Statistically, when looking at the provincial level, there is a strong correlation between the share Yaku Pérez received in the first round and the share of null votes in the runoff. In some Andean provinces (Azuay, Bolívar, Cañar, and Cotopaxi), 30 percent of the voters cast invalid ballots (Galindo 2021). As a consequence, Lasso, who is not only from Guayaquil but clearly represents the coastal politicoeconomic elite, prevailed in most highland and Amazon provinces, while the Correísta candidate Arauz, who is from Quito, won in almost all coastal provinces (El Comercio 2021). Very clearly, the division between anti- and pro-Correístas continues to cut across and thereby offset the traditional regional divide.

32. According to Pástor (2021), the key economic groups that supported the Lasso campaign belong to the export, the financial, and the agroindustrial sectors. Business support for Arauz, in contrast, came mainly from importers and merchants.

33. Keiko Fujimori represented the more socially conservative and authoritarian style of her father, but Kuczynski was more of a classic liberal, in both the political and economic sense.

34. Fujimori's electoral victory in Congress owed much to the tactical alliances forged with regional politicians and their parties. As the result of the presidential election showed, her own support base was much more limited.

35. Kuczynski was accused of receiving advisory fees from Odebrecht while he was minister of economy and finance under the Toledo administration, through companies he owned, notably Westfield Capital.

36. Criticism of the airport project started when private investors asked for government financial support in preference to raising their own finance through the banking system. Kuczynski, keen to push ahead with the project, was widely criticized for authorizing an addendum to the project in which the state assumed the additional costs of US$265 million. He justified himself by arguing that the people of Cuzco deserved swift completion in order to boost tourism (Caballero 2019, 134).

37. Cecilia Blume, a close associate of Kuczynski's since his time as minister under Toledo, was associated with the practice. Zavala's sister,

María Ximena, worked for the investors in the case of the airport project. In response to criticisms of a possible conflict of interest, Zavala said he would resolve the matter by abstaining from decisions about the project. This just heightened suspicions.

38. The conflict involved textbooks that raised gender rights. Saavedra, a renowned World Bank education expert, was forced to resign under pressure from FP and APRA members of Congress. He was replaced by Martens who pursued his agenda.

39. The constitution enables a president to dissolve Congress if two cabinets in the first four years of a five-year presidential term are denied votes of confidence. The dissolution of Congress in September 2019 was justified by being a consequence of a second vote of no confidence.

40. Caballero (2019, 175) quotes Kuczynski as saying "I never received any support from Odebrecht for my electoral campaigns [2011 and 2016]. Nor did I have any professional connection."

41. Kuczynski's role in the release of Fujimori was vehemently criticized by human rights groups as "buying votes" to protect his position (Sifuentes 2019).

42. The political influence exercised by drug trafficking mafias had long been a salient feature of Peru's politics and the connections linking politicians to the criminal underworld. Politicians required political contributions to fund election campaigns. Drug traffickers needed political cover to pursue their activities. APRA, in particular, was widely suspected of having connections with Peruvian drug mafias, as were certain politicians from FP. The connections between APRA and the drugs underworld were suggested by Alan García's move, during his second presidency, to use his presidential prerogative to pardon large numbers of convicted drug traffickers and to commute the sentences of others (Soberón Garrido 2015).

43. Before becoming vice president, Vizcarra had been the governor of Moquegua. As such, he played a key role in promoting mining investment in this region based on the promotion of good community relations. However, as someone from the provinces, he lacked strong family or other contacts with key elite groups. He himself later faced accusations of corrupt behavior as governor.

44. Las Bambas initially belonged to Glencore, which had managed to negotiate a social license for the project. It was then transferred to MMG in 2014. Communities began supporting the project because of cash advances from the mining canon scheme.

45. Universidad San Pablo of Arequipa published a series of studies and position papers on the Tia Maria conflict. See http://cooperaccion.org.pe/las-bambas-cronica-de-un-conflicto-anunciado-que-parece-no-tener-fin/. And also https://ucsp.edu.pe/tia-maria-no-va-pero-la-gestion-del-conflicto/.

46. Confiep published this communiqué on its website on September 11, 2019. It was instantly reproduced on the Internet and on other social media platforms.

47. The game unfolded in the following way. The FP-APRA congressional majority sought to prevent Prime Minister Salvador del Solar from entering the chamber to demand a vote of confidence. Had a vote been passed it would have enabled Vizcarra immediately to dissolve parliament according to the constitution. In the event del Solar was able to demand a vote, but the majority bloc averted taking a vote. This was taken to betoken a refusal. FP and APRA members then abandoned the floor of the legislature. Vizcarra then issued a decree dissolving Congress.

CONCLUSIONS AND OUTLOOK

1. This finding echoes a similar argument made by Fairfield (2015a, 2015b) with a view to the potentially mutually reinforcing relationship between structural and instrumental business power.

2. In Ecuador this change was gradual at best. According to the World Bank (2020, 20), the fiscal stimulus measures adopted in response to the pandemic in Ecuador represented less than 1 percent of GDP, as compared to 3.5–4.0 percent in Bolivia or Peru.

REFERENCES

Acharya, Amitav, Melisa Deciancio, and Diana Tussie, eds. 2022. *Latin America in Global International Relations*. New York: Routledge.

Acosta, Alberto. 2003. *Breve historia económica del Ecuador*. 2nd ed. Quito: Corporación Editora Nacional.

Acosta, Alberto. 2020. "De la pandemia sanitaria al pandemonio económico." *Ecuador Debate* 109: 7-16.

Acosta, Alberto, and John Cajas. 2018. *Una década desperdiciada: las sombras del correísmo*. Quito: CAAP.

Acosta, Alberto, and John Cajas. 2020a. "El 'hocico de lagarto' ecuatoriano: entre desigualdades coyunturales y estructurales." In *Concentración económica y poder político en América Latina*, edited by Liisa North, Blanca Rubio, Alberto Acosta, and Carlos Pástor, 401-40. Mexico City: Fundación Friedrich Ebert.

Acosta, Alberto, and John Cajas. 2020b. "Rebelión en los Andes: ecos económico-políticos del levantamiento popular ecuatoriano." In *OCTUBRE*, edited by Neptalí Martínez Santi, 149-86. Quito: Editorial El árbol de papel.

Adrianzén, Alberto. 2018. "Las izquierdas, antiguos y modernos." In *DESCO*, edited by *Perú Hoy: sin paradero final*, 37-54. Lima: DESCO.

Adrianzén, Carlos Alberto. 2021. *Los empresarios y la organización de partidos políticos: un estudio de caso*. Universidad San Martin, Instituto de Altos Estudios Sociales, Tesis de Maestria en Ciencia Política.

Agramont, Daniel, and Gustavo Bonifaz. 2018. *El desembarco chino en América Latina y su manifestación en Bolivia*. La Paz: Friedrich-Ebert-Stiftung Bolivia and Plural.

Aguirre, Carlos, and Paulo Drinot. 2017. *The Peculiar Revolution: Rethinking the Peruvian Experiment under Military Rule*. Austin: University of Texas Press.

Aguirre A., Milagros. 2022. Ecuador: colcha de retazos. Quito: Comité Ecuménico de Proyectos (CEP). http://www.cepecuador.org/wp-content/uploads/2022/09/coyuntura_julio_2022-2.pdf.

Almeida, Luis. 2007. "Los hombres de Correa." In *Correa un año . . . : de las promesas a la realidad*, edited by Diario Hoy. Quito: Diario Hoy. http://www.hoy.com.ec/temas/temas2008/correa/correa.htm.

Althaus, Jaime. 2007. *La revolución capitalista en el Perú*. Lima: Fondo de Cultura Económica.

Alvarado Chávez, Mariana. 2022. *Populismo radical en el Perú*. Lima: Pontificia Universidad Católica del Perú.

Álvarez González, Freddy Javier, et al. 2013. *El correísmo al desnudo*. Quito: Montecristi Vive.

Andolina, Robert. 2003. "The Sovereign and Its Shadow: Constituent Assembly and Indigenous Movement in Ecuador." *Journal of Latin American Studies* 35 (4): 721–50.

Anria, Santiago. 2019. *When Movements Become Parties: The Bolivian MAS in Comparative Perspective*. Cambridge: Cambridge University Press.

Arce, Moisés. 2010. *El fujimorismo y la reforma del mercado en la sociedad peruana*. Lima: Instituto de Estudios Peruanos.

Arce, Moisés. 2014. *Resource Extraction and Protest in Peru*. Pittsburgh, PA: University of Pittsburgh Press.

Aricó, José. 2015. *La cola del diablo: itinerario de Gramsci en América Latina*. Buenos Aires: Siglo XXI.

Artaraz, Kepa, Melania Calestini, and Mei L. Trueba, eds. 2021. "Vivir bien/buen vivir and Post-neoliberal Development Paths in Latin America: Scope, Strategies, and the Realities of Implementation." *Latin American Perspectives* 48 (3): 4–261.

Artz, Lee, ed. 2017. *The Pink Tide: Media Access and Political Power in Latin America*. London: Rowman and Littlefield.

Arze Vargas, Carlos. 2008. "The Perverse Effects of Globalization in Bolivia." In *Unresolved Tensions: Bolivia Past and Present*, edited by John Crabtree and Laurence Whitehead, 238–53. Pittsburgh, PA: University of Pittsburgh Press.

Arze Vargas, Carlos, and Javier Gómez. 2013. "Bolivia: ¿El 'proceso de cambio' nos conduce al vivir bien?" In *Promesas en su laberinto: cambios y continuidades en los gobiernos progresistas de América Latina*, edited by

Carlos Arze, Javier Gómez, Pablo Ospina, and Víctor Álvarez, 45-176. La Paz: CEDLA.

Bailey, Warren, and Y. Peter Chung. 1995. "Exchange Rate Fluctuations, Political Risk, and Stock Returns: Some Evidence from an Emerging Market." *Journal of Finance and Quantitative Analysis* 30 (4): 541-60.

Balán, Manuel, and Françoise Montambeault, eds. 2020. *Legacies of the Left Turn in Latin America: The Promise of Inclusive Citizenship.* Notre Dame, IN: University of Notre Dame Press.

Banco Central de Reserva del Perú. 1980. *Memoria.* Lima: Banco Central de Reserva del Perú. https://www.bcrp.gob.pe/docs/Publicaciones/Memoria/Memoria-BCRP-1980.pdf.

Banco Central de Reserva del Perú. 1990. *Memoria.* Lima: Banco Central de Reserva del Peru. https://www.bcrp.gob.pe/docs/Publicaciones/Memoria/1990/Memoria-BCRP-1990-7.pdf.

Banco Central de Reserva del Perú. 2015. *Memoria.* Lima: Banco Central de Reserva del Perú. https://www.bcrp.gob.pe/docs/Publicaciones/Memoria/2015/memoria-bcrp-2015-8.pdf.

Banco Mundial and Vice Presidencia de la República de Colombia. 2002. *Corrupción, desempeño institucional y gobernabilidad: desarrollando una estrategia anticorrupción en Colombia.* Bogotá: Vice Presidencia de Colombia.

Barndt, William T. 2014. "Corporation-Based Parties: The Present and Future of Business Politics in Latin America." *Latin American Politics and Society* 56 (3): 1-22.

Barragán, Rossana. 2008. "Oppressed or Privileged Regions? Some Historical Reflections on the Use of State Resources." In *Unresolved Tensions: Bolivia Past and Present*, edited by John Crabtree and Laurence Whitehead, 83-103. Pittsburgh, PA: University of Pittsburgh Press.Bartell, Ernest, and Leigh Payne, eds. 1995. *Business and Democracy in Latin America.* Pittsburgh, PA: University of Pittsburgh Press.

Bayas-Erazo, Matias. 2020. "Understanding Ecuador's Growth Prospects in the Aftermath of the Citizens' Revolution." In *Assessing the Left Turn in Ecuador*, edited by Francisco Sánchez and Simón Pachano, 213-30. Cham: Palgrave Macmillan.

Bebbington, Anthony, ed. 2007. *Minería, movimientos sociales y respuestas campesinas.* Lima: IEP-CEPES.

Becker, Marc. 2013. "The Stormy Relations between Rafael Correa and Social Movements in Ecuador." *Latin American Perspectives* 40 (3): 43-62.

Beckerman, Paul. 2002. "Longer-Term Origins of Ecuador's 'Predollarization' Crisis." In *Crisis and Dollarization in Ecuador: Stability, Growth, and Social Equity*, edited by Paul Beckerman and Andrés Solimano, 17-80. Washington, DC: World Bank.

Beckerman, Paul, and Andrés Solimano, eds. 2002. *Crisis and Dollarization in Ecuador: Stability, Growth, and Social Equity*, Washington, DC: World Bank.

Ben-Porath, Yoram. 1980. "The 'F' Connection: Family, Friends and Firms and the Organization of Exchange." *Population and Development Review* 6 (1): 1-30.

Bercerra, Martín and Guillermo Mastrini. 2017. *La concentración infocomunicacional en América Latina (2000-2015): Nuevos medios y tecnologías, menos actores.* Bernal: Universidad Nacional de Quilmes, Observacom.

Bernhagen, Patrick. 2017. *The Political Power of Business: Structure and Information in Public-Policy-Making.* New York: Routledge.

Blofield, Merike. 2011a. "Desigualdad y política en América Latina." *Journal of Democracy en Español* 3: 58-73.

Blofield, Merike, ed. 2011b. *The Great Gap: Inequality and the Politics of Redistribution in Latin America.* University Park, PA: Penn State University Press.

Boloña, Carlos. 1993. *Cambio de rumbo.* Lima: Instituto de Economía de Libre Mercado.

Bowen, James D. 2014. "The Right and Nonparty Forms of Representation and Participation: Bolivia and Ecuador Compared." In *The Resilience of the Latin American Right*, edited by Juan Pablo Luna and Cristóbal Rovira Kaltwasser, 94-116. Baltimore, MD: Johns Hopkins University Press.

Bowen, Sally, and Richard Bauer. 1997. *The Bolivian Formula: From State Capitalism to Capitalisation.* Santiago: McGraw-Hill.

Bril-Mascarenhas, Tomás, and Antoine Maillet. 2019. "How to Build and Wield Business Power: The Political Economy of Regulation in Chile." *Latin American Politics and Society* 61 (10): 101-25.

Brockmann Quiroga, Erika. 2020. "Tentativa de toma gradual del poder: prorroguismo fallido y transiciones." In *Crisis y cambio político en Bolivia: octubre y noviembre de 2019*, edited by Fernando Mayorga, 29-60. La Paz: CESU-UMSS.

Bull, Benedicte, Fulvio Castellani, and Yuri Kalahari. 2013. *Business Groups and Transnational Capitalism in Central America: Political and Economic Strategies.* London: Palgrave.

Burbano de Lara, Felipe. 2006. "Estrategias para sobrevivir a la crisis del Estado: empresarios, política y partidos en Ecuador." In *Neoliberalismo y sectores dominantes: tendencias globales y experiencias nacionales*, edited by Eduardo M. Basualdo and Enrique Arceo, 293-316. Buenos Aires: CLACSO.

Burbano de Lara, Felipe. 2020. "La patria ya es de todos: Pilgrimages, Charisma, Territory, and the Return of the State." In *Assessing the Left Turn in Ecuador*, edited by Francisco Sánchez and Simón Pachano, 41-66. Cham: Palgrave Macmillan.

Burchardt, Hans-Jürgen. 2012. "¿Por qué América Latina es tan desigual? Tentativas de explicación desde una perspectiva inusual." *Nueva Sociedad* 239: 137-50.

Burchardt, Hans-Jürgen, and Kristina Dietz. 2014. "(Neo-)extractivism—A New Challenge for Development Theory from Latin America." *Third World Quarterly* 35 (3): 468-86.

Burdick, John, Philip Oxhorn, and Kenneth M. Roberts, eds. 2009. *Beyond Neoliberalism in Latin America? Societies and Politics at the Crossroads.* New York: Palgrave Macmillan.

Caballero, Víctor. 2012. "La negocación de conflictos sociales 2006-2010: tres modelos para armar." Pontificia Universidad Católica del Perú, Departamento de Ciencias Sociales, Cuaderno de Trabajo no. 17.

Caballero, Víctor. 2019. *Mototaxi: auge y caída de Fuerza Popular.* Lima: Penguin Random Books Grupo Editorial.

Cabral, Marcelo, and Regiane Oliveira. 2017. *O principe: uma biografia não autorizada de Marcelo Odebrecht.* São Paulo: Astral Cultural.

Cagé, Julia. 2018. *Le Prix de la démocratie: une démonstration implacable.* Paris: Fayard.

Cameron, Maxwell. 2009. "El giro a la izquierda frustrado en Perú: el caso de Ollanta Humala." *Convergencia*, 16: 275-302.

Cameron, Maxwell. 2021. "The Return of the Oligarchy? Threats to Representative Democracy in Latin America." *Third World Quarterly* 42 (4). Online edition (January 11).

Cameron, Maxwell A., and Eric Hershberg, eds. 2010. *Latin America's Left Turns: Politics, Policies, and Trajectories of Change.* Boulder, CO: Lynne Rienner.

Cañete, Rosa. 2018. *Democracia capturada: el gobierno de unos pocos.* Barcelona: Oxfam International y CLACSO.

Cannon, Barry. 2016. *The Right in Latin America: Elite Power, Hegemony and the Struggle for the State.* New York: Routledge.

Cannon, Barry, and Peadar Kirby, eds. 2012. *Civil Society and the State in Left-Led Latin America: Challenges and Limitations to Democratization.* London: Zed Books.

Capoccia, Giovanni, and R. Daniel Kelemen. 2007. "The Study of Critical Junctures: Theory, Narrative, and Counterfactuals in Historical Institutionalism." *World Politics* 59 (3): 341-69.

Cárdenas, Julián, and Francisco Robles-Rivera. 2020. *Business Elites in Panama: Sources of Power and State Capture in Panama.* United Nations: UNRISD (Occasional Papers 12).

Cardoso, Fernando Henrique, and Enzo Faletto. 1968. *Dependencia y desarrollo en America Latina*. México: Siglo XXI Editores.

Casas-Zamora, Kevin. 2005. *Paying for Democracy*. Oxford: Oxford University Press.

Castañeda, Jorge G. 1993. *Utopia Unarmed: The Latin American Left after the Cold War*. New York: Knopf.

Castellani, Ana. 2018. "Lobbies y puerta giratoria: los riesgos de la captura en la decision pública." *Nueva Sociedad* 276: 49-61.

Cateriano, Pedro. 2021. *Sin anestesia: una década de lucha por la democracia*. Lima: Planeta.

Cave, Tamarin, and Christopher Rowell. 2015. *A Quiet World of Lobbying: Crony Capitalism and Broken Politics in Britain*. London: Penguin Random House.

Chiasson-LeBel, Thomas. 2019. "Neoliberalism in Ecuador after Correa: A Surprise Turn or according to Economic Elites' Plan?" *European Review of Latin American and Caribbean Studies* 108: 153-74.

Chiasson-LeBel, Thomas. 2020. "Tres períodos de relaciones entre las élites y el Estado: una comparación entre los casos de Venezuela y Ecuador." In *Concentración económica y poder político en América Latina*, edited by Liisa North, Blanca Rubio, Alberto Acosta, and Carlos Pástor, 93-136. Mexico City: Fundación Friedrich Ebert.

Chiasson-LeBel, Thomas, and Manuel Larrabure, eds. 2019. "Elite and Popular Responses to a Left in Crisis." Special Collection of the *European Review of Latin American and Caribbean Studies* no. 108.

CIUP (Centro de Investigaciones de la Universidad del Pacífico). 2022. "Precariedad laboral en el Perú de la post pandemia." *Punto de Equilibrio* 25, May 5, 2022. https://ciup.up.edu.pe/analisis/punto-de-equilibrio-25-precariedad-laboral-en-el-peru-de-la-post-pandemia.

Clark, Patrick, and Jacobo García. 2018. "Left Populism, State Building, Class Compromise, and Social Conflict in Ecuador's Citizens' Revolution." *Latin American Perspectives* 224 (46): 230-46.

Collier, Ruth Berins, and David Collier. 2002. *Shaping the Political Arena: Critical Junctures, the Labor Market and Regime Dynamics in Latin America*. Notre Dame, IN: University of Notre Dame Press.

Colque, Gonzalo, Efraín Tinta, and Esteban Sanjinés. 2016. *Segunda reforma agraria: una historia que incomoda*. La Paz: Tierra.

Conaghan, Catherine. 1988. *Restructuring Domination: Industrialists and the State in Ecuador*. Pittsburgh, PA: University of Pittsburgh Press.

Conaghan, Catherine. 1995a. "Politicians against Parties: Discord and Disconnection in Ecuador's Party System." In *Building Democratic Institutions: Party Systems in Latin America*, edited by Scott Mainwaring and Timothy R. Scully, 434-58. Stanford, CA: Stanford University Press.

Conaghan, Catherine. 1995b. "The Private Sector and the Public Transcript: The Political Mobilization of Business in Bolivia." In *Business and Democracy in Latin America*, edited by Ernest Bartell and Leigh Payne, 105-40. Pittsburgh, PA: University of Pittsburgh Press.

Conaghan, Catherine. 2005. *Fujimori's Peru: Deception in the Public Sphere.* Pittsburgh, PA: University of Pittsburgh Press.

Conaghan, Catherine M. 2011. "Ecuador: Rafael Correa and the Citizens' Revolution." In *The Resurgence of the Latin American Left*, edited by Steven Levitsky and Kenneth M. Roberts, 260-82. Baltimore, MD: Johns Hopkins University Press.

Conaghan, Catherine, and Carlos de la Torre. 2008. "The Permanent Campaign of Rafael Correa: Making Ecuador's Plebiscitary Presidency." *International Journal of Press/Politics* 13, no 3: 267-84.

Conaghan, Catherine, and James Malloy. 1994. *Unsettling Statecraft: Democracy and Neoliberalism in the Central Andes.* Pittsburgh, PA: University of Pittsburgh Press.

Conaghan, Catherine M., James M. Malloy, and Luis A. Abugattas. 1990. "Business and the 'Boys': The Politics of Neoliberalism in the Central Andes." *Latin American Research Review* 25 (2): 3-30.

Contreras, Carlos, and Marcos Cueto. 2000. *Historia del Perú contemporáneo.* Lima: Instituto de Estudios Peruanos.

Córdova, Daniel. 2010. *Los nuevos héroes peruanos: lecciones de vida de los emprendedores que derrotaron la pobreza.* Lima: Planeta.

Coronel, Valeria, Soledad Stoessel, Julio César Guanche, and María Luciana Cadahia. 2019. "Captura y descorporativización estatal de las élites financieras en Ecuador." *Colombia Internacional* 100: 147-74.

Correa Leite, José, Janaina Uemura, and Filomena Siqueira, eds. 2018. *O eclipse do progressismo: a esquerda latino-americana em debate.* São Paulo: Elefante.

Cortés, Hernán and Deborah Itriago. 2018. *El fenómeno de la captura: desenmascarando el Estado.* Barcelona: OXFAM Intermon.

COVID-19 Excess Mortality Collaborators. 2022. "Estimating Excess Mortality due to the COVID-19 Pandemic: A Systematic Analysis of COVID-19-Related Mortality, 2020-21." *Lancet* 399 (10334): 1513-36.

Crabtree, John. 1987. *The Great Tin Crash.* London: Latin America Bureau.

Crabtree, John. 1992. *Peru under García: An Opportunity Lost.* Basingstoke: Macmillan.

Crabtree, John. 2005. *Patterns of Protest: Politics and Social Movements in Bolivia.* London: Latin America Bureau.

Crabtree, John, and Ann Chaplin. 2013. *Bolivia: Processes of Change*. London: Zed Books.

Crabtree, John, and Francisco Durand. 2017. *Peru: Power Elites and Political Capture*. London: Zed Books.

Crabtree, John, and Laurence Whitehead, eds. 2001. *Towards Democratic Viability: The Bolivian Experience*. Basingstoke: Palgrave.

Criollo, Gonzalo. 2018. *Ley de Plusvalía luego de la consulta popular: el quiebre a la derecha de Moreno*. Quito: Friedrich-Ebert-Stiftung (FES) Ecuador. https://library.fes.de/pdf-files/bueros/quito/14411.pdf.

Cuba, Elmer. 2008. "El despegue del Perú." In *Perú en el siglo XXI*, edited by Luis Pásara, 343–60. Lima: Fondo Editorial de la PUCP.

Culpepper, Pepper. 2015. "Structural Power and Political Power in the Post-crisis Era." *Business and Politics* 17 (3): 392–409.

Cuvi, Juan. 2021. "¿Cómo volvió la derecha al poder en Ecuador?" *Nueva Sociedad*, April. https://nuso.org/articulo/como-volvio-la-derecha-al-poder-en-ecuador.

Dammert, Manuel. 2009. *La República lobbysta: amenaza contra la Democracia Peruana en el siglo XXI*. Lima: Edición del autor.

Dargent, Eduardo. 2015. *Technocracy and Democracy in Latin America: The Experts Running Government*. New York: Cambridge University Press.

Dargent, Eduardo, and Stephanie Rousseau. 2022. "Choque de poderes y degradación institucional: cambio de sistema sin cambio de reglas en el Perú 2016-2022." *Política y Gobierno* 29 (2): 1–28.

De Echave, José. 2016. "La minería ilegal en el Perú: entre la informalidad y el delito." *Nueva Sociedad* 263, 131–44.

Degregori, Carlos Iván. 2012. *How Difficult It Is to Be God: Shining Path's Politics of War in Peru*. Madison: Wisconsin University Press.

De la Torre, Augusto, Simón Cueva, and María Alexandra Castellanos-Vásconez. 2020. "The Macroeconomics of the Commodities Boom in Ecuador: A Comparative Perspective." In *Assessing the Left Turn in Ecuador*, edited by Francisco Sánchez and Simón Pachano, 163–212. Cham: Palgrave Macmillan.

De la Torre, Carlos. 1993. *La seducción velasquista*. Quito: Ediciones Libri Mundi.

De la Torre, Carlos. 2013. "Technocratic Populism in Ecuador." *Journal of Democracy* 24 (3): 33–46.

De la Torre, Carlos. 2020. "Rafael Correa's Technopopulism in Comparative Perspective." In *Assessing the Left Turn in Ecuador*, edited by Francisco Sánchez and Simón Pachano, 91–114. Cham: Palgrave Macmillan.

DESCO (Centro de Estudios y Promoción del Desarrollo). 2012. *Perú hoy: la gran continuidad*. Lima: DESCO, Serie Perú Hoy.

DESCO. 2013. *Perú hoy: el Perú subterráneo*. Lima: DESCO, Serie Perú Hoy.

De Soto, Hernando. 1986. *El otro sendero: la revolución informal.* Lima: Instituto de Libertad y Democracia.

De Soto, Hernando. 1989. *The Other Path: The Economic Answer to Terrorism.* New York: Basic Books.

Deutsch, Karl. W. 1963. *The Nerves of Government: Models of Political Communication and Control.* London: Free Press of Glencoe.

Diamond, Larry, and Marc F. Plattner, eds. 1995. *Economic Reform and Democracy.* Baltimore, MD: Johns Hopkins University Press.

Dietz, Henry. 2019. *Population Growth, Social Segregation and Voting Behavior in Lima, Peru, 1940-2016.* Notre Dame, IN: University of Notre Dame.

Domínguez, Jorge I. 1998. "Free Politics and Free Markets in Latin America." *Journal of Democracy* 9 (4): 70-84.

Drake, Paul. 1989, *The Money Doctor in the Andes: US Advisors, Investors and Economic Reform from World War 1 to the Great Depression.* Durham, NC: Duke University Press.

Driscoll, Amanda. 2017. "Bolivia's 'Democracy in Transition': More Questions than Answers in 2016." *Revista de Ciencia Política* 37 (2): 255-79.

Dunkerley, James. 1984. *Rebellion in the Veins.* London: Verso.

Dunkerley, James. 1990. *Political Transition and Economic Stabilisation, Bolivia, 1982-1989.* London: Institute of Latin American Studies.

Durand, Francisco. 2003. *Riqueza económica y pobreza política.* Lima: Fondo Editorial de la PUCP.

Durand, Francisco. 2010a. "Corporate Rents and the Capture of the Peruvian State." In *Business, Politics and Public Policy*, edited by Marques Carlos and Peter Utting, 184-207. London: Palgrave Macmillan.

Durand, Francisco. 2010b. *La mano invisible en el Estado: critica a los neoliberales criollos.* Lima: Fondo Editorial del Pedagógico San Marcos.

Durand, Francisco. 2012. "El señor de los Anillos." *Quehacer* 185: 8-23.

Durand, Francisco. 2013. *Los Romero: fe, fama y fortuna.* Lima: Ediciones Virrey and DESCO.

Durand, Francisco. 2017a. *Los doce apóstoles de la economía peruana: una mirada social a los grupos de poder limeños y provincianos.* Lima: Fondo Editorial de la PUCP.

Durand, Francisco. 2017b. *Juegos del poder: política tributaria y lobby en el Perú, 2011-2017.* Lima: Oxfam.

Durand, Francisco. 2018a. *Decretismo y captura: un breve balance con referencia al decretismo económico.* Lima: Fundacion Friedrich Ebert, working paper.

Durand, Francisco. 2018b. *Odebrecht: la empresa que capturaba gobiernos.* Lima: Fondo Editorial de la PUCP.

Durand, Francisco. 2019. *La captura del Estado en América Latina: reflexiones teóricas.* Lima: Fondo Editorial de la PUCP.

Durand, Francisco, Julián Cárdenas, and Emilio Salcedo. 2022. *La crisis de las AFP: poder y malestar previsional.* Lima: Fondo Editorial de la PUCP.

Durand, Francisco, and Emilio Salcedo. 2020. *El dinero de la democracia: quien financia a los partidos.* Lima: Fondo Editorial de la PUCP.

Durand, Francisco, and Eduardo Silva, eds. 1998. *Organized Business, Democracy and Economic Change in Latin America.* Miami, FL: North-South Center.

Eaton, Kent. 2011. "Conservative Autonomy Movements." *Comparative Politics* 43 (3): 291–310.

Eaton, Kent. 2017. *Territory and Ideology in Latin America.* Oxford: Oxford University Press.

Eckstein, Susan Eva, and Timothy P. Wickham-Crowley, eds. 2003. *Struggles for Social Rights in Latin America.* New York: Routledge.

ECLAC (Economic Commission for Latin America and the Caribbean). 2019. "Economic Survey of Latin America and the Caribbean 2019." Santiago: ECLAC. https://www.cepal.org/en/publications/44675-economic-survey-latin-america-and-caribbean-2019-new-global-financial-context.

ECLAC. 2020. "Economic Survey of Latin America and the Caribbean 2020: Ecuador." https://repositorio.cepal.org/bitstream/handle/11362/46071/16/ES2020_Ecuador_en.pdf.

ECLAC. 2022a. Cepalstat Statistical Databases and Publications. https://statistics.cepal.org/portal/cepalstat/dashboard.html?indicator_id=2207&area_id=1318&lang=en.

ECLAC. 2022b. *Los impactos socio demográficos de la pandemia COVID-19 en América Latina y el Caribe.* Santiago de Chile: CEPAL.

Edwards, Sebastián. 1995. *Crisis and Reform in Latin America: From Despair to Hope.* Washington, DC: World Bank.

El Comercio. 2017a. "El frente económico abre las puertas al sector empresarial." May 24. https://www.elcomercio.com/actualidad/ecuador-frenteeconomico-empresarios-politica-gabinete.html.

El Comercio. 2017b. "¿Quiénes son los integrantes del Gabinete de Lenín Moreno?" May 23. https://www.elcomercio.com/actualidad/ecuador-miembros-gabineteministerial-leninmoreno-gobierno.html.

El Comercio. 2018. "Ecuador relanza su agenda comercial con Estados Unidos." February 5. https://www.elcomercio.com/actualidad/ecuador-relanza-agendacomercial-eeuu-negocios.html.

El Comercio. 2021. "Guillermo Lasso se impuso en los tres cantones más poblados del país." April 13. https://www.elcomercio.com/actualidad/lasso-quito-guayaquil-cuenca-cne.html.

El Deber. 2019. "CAO pide unidad ante llamado a renuncia de líderes empresariales." November 12. https://eldeber.com.bo/el-deber/cao-pide-unidad-ante-llamado-a-renuncia-de-lideres-empresariales_156326.

Ellner, Steve. 2019. "Introduction: Pink-Tide Governments—Pragmatic and Populist Responses to Challenges from the Right." *Latin American Perspectives*, 46 (1): 4–22.

Ellner, Steve, ed. 2020. *Latin America's Pink Tide: Breakthroughs and Shortcoming*. Lanham, MD: Rowman and Littlefield.

El Universo. 2017a. "Gobierno crea Consejo Consultivo Productivo, con Jorge Glas a la cabeza." June 22. https://www.eluniverso.com/noticias/2017/06/22/nota/6243256/gobierno-crea-consejo-consultivo-productivo-jorge-glas-cabeza.

El Universo. 2017b. "Proponle al Futuro es la apuesta de empresarios por la inversión y el agro." March 25. https://www.eluniverso.com/noticias/2017/03/25/nota/6106123/proponle-futuro-es-apuesta-empresarios-inversion-agro.

El Universo. 2019. "Bancadas en la Asamblea de Ecuador anticipan rechazo a aumento de impuestos." https://www.eluniverso.com/noticias/2019/10/01/nota/7542550/bancadas-anticipan-rechazo-impuestos.

Escobar, Arturo. 2010. "Latin America at a Crossroads: Alternative Modernizations, Post-liberalism, or Post-development?" *Cultural Studies* 24 (1): 1–65.

Espinoza Molina, Fran. 2015. *Bolivia: la circulación de sus élites (2006-2014)*. Santa Cruz: Editorial El País.

Etchemendy, Sebastián. 2011. *Models of Economic Liberalization: Business, Workers, and Compensation in Latin America, Spain, and Portugal*. Cambridge: Cambridge University Press.

Fairfield, Tasha. 2015a. *Private Wealth and Public Revenue in Latin America: Business Power and Tax Politics*. Cambridge: Cambridge University Press.

Fairfield, Tasha. 2015b. "Structural Power in Comparative Political Economy: Perspectives from Policy Formulation in Latin America." *Business and Politics* 17 (3): 411–41.

Falleti, Tulia G., and Emilio A. Parrado, eds. 2018. *Latin America since the Left Turn*. Philadelphia: University of Pennsylvania Press.

Fazekas, Mihály, and Itsván János Tóth. 2016. "From Corruption to State Capture: A New Analytical Framework with Empirical Application from Hungary." *Political Research Quarterly* 69 (3): 320–34.

Field, Thomas. 2014. *From Development to Dictatorship: Bolivia and the Alliance for Progress in the Kennedy Era*. Ithaca, NY: Cornell University Press.

Fierro Carrión, Luis. 1991. *Los grupos financiero en el Ecuador*. Quito: CEDEP.

Fitzgerald, Valpy. 1979. *The Political Economy of Peru, 1956-78: Economic Development and the Restructuring of Capital*. Cambridge: Cambridge University Press.

Foweraker, Joe. 2018. *Demystifying Democracy in Latin America and Beyond.* New York: Lynne Rienner.

Francke, Pedro. 2006. "Institutional Change and Social Programs." In *Making Institutions Work in Peru*, edited by John Crabtree, 89–112. London: ILAS.

Freeland, Chrysta. 2000. *Sale of the Century: The Inside Story of the Second Russian Revolution.* New York: Penguin.

Fuchs, Doris. 2007. *Business Power in Global Governance.* New York: Lynne Rienner.

Fuchs, Doris, and Markus M. L. Lederer. 2007. "Business Power and Global Governance." *Business and Politics* 9 (3): 1–12.

Fuentes Knight, Juan Alberto. 2016. "State Capture and Fiscal Policy in Latin America." *Plaza Pública*, June 3. https://www.plazapublica.com.gt/content/state-capture-and-fiscal-policy-latin-america.

Galindo, Jorge. 2021. "Yaku Pérez y los casi dos millones de votos nulos en las elecciones ecuatorianas." *El País*, April 12. https://elpais.com/internacional/2021-04-12/yaku-perez-y-los-casi-dos-millones-de-votos-nulos-en-las-elecciones-ecuatorianas.html.

Gamarra, Eduardo A. 1994. "Crafting Political Support for Stabilization: Political Pacts and the New Economic Policy in Bolivia." In *Democracy, Markets, and Structural Reform in Latin America: Argentina, Bolivia, Brazil, Chile, and Mexico*, edited by William C. Smith, Carlos H. Acuña, and Eduardo A. Gamarra, 105–27. New Brunswick, NJ: Transaction.

Garay, Luis Jorge, and Eduardo Salcedo-Albarán. 2012. *Narcotráfico, corrupción y estados.* Bogotá: Debate.

García Gallegos, Bertha. 2003. "Petroleo, estado y proyecto militar." *Ecuador Debate* 58: 111–34.

García Laguardia, Jorge M. 2001. "Dinero y política: la cuadratura del círculo en América Latina." *Revista IIDH* 34–35: 521–50.

García Pascual, Francisco. 2003. "¿De la 'década perdida' a otra 'decada perdida'? El impacto del ajuste estructural en Ecuador y en América Latina, 1980–2002." In *Estado, etnicidad y movimientos sociales en América Latina: Ecuador en crisis*, edited by Víctor Bretón and Francisco García, 57–106. Barcelona: Icaria.

Gargurevich, Juan. 2021. *Velasco y la prensa, 1968–1975.* Lima: Fondo Editorial de la PUCP.

Garín, Renato, and Patricio Morales. 2016. *Elites y regulación de intereses: lobby y puerta giratoria.* Santiago: Centro de Análisis e Inversión Política.

Gates, Leslie C. 2009. "Theorizing Business Power in the Semi-periphery: Mexico." *Theory and Society* 38 (1): 39–57.

Gestión. 2020. "Reactivación de proyectos Conga y Tía María 'tiene que darse en algún momento,' dice el Minem." May 17. https://gestion.pe/

economia/coronavirus-peru-reactivacion-de-proyectos-conga-y-tia
-maria-tienen-que-darse-en-algun-momento-sostiene-titular-del-mi
nem-covid-19-nndc-noticia.

Giddens, Anthony. 1984. *The Constitution of Society: Outline of the Theory of Structuration*. Berkeley: University of California Press.

Gilens, Martin. 2012. *Affluence and Influence: Economic Inequality and Political Power*. Princeton, NJ: Princeton University Press.

Gonzales de Olarte, Efraín. 1998. *El neoliberalismo a la peruana: economía política del ajuste estructural, 1990-1997*. Lima: Instituto de Estudios Peruanos.

Gramsci, Antonio. 1980. *Notas sobre Maquiavelo, sobre la política y sobre el Estado moderno*. Madrid: Nueva Visión.

Gray Molina, George. 2001. "Exclusion, Participation and Democratic State Building." In *Towards Democratic Viability: The Bolivian Experience*, edited by John Crabtree and Laurence Whitehead, 63-82. Basingstoke: Palgrave.

Gray Molina, George. 2010. "The Challenge of Progressive Change under Evo Morales." In *Leftist Governments in Latin America: Successes and Shortcomings*, edited by Kurt Weyland, Raúl L. Madrid, and Wendy Hunter, 57-76. Cambridge: Cambridge University Press.

Grebe López, Horst. 2001. "The Private Sector and Democratisation." In *Towards Democratic Viability: The Bolivian Experience*, edited by John Crabtree and Laurence Whitehead, 160-78. Basingstoke: Palgrave.

Grupo Permanente de Trabajo sobre Alternativas al Desarrollo. 2011. *Más allá del desarrollo*. Quito: Fundación Rosa Luxemburg and Abya Yala.

Gudynas, Alejandro. 2015. *Extractivismos: ecología, economía y política de un modo de entender el desarrollo y la naturaleza*. Cochabamba: CEDIB.

Guerrero, Andrés. 1980. *Los oligarcas del cacao: ensayo sobre la acumulación originaria en el Ecuador*. Quito: Editorial El Conejo.

Guillén, Renzo. 2020. *"Los Cuellos Blancos del Puerto": un caso de cooptación institucional judicial*. Tesis de Licenciatura, Ciencia Política y Gobierno, PUCP.

Haggard, Stephan, and Robert R. Kaufman. 1992. *The Politics of Economic Adjustment: International Constraints, Distributive Conflicts, and the State*. Princeton, NJ: Princeton University Press.

Haggard, Stephan, and Robert R. Kaufman. 1995. *The Political Economy of Democratic Transitions*. Princeton, NJ: Princeton University Press.

Heilman, Lawrence C. 2017. *USAID in Bolivia: Partner or Patrón?* Boulder, CO: First Forum Press.

Hellman, Joel, and Daniel Kaufmann. 2001. "Confronting the Challenge of State Capture in Transition Economies." *Finance and Development* 38 (3). https://www.imf.org/external/pubs/ft/fandd/2001/09/hellman.htm.

Hey, Jeanne A. K., and Thomas Klak. 1999. "From Protectionism towards Neoliberalism: Ecuador across Four Administrations (1981-1996)." *Studies in Comparative International Development* 34 (3): 66-97.

Hirschman, Albert O. 1970. *Exit, Voice and Loyalty.* Cambridge, MA: Harvard University Press.

Hughes, Sallie, and Paola Prado. 2011. "Media Diversity and Social Inequality in Latin America." In *The Great Gap: Inequality and the Politics of Redistribution in Latin America*, edited by Merike Blofield, 109-46. University Park, PA: Penn State University Press.

Huntington, Samuel P. 1991. *The Third Wave: Democratization in the Late Twentieth Century.* Norman: University of Oklahoma Press.

Ibarra, Hernán. 2015. "¿Declive de la Revolución Ciudadana?" *Ecuador Debate* 95: 7-26.

Ibarra, Hernán. 2016. "Génesis y significado de la Reforma Agraria de 1964." In *50 años de reforma agraria: cuestiones pendientes y miradas alternativas*, edited by Francisco Rhon Dávila and Carlos Pástor Pazmiño, 21-61. Quito: Universidad Andina Simón Bolívar and Ediciones La Tierra.

IDEA Internacional, ed. 2010. *Miradas: nuevo texto constitucional.* La Paz: IDEA Internacional, Vicepresidencia del Estado Plurinacional de Bolivia and Universidad Mayor de San Andrés.

Iguíñiz, Javier. 1998. "The Economic Strategy of the Fujimori Government." In *Fujimori's Peru: The Political Economy*, edited by John Crabtree and Jim Thomas, 24-40. London: ILAS.

ILDIS and La Tendencia, eds. 2008. *Análisis nueva constitución.* Quito: Instituto Latinoamericano de Investigaciones Sociales (ILDIS) & Revista La Tendencia.

IMF (International Monetary Fund). 2015. *Peru: Staying the Course of Economic Success.* Washington, DC: IMF.

Innes, Abby. 2014. "The Political Economy of State Capture in Central Europe." *Journal of Common Market Studies* 52 (1): 88-104.

Isaacs, Anita. 1993. *Military Rule and Transition in Ecuador, 1972-92.* Basingstoke: Macmillan.

Isaacs, Anita. 1996. "Ecuador: Democracy Standing the Test of Time?" In *Constructing Democratic Governance: South America in the 1990s*, edited by Jorge I. Domínguez and Abraham F. Lowenthal, 42-57. Baltimore, MD: Johns Hopkins University Press.

Jansen, Robert. 2017. *Revolutionizing Repertoires: The Rise of Populist Mobilization in Peru.* Chicago: University of Chicago Press.

John, S. Sandor. 2009. *Bolivia's Radical Tradition: Permanent Revolution in the Andes.* Tucson: University of Arizona Press.

Johnston, Hank, and Paul Almeida, eds. 2006. *Latin American Social Move-*

ments: Globalization, Democratization, and Transnational Networks. Lanham: Rowman and Littlefield.

Kapiszewski, Diana, Steven Levitsky, and Deborah J. Yashar, eds. 2021. *The Inclusionary Turn in Latin American Democracies*. Cambridge: Cambridge University Press.

Karcher, Sebastian, and Ben Ross Schneider. 2012. "Business Politics in Latin America: Investigating Structures, Preferences and Influence." In *Routledge Handbook of Latin American Politics*, edited by Peter Kingstone and Deborah Yashar, 273-84. New York: Taylor and Francis.

Kaup, Brent. 2010. "The Constraints on Natural-Gas-Led Development in Bolivia." *Latin American Perspectives* 37 (3): 123-38.

King, Katiuska, and Pablo Samaniego. 2019. "The Crisis Narrative of Ecuador's Lenin Moreno Has Obscured the Real Winners and Losers of Recent Economic Policy." *LSE Latin America and Caribbean Centre*, September 12. https://blogs.lse.ac.uk/latamcaribbean/2019/09/12/the-crisis-narrative-of-ecuadors-lenin-moreno-has-obscured-the-real-winners-and-losers-of-recent-economic-policy.

Kingstone, Peter R. 2018. "The Rise and Fall (and Rise Again?) of Neoliberalism in Latin America." In *The SAGE Handbook of Neoliberalism*, edited by Damien Cahill, Melinda Cooper, Martijn Konings, and David Primrose, 201-18. London: SAGE.

Kitzberger, Philip. 2016. "Counterhegemony in the Media under Rafael Correa's Citizens' Revolution." *Latin American Perspectives* 43 (1): 53-70.

Klarén, Peter Flindell. 2000. *Peru: Society and Nationhood in the Andes*. Oxford: Oxford University Press.

Klein, Herbert, 1971. "Prelude to the Revolution." In *Beyond the Revolution: Bolivia since 1952*, edited by James Malloy and Richard Thorn, 25-52. Pittsburgh, PA: University of Pittsburgh Press.

Klein, Herbert. 2003. *A Concise History of Bolivia*. New York: Cambridge University Press.

Knight, Peter. 1975. "New Forms of Economic Organization in Peru: Toward Workers' Self Management." In *The Peruvian Experiment: Continuity and Change under Military Rule*, edited by Abraham Lowenthal, 350-401. Princeton, NJ: Princeton University Press.

Kuczynski, Pedro Pablo. 1977. *Peruvian Democracy under Economic Stress*. Princeton, NJ: Princeton University Press.

Kuczynski, Pedro Pablo, and John Williamson. 2003. *After the Washington Consensus: Restarting Growth in Latin America*. Washington, DC: Institute for International Economics.

Kurtz, Marcus J. 2004. "The Dilemmas of Democracy in the Open Economy: Lessons from Latin America." *World Politics* 56 (1): 262-302.

Kwak, James. 2014. "Cultural Capture and the Financial Crisis." In *Preventing Capture: Special Interest Influence in Legislation and How to Limit It*, edited by Daniel Carpenter and David Moss, 71-98. Cambridge, MA: Harvard University Press.

Labarthe, Sunniva, and Marc Saint-Upéry. 2017. "Leninismo versus correísmo: la 'tercera vuelta' en Ecuador." *Nueva Sociedad* 272: 29-42.

Lalander, Rickard, Magnus Lembke, and Pablo Ospina Peralta. 2019. "Political Economy of State-Indigenous Liaisons: Ecuador in Times of Alianza PAIS." *European Review of Latin American and Caribbean Studies* 108: 193-220.

Lalander, Rickard, and Pablo Ospina Peralta. 2012. "Movimiento indígena y revolución ciudadana en Ecuador." *Cuestiones Políticas* 28 (48): 13-50.

Latinobarómetro. 2021. "Análisis de datos." (Online analysis.) https://www.latinobarometro.org/latOnline.jsp.

Lazzarini, Sergio G. 2011. *Capitalismo de lazos: os donos de Brasil e suas conexoes*. São Paulo: Campus.

León, Raffaela. 2019. *Vizcarra: retrato de un poder en construccion*. Lima: Debate.

León Trujillo, Jorge. 2003. "Un sistema político regionalizado y su crisis." In *Estado, etnicidad y movimientos sociales en América Latina: Ecuador en crisis*, edited by Víctor Bretón and Francisco García, 25-55. Barcelona: Icaria.

León Trujillo, Jorge, and Juan P. Pérez. 1986. "Crisis y movimiento sindical en Ecuador: las huelgas nacionales del FUT (1981-1983)." In *Movimientos sociales en el Ecuador*, edited by Luis Verdesoto, 93-150. Buenos Aires: CLACSO.

Levitsky, Steven, and Kenneth Roberts, eds. 2011. *The Resurgence of the Latin American Left*. Baltimore, MD: Johns Hopkins University Press.

Levitsky, Steven, and Mauricio Zavaleta. 2016. "Why No Party-Building in Peru?" In *Challenges of Party-Building in Latin America*, edited by Steven Levitsky, James Loxton, Brandon Philip Van Dyck, and Jorge Domínguez, 413-39. Cambridge: Cambridge University Press.

Lindblom, Charles. 1977. *Politics and Markets: The World's Economic-Political Systems*. New York: Basic Books.

Lipietz, Alain. 1987. *Mirages and Miracles: The Crisis of Global Fordism*. London: Verso.

López Jiménez, Sinesio. 2012. "Si Humala no hubiera tirado la toalla antes de pelear." *El Zorro de Abajo*, May 18. http://blog.pucp.edu.pe/blog/sinesio/2012/05/18/si-humala-no-hubiera-tirado-la-toalla-antes-de-pelear.

López L., Baldomero Rafael. 2019. "Influencia del neoliberalismo en los principios y valores de las elites empresariales en la ciudad de Lima, Perú." *Entramado* 15 (2): 202-15.

López Segrera, Francisco. 2016. *América Latina: crisis del posneoliberalismo y ascenso de la nueva derecha*. Buenos Aires: CLACSO.

Lora, Eduardo. 2001. *Las reformas estructurales en América Latina: qué se ha reformado y cómo medirlo*. IADB Research Department working paper no. 462. Washington, DC: Inter-American Development Bank.

Lora, Guillermo. 1977. *A History of the Bolivian Labour Movement*. Cambridge: Cambridge University Press.

Love, Joseph. 2005. "The Rise and Fall of Structuralism." In *Economic Doctrines in Latin America: Origins, Embedding and Evolution*, edited by Valpy Fitzgerald and Rosemary Thorp, 157-81. Basingstoke: Macmillan.

Lowenthal, Abraham. 1975. *The Peruvian Experiment: Continuity and Change under Military Rule*. Princeton, NJ: Princeton University Press.

Lukes, Steven. 2005. *Power: A Radical View*. New York: Macmillan.

Luna, Juan Pablo, and Cristóbal Rovira Kaltwasser, eds. 2014. *The Resilience of the Latin American Right*. Baltimore, MD: Johns Hopkins University Press.

Macaroff, Anahí. Forthcoming. "De banquero a presidente: las élites económicas ecuatorianas y sus mecanismos de incidencia política." In *Elites empresariales, Estado y dominación en América Latina: persistencias y resistencias en la época post Covid*, edited by Francisco Robles, Ines Nercesian, and Miguel Serna. Buenos Aires: CLACSO.

Macdonald, Laura, and Arne Ruckert, eds. 2009. *Post-neoliberalism in the Americas*. Basingstoke: Palgrave Macmillan.

Madariaga, Aldo. 2020. *Neoliberal Resilience: Lessons in Democracy and Development from Latin America and Eastern Europe*. Princeton, NJ: Princeton University Press.

Madrid, Raúl. 2011. "Bolivia: Origins and Policies of the Movimiento al Socialismo." In *The Resurgence of the Latin American Left*, edited by Steven Levitsky and Kenneth M. Roberts, 239-59. Baltimore, MD: Johns Hopkins University Press.

Madrid, Raúl L., Wendy Hunter, and Kurt Weyland. 2010. "The Policies and Performance of the Contestatory and Moderate Left." In *Leftist Governments in Latin America: Successes and Shortcomings*, edited by Kurt Weyland, Raúl L. Madrid, and Wendy Hunter, 140-80. Cambridge: Cambridge University Press.

Mahoney, James. 2001. *The Legacies of Liberalism: Path Dependence and Political Regimes in Central America*. Baltimore, MD: Johns Hopkins University Press.

Maiguashca, Juan, and Liisa North. 1991. "Orígenes y significado del velasquismo: lucha de clases y participación política en el Ecuador, 1920-1972." In *La cuestión regional y el poder*, edited by Rafael Quintero, 89-159. Quito: Corporación Editora Nacional.

Maillet, Antoine, Bastián González-Bustamante, and Alejandro Olivares L. 2016. *¿Puerta giratoria? análisis de la circulación público-privada en Chile (2000-2014).* Working paper no. 7/2016. Santiago: PNUD.

Malloy, James, and Richard Thorn. 1971. *Beyond the Revolution: Bolivia since 1952.* Pittsburgh, PA: University of Pittsburgh Press.

Mantilla B., Sebastián, and Santiago Mejía R., eds. 2012. *Rafael Correa: balance de la revolución ciudadana.* Quito: Editorial Planeta del Ecuador.

Manzetti, Luigi. 2009. *Neoliberalism, Accountability and Reform Failures in Emerging Markets: Eastern Europe, Russia, Argentina, and Chile in Comparative Perspective.* University Park, PA: Penn State University Press.

Marandici, Ion. 2017. "Oligarchic State Capture in Post-communist Societies." PhD diss., Rutgers University, New Brunswick, New Jersey.

Martínez Santi, Neptalí, ed. 2020. *OCTUBRE.* Quito: Editorial El árbol de papel.

Mattei, Ugo, and Laura Nader. 2013. *Saqueo: cuando el estado de derecho es ilegal—traducción de Alvaro Bonilla y Roger Merino.* Lima: Palestra Editores.

Mayorga, Fernando. 2003. "Neopopulismo y democracia en Bolivia." *Revista de Ciencia Política* 23 (1): 99-118.

Mayorga, Fernando. 2006. "Nacionalismo e indigenismo en el MAS: los desafíos de la articulación hegemónica." *Decursos: Revista de Ciencias Sociales* 8, nos. 15-16: 135-64.

Mayorga, Fernando. 2009. *Antinomias: el azaroso camino de la reforma política.* Cochabamba: CESU-UMSS.

Mayorga, Fernando, ed. 2020a. *Crisis y cambio político en Bolivia, octubre y noviembre de 2019: La democracia en una encrucijada.* La Paz: CESU-UMSS.

Mayorga, Fernando. 2020b. "Derrota política del MAS y proyecto de restauración oligárquico-señorial." In *Crisis y cambio político en Bolivia, octubre y noviembre de 2019: La democracia en una encrucijada*, edited by Fernando Mayorga, 1-28. La Paz: CESU-UMSS.

Mayorga, Fernando. 2020c. "El MAS-IPSP ante un nuevo contexto político: de 'partido de gobierno' a 'instrumento político' de las organizaciones populares." In *Nuevo Mapa de Actores en Bolivia: crisis, polarización e incertidumbre (2019-2020)*, edited by Jan Souverein and José Luis Exeni Rodríguez, 1-34. La Paz: Friedrich-Ebert-Stiftung Bolivia.

McClintock, Cynthia, and Abraham Lowenthal. 1983. *The Peruvian Experiment Reconsidered.* Princeton, NJ: Princeton University Press.

Mejía Acosta, Andrés. 2006. "Crafting Legislative Ghost Coalitions in Ecuador: Informal Institutions and Economic Reform in an Unlikely Case." In *Informal Institutions and Democracy: Lessons from Latin America*, edited by Gretchen Helmke and Steven Levitsky, 59-84. Baltimore. MD: Johns Hopkins University Press.

Mejía Acosta, Andrés. 2009. *Informal Coalitions and Policymaking in Latin America: Ecuador in Comparative Perspective*. New York: Routledge.

Meléndez, Carlos, and Paolo Moncagatta. 2017. "Ecuador: Una década de correísmo." *Revista de Ciencia Política* 37 (2): 413–47.

Moldiz Mercado, Hugo. 2020. *Golpe de estado en Bolivia: la soledad de Evo Morales*. Havana: Ocean Sur.

Molina, Fernando. 2017. *Breve historia de la Banca (1957-2017): Seis décadas de aporte al desarrollo de Bolivia*. La Paz: ASOBAN.

Molina, Fernando. 2019. *Modos de privilegio: alta burguesía y alta gerencia en la Bolivia contemporánea*. La Paz: Vicepresidencia del Estado, CIS, Oxfam.

Molina, Fernando. 2020. "La rebelión de los blancos: Causas raciales de la caída de Evo Morales." In *Crisis y cambio político en Bolivia, octubre y noviembre de 2019: la democracia en una encrucijada*, edited by Fernando Mayorga, 141-62. La Paz: CESU-UMSS.

Molina, Fernando. 2021. *Historia contemporánea de Bolivia: de la reinstalación de la democracia al nacimiento del Estado Plurinacional—segunda edición corregida y aumentada*. La Paz: Libros Nómadas.

Molina, Fernando, and Susana Bejarano. 2020. "La transformación restauradora del campo mediático: el alineamiento de los medios de comunicación con el bloque de poder postevista en noviembre de 2019." In *Nuevo Mapa de Actores en Bolivia: crisis, polarización e incertidumbre (2019-2020)*, edited by Jan Souverein and José Luis Exeni Rodríguez, 165-200. La Paz: Friedrich-Ebert-Stiftung Bolivia.

Morales, Juan Antonio. 2001. "Economic Vulnerability in Bolivia." In *Towards Democratic Viability: The Bolivian Experience*, edited by John Crabtree and Laurence Whitehead, 41-60. Basingstoke: Palgrave.

Morales, Juan Antonio. 2008. "Bolivia in a Global Setting: Economic Ties." In *Unresolved Tensions: Bolivia Past and Present*, edited by John Crabtree and Laurence Whitehead, 217-38. Pittsburgh, PA: University of Pittsburgh Press.

Morales, Juan Antonio, and Jeffrey Sachs. 1990. "Bolivia's Economic Crisis." In *Developing Country Debt and Economic Performance, Vol. 2, Country Studies—Argentina, Bolivia, Brazil, Mexico*, edited by Jeffrey Sachs, 157-268. Chicago: University of Chicago Press.

Morley, Samuel A., Roberto Machado, and Stefano Pettinato. 1999. *Indexes of Structural Reform in Latin America*. Reformas Económicas no. 12. Santiago: ECLAC.

Mudde, Cas. 2019. *The Far Right Today*. Cambridge, UK: Polity.

Muñoz Jaramillo, Francisco, ed. 2014. *Balance crítico del gobierno de Rafael Correa*. Quito: Universidad Central del Ecuador.

Naranjo, Alexis. 1993. "Las cámaras de la producción y la política: Ecuador 1980-1990." *Ecuador Debate* 31: 155-68.

Navas Alvear, Marco. 2012. *Lo público insurgente: crisis y construcción de la política en la esfera pública*. Quito: CIESPAL.

Nelson, Marcel. 2019. "Walking the Tightrope of Socialist Governance: A Strategic-Relational Analysis of Twenty-First-Century Socialism." *Latin American Perspectives* 46 (1): 46-65.

Nercesian, Ines. 2020. *Presidentes empresarios y estados capturados: America Latina en el siglo XXI*. Buenos Aires: Teseo.

North, Liisa. 2006. "Militares y estado en Ecuador ¿construcción militar y desmantelamiento civil?" *Íconos* 10 (3): 85-95.

North, Liisa L., and Timothy D. Clark, eds. 2018. *Dominant Elites in Latin America: From Neo-Liberalism to the "Pink Tide."* London: Palgrave Macmillan.

OAS (Organization of American States). 2008. *Política, dinero y poder: un dilema para las democracias de América Latina*. Mexico City: Organización de los Estados Americanos.

O'Donnell, Guillermo. 1973. *Modernization and Bureaucratic Authoritarianism: Studies in South American Politics*. Berkeley: University of California at Berkeley.

O'Donnell, Guillermo, and Philippe Schmitter. 1986. *Transitions from Authoritarian Rule: Tentative Conclusions about Uncertain Democracies*. Baltimore, MD: Johns Hopkins University Press.

Olivares, Alejandro, and Pablo Medina. 2020. "La persistente debilidad institucional de Ecuador: protestas, elecciones y divisiones políticas durante el 2019." *Revista de Ciencia Política* 40 (2): 315-49.

Omelyanshuk, Oleksiy. 2001. "Explaining State Capture and Capture Modes: The Cases of Russia and Ukraine." *Paper*. Central European University, Vienna.

Ormachea S., Enrique, and Nilton Ramirez F. 2013. *Políticas agrarias del gobierno del MAS o la agenda del "poder empresarial-hacendal."* La Paz: CEDLA.

Ospina Peralta, Pablo. 2013. "Estamos haciendo mejor las cosas con el mismo modelo antes que cambiarlo." In *Promesas en su laberinto: cambios y continuidades en los gobiernos progresistas de América Latina*, edited by Carlos Arze, Javier Gómez, Pablo Ospina, and Víctor Álvarez, 177-278. La Paz: CEDLA.

Ospina Peralta, Pablo. 2015. *Grandes empresas, crisis económica y revolución ciudadana*. Análisis de Coyuntura, November. Quito: Comité Ecuménico de Proyectos (CEP).

Ospina Peralta, Pablo. 2016. "La aleación inestable: origen y consolidación de un Estado transformista: Ecuador, 1920-1960." PhD diss., University of Amsterdam, Netherlands.

Ospina Peralta, Pablo. 2019. "Ecuador contra Lenín Moreno." *Nueva Sociedad*, October. https://nuso.org/articulo/ecuador-lenin-moreno.

OXFAM. 2022. "Primera encuesta nacional de percepción de desigualdades." Lima: OXFAM and IEP. https://peru.oxfam.org/ENADES-2022.

Oxhorn, Philip, and Graciela Ducatenzeiler, eds. 1998. *What Kind of Democracy? What Kind of Market? Latin America in the Age of Neoliberalism.* University Park, PA: Penn State University Press.

Oxhorn, Philip, and Pamela K. Starr, eds. 1999. *Markets and Democracy in Latin America: Conflict or Convergence?* Boulder, CO: Lynne Rienner.

Pachano, Simón. 2006. "Ecuador: The Provincialization of Representation." In *The Crisis of Democratic Representation in the Andes,* edited by Scott Mainwaring, Ana María Bejarano, and Eduardo Pizarro Leongómez, 100-131. Stanford, CA: Stanford University Press.

Pachano, Simón. 2012. "RC-R'C' = 0." In *Rafael Correa: balance de la revolución ciudadana,* edited by Sebastián Mantilla B. and Santiago Mejía R., 43-74. Quito: Editorial Planeta del Ecuador.

Paredes, Carlos. 2021. *El perfil del lagarto.* Lima: Planeta.

Paredes, Carlos, and Jeffrey Sachs, eds. 1991. *Estabilización y crecimiento en el Perú.* Lima: Grupo de Analisis para el Desarrollo (GRADE).

Pásara, Luis. 2019. *De Montesinos a los Cuellos Blancos del Puerto: la persistente crisis de la justicia peruana.* Lima: Planeta.

Pásara, Luis, and Carlos Indacochea. 2014. *Cipriano como actor político.* Lima: Instituto de Estudios Peruanos.

Pástor Pazmiño, Carlos. 2019. *Los grupos económicos en el Ecuador: acumulación de capital y captura del Estado—segunda edición.* Quito: Ediciones La Tierra.

Pástor Pazmiño, Carlos. 2021. "¿Por quién votar? Elecciones presidenciales en el Ecuador 2021." *Ecuador Today,* February 1. https://ecuadortoday .media/2021/02/01/por-quien-votar-elecciones-presidenciales-en-el-ec uador-2021.

Paz y Miño Cepeda, Juan J. 2012. El gobierno de la revolución ciudadana: una visión histórica. In *Rafael Correa: Balance de la revolución ciudadana,* edited by Sebastián Mantilla B. and Santiago Mejía R., 23-41. Quito: Editorial Planeta del Ecuador.

Pearce, Adrian, ed. 2011. *Evo Morales and the Movimiento al Socialismo in Bolivia: The First Term in Context, 2005-2009.* London: Institute for the Study of the Americas.

Peña Claros, Claudia. 2010. "Un pueblo eminente: Autonomist Populism in Santa Cruz." *Latin American Perspectives* 37 (4): 125-39.

Peru Top Publications. 2014. *Peru: The Top 1,000 Companies.* Lima: Top Publications.

Plan V. 2021. "Guillermo Lasso, el hombre que se hizo a sí mismo." *Plan V,* February 9. https://www.planv.com.ec/historias/perfiles/guillermo -lasso-el-hombre-que-se-hizo-si-mismo.

PNUD (Programa de las Naciones Unidas para el Desarrollo), ed. 2010. *Mutaciones del campo político en Bolivia*. La Paz: PNUD Bolivia.

PNUD. 2018. *Desiguales: orígenes, cambios y desafíos de la brecha social en Chile*. Santiago de Chile: PNUD.

Ponce, Karina, Andrés Vasquez, Pablo Vivanco, and Ronaldo Munck. 2020. "The October 2019 Indigenous and Citizens' Uprising in Ecuador." *Latin American Perspectives* 47 (5): 9-19.

Pop-Eleches, Grigore. 2009. *From Economic Crisis to Reform: IMF Programs in Latin America and Eastern Europe*. Princeton, NJ: Princeton University Press.

Portantiero, José Carlos. 1999. *Los usos de Gramsci*. Buenos Aires: Grijalbo.

Portocarrero, Felipe, and Cynthia Sanborn, eds. 2006. *Philanthropy and Social Change in Latin America*. Cambridge, MA: David Rockefeller Center for Latin American Studies, Harvard University.

Posada-Carbó, Eduardo, and Carlos Malamud, eds. 2005. *The Financing of Politics: Latin America and European Perspectives*. London: Institute for the Study of the Americas.

Postero, Nancy. 2017. *The Indigenous State: Race, Politics, and Performance in Plurinational Bolivia*. Oakland: University of California Press.

Quiliconi, Cintia, and Renato Rivera Rhon. 2022. "The Latin American School of IPE: A Road from Development to Regionalism." In *Latin America in Global International Relations*, edited by Amitav Acharya, Melisa Deciancio, and Diana Tussie, 144-62. New York: Routledge.

Quijano, Anibal. 2000. *Colonialidad del poder, eurocentrismo y América Latina*. Buenos Aires: CLACSO.

Quintero, Rafael, and Erika Silva. 1998a. *Ecuador: Una nación en ciernes. Tomo I*. Quito: Abya-Yala.

Quintero, Rafael, and Erika Silva. 1998b. *Ecuador: Una nación en ciernes. Tomo II*. Quito: Abya-Yala.

Ramírez Gallegos, Franklin. 2012. "Perspectivas del proceso de democratización en Ecuador: cambio político e inclusión social (2005-2010)." In *Democracias en transformación ¿Qué hay de nuevo en los Estados andinos?*, edited by Anja Dargatz and Moira Zuazo, 103-54. La Paz: Friedrich-Ebert-Stiftung Bolivia.

Ramírez Gallegos, Franklin. 2016. "Political Change, State Autonomy, and Post-neoliberalism in Ecuador, 2007-2012." *Latin American Perspectives* 43 (1): 143-57.

Ramírez Gallegos, Franklin. 2019. "Las masas en octubre: Ecuador y las colisiones de clase." *Nueva Sociedad* 284: 15-27.

Ramírez Gallegos, Franklin. 2021. "Elecciones Ecuador 2021: entre la despolarización lenta y el retorno de la gran batalla." *Análisis Carolina* 13/2021.

https://www.fundacioncarolina.es/wp-content/uploads/2021/04/AC -13.2021.pdf.

Remmer, Karen. 1998. "The Politics of Neoliberal Economic Reform in South America, 1980-94." *Studies in Comparative Development* 33 (2): 3-29.

Rivera Vélez, Fredy, and Franklin Ramírez Gallegos. 2005. "Ecuador: Democracy and Economy in Crisis." In *The Andes in Focus: Security, Democracy and Economic Reform*, edited by Russell Crandall, Guadalupe Paz, and Riordan Roett, 121-49. Boulder, CO: Lynne Rienner.

Roberts, Kenneth M. 1995. "Neoliberalism and the Transformation of Populism in Latin America: The Peruvian Case." *World Politics*, 48 (1): 82-116.

Roberts, Kenneth M. 2008. "The Mobilization of Opposition to Economic Liberalization." *Annual Review of Political Science* 11: 327-49.

Roberts, Kenneth M. 2018. "Introduction to Part III: Political Parties in Latin America's Second Wave of Incorporation." In *Reshaping the Political Arena in Latin America: From Resisting Neoliberalism to the Second Incorporation*, edited by Eduardo Silva and Federico M. Rossi, 211-21. Pittsburgh, PA: University of Pittsburgh Press.

Robles, Francisco, Ines Nercesian, and Miguel Serna, eds. Forthcoming. *Elites empresariales, Estado y dominación en América Latina: persistencias y resistencias en la época post Covid*. Buenos Aires: CLACSO.

Roca, José Luis. 2001. Economía y sociedad en el Oriente Boliviano (siglos XVI-XX). Santa Cruz de la Sierra: Editorial Oriente.

Rojas Ortuste, Gonzalo. 2009. *Cultura política de las élites en Bolivia, 1982-2005*. La Paz: CIPCA and Fundación Friedrich Ebert.

Romero, Carlos, Carlos Böhrt, and Raúl Peñaranda. 2009. *Del conflicto al diálogo: memorias del acuerdo constitucional*. La Paz: fBDM and FES-ILDIS.

Romero, Teresa. 2021. "Perú: Informal Employment Share 2010-2021." *Statista* (October). https://www.statista.com/statistics/1039975/informal-em ployment-share-peru.

Rosales, Antulio. 2020. "Structural Constraints in Times of Resource Nationalism: Oil Policy and State Capacity in Post-neoliberal Ecuador." *Globalizations* 17 (1): 77-92.

Rospigliosi, Fernando 2006. "The Blocking of Reform in the Security Services." In *Making Institutions Work in Peru: Democracy, Development and Inequality since 1980*, edited by John Crabtree, 66-88. London: Institute for the Study of the Americas.

Ruckert, Arne, Laura Macdonald, and Kristina R. Proulx. 2017. "Post-neoliberalism in Latin America: A Conceptual Review." *Third World Quarterly* 38 (7): 1583-1602.

Rueschemeyer, Dietrich, Evelyne Huber Stephens, and John D. Stephens, eds. 1992. *Capitalist Development and Democracy.* Chicago: University of Chicago Press.

Sacher, William. 2017. *Ofensive megaminera china en los Andes: acumulación por desposesión en el Ecuador de la "Revolución Ciudadana."* Quito: Abya Yala.

Sachs, Jeffrey. 2011. *The Price of Civilization: Reawakening American Virtue and Prosperity.* New York: Vintage.

Salgado, Wilma. 2018. "Paquetazo para 'toda una vida': Ley Orgánica para el Fomento Productivo." *Ecuador Debate* 104: 7–23.

Salgado, Wilma. 2019. "Ecuador: Society's Reaction to IMF Austerity Package." *NACLA*, October 14. https://nacla.org/news/2019/10/14/ecuador-so cietys-reaction-imf-austerity-package-indigenous.

Sánchez, Francisco, and Simón Pachano, eds. 2020. *Assessing the Left Turn in Ecuador.* Cham: Palgrave Macmillan.

Scherer, Andrea, and Guido Palazzo. 2011. "The New Political Role of Business in a Globalized World: A Review of CSR and Its Implications for the Firm." *Governance and Democracy: Journal of Management Studies* 48 (4): 899–931.

Schiffrin, Anna, ed. 2017. *In the Service of Power: Media Capture and the Threat to Democracy.* Washington, DC: National Endowment for Democracy (NED).

Schneider, Ben Ross. 2004. *Business Politics and the State in the Twentieth-Century Latin America.* New York: Cambridge University Press.

Schneider, Ben Ross. 2010. "Business Politics in Latin America: Patterns of Fragmentation and Centralization." In *The Oxford Handbook of Business and Government*, edited by David Coen, Graham K. Wilson, and Graham Wilson, 307–29. New York: Oxford University Press.

Schneider, Ben Ross. 2013. *Hierarchical Capitalism in Latin America: Business, Labor and the Challenges of Equitable Development.* New York: Cambridge University Press.

Schützhofer, Timm B. 2016. "Ecuador's Fiscal Policies in the Context of the Citizens' Revolution: A 'Virtuous Cycle' and Its Limits." *DIE Discussion Paper* no. 15/2016. https://www.die-gdi.de/uploads/media/DP_15.2016 .pdf.

Schützhofer, Timm B. 2019. "Elected Left, Governing Right: In Ecuador, President Lenín Moreno Has Allied with His Political Opponents to Implement a Conservative Economic Agenda." *NACLA*, March 13. https:// nacla.org/news/2019/03/15/elected-left-governing-right.

Seminario, Bruno. 2015. *El desarrollo de la economía peruana en la era moderna.* Lima: Universidad del Pacífico.

Shadlen, Kenneth. 2000. "Neoliberalism, Corporativism and Small Business Activism in Mexico." *Latin American Research Review* 35 (2): 73–106.

Sifuentes, Marco. 2019. *K.O.P.P.K.: caída pública y vida secreta de Pedro Pable Kuczysnki*. Lima: Planeta.

Silva, Eduardo. 2009. *Challenging Neoliberalism in Latin America*. Cambridge: Cambridge University Press.

Silva, Eduardo. 2018. "Social Movements and the Second Incorporation in Bolivia and Ecuador." In *Reshaping the Political Arena in Latin America: From Resisting Neoliberalism to the Second Incorporation*, edited by Eduardo Silva and Federico M. Rossi, 32-59. Pittsburgh, PA: University of Pittsburgh Press.

Silva, Eduardo, and Federico M. Rossi, eds. 2018. *Reshaping the Political Arena in Latin America: From Resisting Neoliberalism to the Second Incorporation*. Pittsburgh, PA: University of Pittsburgh Press.

Smith, William C., Carlos H. Acuña, and Eduardo A. Gamarra, eds. 1994. *Latin American Political Economy in the Age of Neoliberal Reform: Theoretical and Comparative Perspectives for the 1990s*. New Brunswick, NJ: Transaction.

Soberón Garrido, Ricardo. 2015. *Diagnóstico del narcotráfico: mecanismos de infiltración e impactos en el sistema y actores políticos peruanos*. Lima: Congresos de la República.

Souverein, Jan, and José Luis Exeni Rodríguez, eds. 2020. *Nuevo Mapa de Actores en Bolivia: crisis, polarización e incertidumbre (2019-2020)*. La Paz: Friedrich-Ebert-Stiftung Bolivia.

Stallings, Barbara. 1983. "International Capitalism and the Peruvian Military Government." In *The Peruvian Experiment Reconsidered*, edited by Cynthia McClintock and Abraham Lowenthal, 144-80. Princeton, NJ: Princeton University Press.

Stallings, Barbara. 2020. *Dependency in the Twenty-First Century? The Political Economy of China-Latin America Relations*. Cambridge: Cambridge University Press.

Stefanoni, Pablo and Hervé Do Alto. 2006. *La revolución de Evo Morales: de la coca al palacio*. Buenos Aires: Capital Intelectual.

Stepan, Alfred. 1978. *The State and Society: Peru in Comparative Perspective*. Princeton, NJ: Princeton University Press.

Stern, Steve, ed. 1998. *Shining and Other Paths: War and Society in Peru, 1980-95*. Durham, NC: Duke University Press.

Stigler, George J. 1971. "The Theory of Economic Regulation." *Bell Journal of Economics and Management Science* 2 (1): 3-21.

Stokes, Susan C. 2004. *Mandates and Democracy: Neoliberalism by Surprise in Latin America*. Cambridge: Cambridge University Press.

Svampa, Maristella. 2019. *Las fronteras del neoextractivismo en América Latina: conflictos socioambientales, giro ecoterritorial y nuevas dependencias*. Bielefeld: Bielefeld University Press.

Távara, José. 2006. "La regulación del poder de mercado y la transición a la democracia." In *Construir instituciones: democracia, desarrollo y desigualdad en el Perú desde 1980*, edited by John Crabtree, 211-36. Lima: CIUP, IEP y PUCP.

Thorn, Richard. 1971. "The Economic Transformation." In *Beyond the Revolution: Bolivia since 1952*, edited by James Malloy and Richard Thorn, 157-216. Pittsburgh, PA: University of Pittsburgh Press.

Thorp, Rosemary. 1998. *Progress, Poverty and Exclusion: An Economic History of Latin America in the Twentieth Century*. Washington, DC: Inter-American Development Bank.

Thorp, Rosemary, and Geoffrey Bertram. 1978. *Peru, 1890-1977*. London: Macmillan.

Thoumi, Francisco, and Merilee Grindle. 1992. *La política de la economía del ajuste: la actual experiencia ecuatoriana*. Quito: FLACSO.

Tórrez, Yuri F. 2020. "Oposición no partidaria al MAS-IPSP: antes, durante y después de la crisis de octubre-noviembre." In *Nuevo Mapa de Actores en Bolivia: Crisis, polarización e incertidumbre (2019-2020)*, edited by Jan Souverein and José Luis Exeni Rodríguez, 77-138. La Paz: Friedrich-Ebert-Stiftung Bolivia.

Tsolakis, Andreas. 2011. *The Reform of the Bolivian State: Domestic Politics in a Context of Globalization*. Boulder, CO: First Forum.

Tuesta, Fernando, ed. 2017. *Perú: elecciones 2016: un país dividido y un resultado inesperado*. Lima: Pontificia Universidad Católica del Perú.

US Department of Justice. 2016. *Odebrecht Plea Agreement*. New York: Department of Justice.

Van Cott, Donna Lee. 2005. *From Movements to Parties in Latin America: The Evolution of Ethnic Politics*. Cambridge: Cambridge University Press.

Vergara-Camus, Lenadro, and Cristóbal Kay. 2017. "The Agrarian Political Economy of Left-Wing Governments in Latin America: Agribusiness, Peasants and the Limits of Neo-developmentalism." *Journal of Agrarian Change* 17 (2): 415-37.

Villena, Claudia. 2020. *El Club de la Construcción: una aproximación al estudio de la corrupción en las obras públicas del Perú (2002-2016)*. Tesis de Licenciatura, Ciencia Política y Gobierno, PUCP.

Webber, Jeffery R. 2016. "Evo Morales and the Political Economy of Passive Revolution in Bolivia, 2006-15." *Third World Quarterly* 37 (10): 1855-76.

Webber, Jeffery R. 2017. "Evo Morales, Transformismo, and the Consolidation of Agrarian Capitalism in Bolivia." *Journal of Agrarian Change* 17 (2): 330-47.

Weisbrot, Mark, and Andrés Arauz. 2019. *"Headwinds to Growth": The IMF Program in Ecuador*. Washington, DC: Center for Economic and Policy Research (CEPR).

Weyland, Kurt. 1996. "Neopopulism and Neoliberalism in Latin America:

Unexpected Affinities." *Studies in Comparative International Development* 31 (3): 3-31.

Weyland, Kurt. 2002. *The Politics of Market Reform in Fragile Democracies*. Princeton, NJ: Princeton University Press.

Weyland, Kurt, Raúl L. Madrid, and Wendy Hunter, eds. 2010. *Leftist Governments in Latin America: Successes and Shortcomings*. Cambridge: Cambridge University Press.

Whitehead, Laurence. 1975. "The State and Sectional Interests: The Bolivian Case." *European Journal of Political Research* 3: 115-46.

Williamson, John, ed. 1990. *Latin American Adjustment: How Much Has Happened?* Washington, DC: Institute for International Economics.

Wise, Carol. 2003. *Reinventing the State: Economic Strategy and Institutional Change in Peru*. Ann Arbor: University of Michigan Press.

Wise, Carol. 2020. *Dragonomics: How Latin America Is Maximizing (or Missing Out On) China's International Development Strategy*. New Haven, CT: Yale University Press.

Wolff, Jonas. 2003. *Bestimmungsfaktoren und Konsequenzen der offiziellen Dollarisierung in Lateinamerika: Eine politökonomische Analyse unter besonderer Berücksichtigung Ecuadors*. Hamburg: Institut für Iberoamerika-Kunde.

Wolff, Jonas. 2007. "(De-)Mobilising the Marginalised: A Comparison of the Argentine Piqueteros and Ecuador's Indigenous Movement." *Journal of Latin American Studies* 39 (1): 1-29.

Wolff, Jonas. 2009. "De-idealizing the Democratic Civil Peace: On the Political Economy of Democratic Stabilisation and Pacification in Argentina and Ecuador." *Democratization* 16 (5): 998-1026.

Wolff, Jonas. 2012. "New Constitutions and the Transformation of Democracy in Ecuador and Bolivia." In *New Constitutionalism in Latin America: Promises and Practices*, edited by Detlef Nolte and Almut Schilling-Vacaflor, 183-202. Farnham, UK: Ashgate.

Wolff, Jonas. 2016. "Business Power and the Politics of Post-neoliberalism: Relations between Governments and Economic Elites in Bolivia and Ecuador." *Journal of Politics and Society* 58 (2): 124-47.

Wolff, Jonas. 2018a. "Ecuador after Correa: The Struggle over the 'Citizens' Revolution.'" *Revista de Ciencia Política* 38 (2): 281-302.

Wolff, Jonas. 2018b. "Las élites políticas y económicas en Bolivia y Ecuador: convivir con gobiernos posneoliberales." In *Élites en las Américas: diferentes perspectivas*, edited by Adriano Codato and Fran Espinoza, 73-114. Curitiba: Editora UFPR.

Wolff, Jonas. 2018c. "Political Incorporation in Measures of Democracy: A Missing Dimension (and the Case of Bolivia)." *Democratization* 25 (4): 692-708.

Wolff, Jonas. 2019. "The Political Economy of Bolivia's Post-neoliberalism: Policies, Elites, and the MAS Government." *European Review of Latin American and Caribbean Studies (ERLACS)* 108: 109-29.

Wolff, Jonas. 2020a. "Las élites económicas en la Bolivia contemporánea." In *Nuevo Mapa de Actores en Bolivia: crisis, polarización e incertidumbre (2019-2020)*, edited by Jan Souverein and José Luis Exeni Rodríguez, 139-63. La Paz: Friedrich-Ebert-Stiftung Bolivia.

Wolff, Jonas. 2020b. "Organized Labor and Political Change in Latin America: An Overview." In *Socioeconomic Protests in MENA and Latin America: Egypt and Tunisia in Interregional Comparison*, edited by Irene Weipert-Fenner and Jonas Wolff, 107-21. Cham: Palgrave Macmillan.

Wolff, Jonas. 2020c. "The Turbulent End of an Era in Bolivia: Contested Elections, the Ouster of Evo Morales, and the Beginning of a Transition towards an Uncertain Future." *Revista de Ciencia Política* 40 (2): 163-86.

Wolff, Jonas. Forthcoming. "Después de la tormenta: la élite económica boliviana entre la negociación pragmática y el conflicto político latente." In *Elites empresariales, Estado y dominación en América Latina: persistencias y resistencias en la época post Covid*, edited by Francisco Robles, Ines Nercesian, and Miguel Serna. Buenos Aires: CLACSO.

World Bank. 2020. *The Cost of Staying Healthy: Semiannual Report of the Latin America and the Caribbean Region*. Washington, DC: The World Bank.

Yakolev, Andrei. 2006. "The Evolution of Business: State Interaction in Russia, from State Capture to Business Capture." *Europe Asia Studies* 58 (7): 1033-56.

Yashar, Deborah J. 2005. *Contesting Citizenship in Latin America: The Rise of Indigenous Movements and the Postliberal Challenge*. Cambridge: Cambridge University Press.

Zegada, María Teresa. 2019. "El escenario boliviano en 2018: estabilidad económica e incertidumbre institucional." *Revista Ciencia Política* 39 (2): 147-64.

Zegada, María Teresa. 2020. "La crisis del sistema de representación política: los partidos opositores al MAS en el interregno post y preelectoral (2019-2020)." In *Nuevo Mapa de Actores en Bolivia: Crisis, polarización e incertidumbre (2019-2020)*, edited by Jan Souverein and José Luis Exeni Rodríguez, 35-76. La Paz: Friedrich-Ebert-Stiftung Bolivia.

Zegada, María Teresa, and Jorge Komadina. 2014. *El espejo de la sociedad: poder y representación en Bolivia*. La Paz: CERES and Plural.

Zuazo Oblitas, Moira, and Cecilia Quiroga San Martín, eds. 2012. *Lo que unos no quieren recordar es lo que otros no pueden olvidar: Asamblea Constituyente, descolonización e interculturalidad*. 3rd ed. La Paz: Friedrich-Ebert-Stiftung Bolivia.

Zucman, Gabriel. 2014. *La riqueza oculta de las naciones: una investigacion sobre paraisos fiscales*. Barcelona: Pasado y Presente.

INDEX